Sensorimotor Awareness

Sensorimotor Awareness

THEODORE DIMON

ILLUSTRATIONS BY JACKIE COLLINS

DAY STREET PRESS

Published by:
Day Street Press
356 West 123rd Street
New York, New York 10027

Illustrations by Jackie Collins
Book design by Jan Derevjanik

Names: Dimon, Theodore, author.
Title: Sensorimotor Awareness: A Kinesthetic Guide to the
Body in Action
Description: New York: Day Street Press, {2024} Includes
references and index
Summary: A guide to kinesthetic awareness of the
body in action
Library of Congress Control Number: 2024923731
ISBN 979-8-9919489-0-6 (trade paperback);
ISBN 979-8-9919489-1-3 (ebook)
Subjects: LCSH: Musculoskeletal system—anatomy.
Human locomotion. Breathing exercises or breathing work.
Movement. Wellness. Self-help.

Illustration credits
Cover illustration by iStock.com/Grafissimo
Illustrations by Jackie Collins with the exception of the
following:
Figs. 7, 8, 9, 10, 11, 12, 15, 17 (Chap. 1); Fig. 21 (Chap. 6); Figs.
1, 2, 3 (Chap. 15) are by G. David Brown and were originally
published in Anatomy in Action by Theodore Dimon, North
Atlantic Books, 2021.
Fig. 4. Tent (Chap. 1)
https://www.shutterstock.com/image-vector/tent-camping-
outdoor-travel-vector-illustration-721958653
Fig. 5. Geodesic dome (Chap. 1)
Philipp Hienstorfer (https://commons.wikimedia.org/
wiki/File: Biosphere_montreal.JPG). This file is licensed
under the Creative Commons Attribution-Share Alike 4.0
International, 3.0 Unported, 2.5 Generic, 2.0 Generic and
1.0 Generic license (https://creativecommons.org/licenses /
by-sa/4.0/).
Fig. 6. Tensegrity architecture of the rabbit (Chap. 1)
From J. Z. Young. The Life of Mammals. Oxford University
Press. Reproduced with permission of the Licensor through
PLSclear.
All photos by Ted Dimon

CONTENTS

ACKNOWLEDGMENTS

I would like to express my gratitude to a number of people who have helped to bring this book to fruition.

To Serena Woolf, whose invaluable help in the early stages of this book helped me to organize and clarify many of the concepts in this book.

To Rebecca Price, who has been wonderfully encouraging throughout the process of writing this book and who believed in it more than I did.

To Dr. Tara Fenamore, my former graduate student and advisee, who helped me to conceive of a kinesiology curriculum for a subject that is badly in need of clarity and elucidation.

To my friend Seymour Simmons, for his many decades of support and friendship.

G. David Brown, who contributed the introductory illustrations in this book.

To James French, teaching assistant at the Dimon Institute, for his extensive help in developing the online platform now offered at the Dimon Institute, and for his invaluable help in proofreading and editing this book.

Thanks to Jan Derevjanik for her elegant, clear, and coherent layout and design.

Thanks to Genine Yarborough, Marketing Director at the Dimon Institute, for her new perspectives in presenting this work to the larger public.

To Jackie Collins, whose wonderful and thoughtful illustrations have helped to make this book readable, interesting, and intelligible.

To the many students who have supported my work, and whose feedback has been so instrumental in helping me to clarify this subject and to discover new and innovative ways of teaching.

And to my wife Tamara, for her patience, love, and support.

Sensorimotor Awareness: A New Field of Study

This manual is a practical, one-year course of study of the moving body—how it works, how to restore its natural working, and how to become more aware during daily activity. In my last book, *Anatomy in Action*, I described how the various parts and systems of the moving body are designed to work as a complete, holistic structure. This new book contains the practical knowledge that enables a person to become increasingly aware of their own functioning organism in real time—practically and not just theoretically. To my knowledge, outside of the new field of Sensorimotor Awareness there is no method that elucidates the subject of how we are designed to perform everyday actions, how we perform these actions in an unconscious and harmful way, and how it is possible, with dedicated study, to perform these actions more efficiently and consciously.

But why is it necessary to learn to be aware in action? Why not simply treat the problem by learning to stretch or strengthen muscles? Movement systems, as opposed to awareness practices, are based on learned actions and do not address the more fundamental question of how we are designed to move and how to raise this process to a conscious level. The countless numbers of yoga practitioners, dancers, and martial artists who are crippled with back and muscle pain bear witness to this fact. Ask any of these practitioners to show you, in concrete terms, how the back is designed to work when, for instance, you pick something up or bend down, and you will have your answer: they will show you how to stretch or strengthen this or that muscle or how to hold this or that position, but they will not be able to describe, as a matter of practical knowledge, how the back actually works or even what parts make up your back. Even more troubling will be the disparity between what they teach and what they are doing in their own daily lives. Methods may be useful as the foundation for learning specific skills, but they cannot confer awareness of, or knowledge about, how the body is actually designed.

This book, in contrast, is based on practical knowledge about how the back and other systems in the body actually work. Progressing from the anatomical detail described in *Anatomy in Action*, the present work demonstrates how to use these systems in activity and how to stop interfering with them as a matter of practical knowledge. Such knowledge—which is as yet little understood both in the biological sciences and in the movement and somatic disciplines—must be at the heart of any movement and awareness discipline. This book delves into them in depth, giving you the tools necessary to understand how they work and how to improve your bodily functioning in the process.

There is an even deeper reason why movement and somatic disciplines cannot provide the knowledge we need. The vast majority of movements we perform during daily life take place in the context of achieving goals and in response to our intention or decision to act. In this context, the notion of movement as a thing in itself is a kind of abstraction that, in reality, cannot be separated from the way actions take place in the service of actual goals. Movement, in other words, is not just about the body but about how mind and body work as a unified system. Consider what happens, for instance, when you practice a stretching exercise designed to alleviate tight back muscles. You may make some improvement but, the moment you return to normal activities such as walking or sitting in a chair, you will not be able to maintain such improvements or even be aware of what you are doing because the habitual patterns that cause this condition are part and parcel of how we perform these acts. Like all forms of exercise, stretching and bodywork methods treat mind and body as two separate entities, whereas a holistic and truly educational study of the moving body recognizes its essentially psychophysical character and the corresponding need for knowledge and awareness as the true basis for an elucidation of this crucial subject.

As an educational subject, the study of awareness in action is continuous with conscious development as a larger field, filling in the gap between bodily function and higher forms of mindfulness that study the mind alone. As such, this subject serves as the basis for a truly holistic model of awareness in living that spans bodily function and consciousness. Learning to move more efficiently is not simply about kinesthetic awareness but about raising our unconscious and habitual ways of doing things to a more conscious level.

It is important to mention that the theory and practice outlined in this course is derived not from pure science or theory but from direct experience with, and observation of, human movement. Current research tells us a great deal about the working of the human motor system—about muscles and how they work, how they receive impulses from the premotor and motor cortices, the role of afferent feedback from muscles and connective tissues, and much more. All this is highly illuminating, advancing our knowledge of the subject and elucidating the biological underpinnings of everyday actions. But it can tell us little about how to become more conscious of our actions. For this, we must acquire a different kind of knowledge, rooted not just in empirical observation and description of bodily systems but in the observation of harmful patterns, in knowledge of coordinated action, and in self-awareness. This is knowledge of a different kind, based not on the empirical study of the body but on movement itself, as it happens in real time in ourselves. From this kind of observation we will discover and understand new things about the human body—how it works, how we interfere with it and how to restore its working and, above all, how to become more conscious and aware in living.

Awareness of the Self in Action

Our capacity for skillful movement is one of the most remarkable features of being human. Walking upright on two feet, we are capable of traveling long distances and over all kinds of terrain. We can fashion and use tools, sing and speak, build houses, and type at computers. All these abilities are made possible by our amazing brains, coupled with an upright body plan that has freed the arm and hand to function as manipulative instruments.

For most of us—particularly when we are young—the body works remarkably efficiently. With virtually no upkeep, the body does whatever is demanded of it. A child can engage in hours of activity every day, for years on end, with only the occasional injury. But what happens when something goes wrong, as it almost inevitably does in so many of us as we age? Suffering from back and joint pain, muscle aches, and various related difficulties, we take up exercise, stretching, or some other form of rehabilitation, or go to a specialist who can help us to strengthen parts of the body or relieve pain.

But these methods—and the science upon which they are based—tell only part of the story. The body works perfectly when we are young. Why then do we assume that, if we experience pain or dysfunction, something is wrong and needs to be fixed, and that stretching or relaxation will somehow correct the problem? Young children are nearly invulnerable to back, shoulder, and other musculoskeletal problems, not because they are young and healthy but because the body has a natural design that they have not yet interfered with. We can see this in the effortless actions of young children, who walk, clamber, squat, and crawl, with such effortless ease. By the time children are 5 or 6, this situation changes dramatically. At this age children begin to slump and, by the time they are teenagers, the entire musculoskeletal system is a picture of disintegration and disorganization. The system that worked so perfectly when they were younger is lost, and the solution, as we will see in this course, is not simply to treat problems but to learn how the body is actually designed to work and to use it more skillfully. This requires real knowledge of our anatomical design and function, as well as the kinesthetic skills that enable us to identify when we interfere with this system and how to perform actions at a more conscious level.

Beyond Treatment and Cure

The belief that, when something is wrong, we need to treat the problem is deeply embedded in our collective psyche. When we experience back pain or have trouble sitting or standing, the usual assumption is that muscles or joints are working incorrectly and that we must correct these imbalances by strengthening muscles, stretching, or receiving treatments. If the symptoms are really crippling, we seek the help of a professional who can diagnose the problem based on objective diagnosis of bodily tissues.

But the typical aches and pains we attribute to muscles are not diseases that can be treated objectively. If you are suffering from lower back tension, a physical therapist or massage therapist may be able to identify and treat the muscles and fascia and, in this way, provide therapeutic relief. But such treatments do not address the actual cause of the problem, which requires real knowledge of how the fascia, muscles, and bones function as a larger system in action. As I will show in this book, this kind of knowledge requires a new paradigm based on new ways of looking at the body and how it works.

This is is not to say that clinical diagnosis and medical treatment are never warranted in treating musculoskeletal problems. If you woke up this morning with shooting pains in your shoulder and arm, it would be advisable to find someone with the medical and clinical expertise to identify the specific problem and, if necessary, to treat it. Symptoms such as these suggest that something is wrong, and when something is wrong, you need to go to the appropriate expert. But muscle tension as a general problem belongs to a different category of function and requires a new kind of knowledge about how the musculoskeletal system functions and the ability to coordinate the different parts based on this knowledge. This kind of knowledge cannot be acquired through objective or clinical observation alone, any more than the anatomical study or dissection of the larynx can teach us to command the proper use of the voice.

The Unity of Mind and Body

The human organism is a complex machine, and how we use it can profoundly affect our health. If, for instance, we habitually strain joints and shorten muscles, back trouble and joint pain

can develop. Constant rushing and worrying can cause stress-related symptoms. And collapsing while sitting interferes with breathing, muscle tone, and organ function. All of these problems can be medically treated after the fact, but we can understand their causes only by understanding how the organism functions in action based on a comprehensive knowledge of its design. This cannot be achieved simply by exercising, learning about body mechanics, or practicing forms of relaxation. The human body functions as a complex psychophysical whole, and understanding this system requires knowledge about how it is designed to move, how action is produced, and how to gain greater awareness and control of this system in action.

In virtually all the methods in use today, consciousness is used as a kind of therapeutic tool that, in the end, amounts to another form of therapy. A holistic treatment that is based on a theoretical concept of mind-body unity, but which reduces the individual to a passive recipient of bodily treatments, is in fact dualistic, since it cannot truly conceive of a mental and physical process that can be understood and translated into educational growth. Such a theory may embrace mind-body unity at an ideological level, but it fails in practice to articulate a positive theory that utilizes this relationship except in a purely therapeutic sense. To be complete, a truly unified concept of mind and body requires a dynamic understanding of functioning that makes it possible to identify underlying causes and, in so doing, to prevent the problem as a positive process of growth.

Kinesthetic Awareness as a Conscious Faculty

We are all familiar with the kinesthetic sense— the so-called 6th sense that enables us to be aware of bodily position, effort, and movement. We use it to adjust our grip when using a tool or to swing a tennis racket. Sometimes we notice if there is too much tension, and we heighten it when we practice various exercises. But using our kinesthetic awareness in this way is only the tip of the iceberg. The truth is that we are constantly flooded with proprioceptive feedback from connective tissues, joints, and muscles throughout the body, at an almost completely unconscious level. When we coordinate the body, we can raise important elements of this process to a conscious level, making it available in all our activities. This includes the conscious management of bodily systems, standing, sitting and walking, the use of the arms, breathing, and speech. When we understand how the body works and bring about a more coordinated working of the body, this activates an emergent, conscious awareness of the body that supports awareness in action. The result is the highest kind of educational know-how: awareness and knowledge of ourselves, our actions and how to be more conscious and mindful in everything we do.

History

My interest in this subject began when I injured my back in college. I tried a number of methods—relaxation, yoga, meditation, and the Feldenkrais method—but nothing seemed to work. Because I was in good physical shape, I was convinced that there was nothing actually wrong with me. I knew that, because my problem returned whenever I engaged in strenuous activity or sat for long periods, I was doing something harmful, if only I could figure out what this was. During this time, I was introduced to the work of F. Matthias Alexander, an Australian actor who discovered that his own vocal and breathing difficulties were caused by a harmful pattern of tension that interfered with how his body was designed to function naturally. Observing himself in front of a mirror, Alexander noticed that, when he recited, he tightened his neck and pulled his head back. In the process of trying to prevent this harmful pattern, he discovered that the relationship of the head to the trunk, or what he called the "primary control," constitutes a basic organizing principle in movement, and that his manner of vocalizing had interfered with this mechanism. By learning to prevent these tensions, he was able to reinstate the normal working of this mechanism

so that his voice, his breathing, and his general functioning improved. Based on these observations, Alexander devised various procedures for bringing about an improved working of the musculoskeletal system and for helping people to notice and prevent harmful tensions that interfered with it.

In the hope of solving my back problem, I began to have lessons in the Alexander Technique and, soon afterwards, entered a teacher-training program. I knew to begin with that my back muscles were tense, and that this tension was part of a harmful pattern that included pulling my head back and arching my back. I soon discovered that, whenever I moved, I wasn't simply tensing my back muscles or moving awkwardly; the shortened muscles were part of a larger pattern of tension that had interfered with my musculoskeletal system as a whole. What I thought was a back problem was in fact far more complex and extensive—a pattern of muscular activity that was interfering with the normal working of my body. The body, I now learned, had a system of internal postural support, or natural reflexes, that permit us to move and support ourselves effortlessly in whatever we do, without having to think about what muscles we use. In animals, as well as in young children, this system is normally working well; but I had interfered with it to such an extent that it could no longer work properly, forcing my body into a compensatory arrangement that made various parts of the body become rigid and tense and others collapsed and weakened. When I was able to prevent this pattern of response, I found that my back muscles began to naturally lengthen, reinstating a more normal condition of the entire muscular system and restoring the ease and flexibility I had enjoyed, but lost, as a child.

Understanding how to bring about an improved coordination of my body led to an even deeper discovery. Even when I was able to restore the natural working of my musculoskeletal system, the back tension reappeared once I resumed my habitual way of performing actions. The problem, I realized, was not simply that my body worked as a whole but that it operates, when we are actually using it, according to an instinctive process that simply isn't within our control.

It was not enough, then, to change the bodily condition; the process of action itself must be held in check, so as to create the possibility of learning a new response to the "stimulus" of doing something. Only by holding this instinctive process in abeyance, and focusing instead on the process by which we do things, would it be possible to overcome this habitual pattern. When I was able to focus on how I was performing an action, while postponing the "end" toward which I was working, the action would take place with surprising ease and effortlessness. The result was a constant improvement in how I performed tasks and an increasing sense of enjoyment in doing things and learning skills that had become laborious and painful. I began to realize that there had been nothing wrong with my back and that my problem had been caused by unconscious habits that had interfered with the natural functioning of my muscular system.

I had always had an interest in the field of education and, in my teenage years, had thought about starting a school that would model new and innovative ways of teaching children. I now became interested in the study of mind and body, no longer for my personal benefit but as a new and emerging educational field with profound implications for health, psychology, and personal development. Soon after I completed my training program I entered graduate school in education, where I began to explore the study of the self in action as a new subject in educational development. I began to research and write about several aspects of this subject but, even after I completed my graduate studies, several key questions remained. I had seen that my back trouble was part of a larger pattern of interference involving my whole body, and that by reorganizing the head and trunk the system as a whole worked better. But why did the head and trunk serve as an organizing factor in action? Books on kinesiology could explain specific actions, but they did not address the larger question of how the body was organized as a whole. Books on bodywork and functional anatomy hinted at the significance of a global bodily design but, apart from identifying lines of connective tissue and functional muscle

groups, they could not explain how the body was organized to function in action, or how to gain a command of it in activity. Yet clearly the body worked as a coordinated whole, maintaining support against gravity—when it was not interfered with—with a minimum of effort as a kind of automatic system.

Over a number of years I wrote about various aspects of this system, including the body's anatomical design, but I could not fully account for this automatic system until I realized that, to maintain bodily support, muscles do not simply contract to support bones but lengthen between bony contacts. The prevailing view about muscles is that they contract to support posture and to produce movement and that, if they become too tight, they must be balanced by opposing groups, stretched, or treated directly. But muscles don't let go simply because they are tight; nor do they simply function better when they are not overworked. Muscles and bones work together in a partnership, forming a tensegrity structure in which bones and connective tissues provide support with a minimum of effort, based on the ability of muscles and connective tissue to naturally lengthen. Getting muscles or connective tissues to release is not simply a remedy for tightness but a fundamental principle in nature.

Based on these observations, I began to develop a theoretical model for how the musculoskeletal system works as a coordinated whole to produce effortless support as the background for voluntary action, which I called the *postural neuromuscular reflex (PNR) system*, described in detail in *Neurodynamics: The Art of Mindfulness in Action*. With a clear idea of how the PNR system worked, I could also describe how specific parts worked, such as the shoulder girdle, voice, and muscles of the back, which I outlined in my last book, *Anatomy in Action*. How to become aware of oneself, based on knowledge of the PNR system, is the subject of the present work, which details specific techniques for restoring natural function, heightening kinesthetic awareness in action, and gaining a command of these systems at a conscious level.

PART ONE

Overview

1

An Organizing Principle in Movement

As a moving machine, the human body is one of nature's incredible marvels. With it, we can speak, walk, and perform an incredible array of movements. At our slightest wish we can carry out any task, the body acting as a machine that seamlessly carries out our intentions. If the body functions inefficiently, as happens increasingly with age, we exercise, strengthen, or treat parts of the body in the hope that it can continue to operate efficiently in response to our wishes.

The problem with such approaches, however, is that the body does not work in pieces but as a coordinated whole, and the working of the parts depends upon this whole. Look, for instance, at how a typical two-year-old sits and stands and it is immediately evident that, in whatever the child does, the body works perfectly as a coordinated whole. To perform a specific movement such as raising an arm, the child must contract individual muscles and move at particular joints, but these movements take place in the context of this larger whole, which serves as the crucial background for whatever specific actions are taking place.

Understanding the working of this system is essential to a model of awareness that makes it possible to identify in a positive way how the body works and to stop interfering with it. When this system works well, muscles do not strain but are naturally healthy and toned; joints have room and are supported so that they can work with maximum ease; breathing is full and unimpeded; vitality is heightened by improved muscle tone; and circulation is maximized by a lack of excessive contraction in muscles. In short, the key to improved movement and health is not the practice of this or that method but an understanding of how the body is designed to function naturally—that is, with a minimum of strain and effortless grace based on our body's natural design.

Being kinesthetically aware based on an understanding of the musculoskeletal system as a whole represents a critical foundation for a complete model of bodily awareness. We are all familiar with the kinesthetic sense, the so-called 6th sense that enables us to be aware of bodily position, effort, and movement. Although partially conscious, the kinesthetic sense operates at a mostly unconscious level to help adjust and coordinate our actions. When we understand how the musculoskeletal system works and bring about a more coordinated working of the body, the kinesthetic sense becomes more conscious, activating a heightened state of awareness in action. This includes the conscious management of bodily systems, sitting, standing and walking, the use of the arms, breathing and speech. Many of us intuitively understand that the body is designed to work naturally, forming the basis for healthful, efficient functioning. Yet how—or why—the body works in this way has never been fully articulated or understood.

Muscle Length and Tensegrity Design

The usual view of muscles—and the view upon which most theories of movement are based—is that muscles contract to make movement possible. When we lift an object, for instance, we must contract the biceps muscle, which flexes the arm at the elbow. Such a strategy is perfectly acceptable when we are performing a specific task, but it cannot account for how a child can sit, without any apparent effort, for hours at a time (*Fig. 1*). In this case, muscles are clearly maintaining support of the head, spine, trunk, shoulders, and hips, yet there is no strain in any of these muscle groups, which do not seem to tire or to forcibly contract and which, furthermore, remain pliable and toned. When all this is taking place—as it typically does in toddlers—posture is maintained effortlessly as the background for whatever specific movements are needed.

Fig. 1. A young child can sit without strain for long periods.

The answer to this apparent mystery is that muscles maintain support of body parts, but they do so in the context of length. To keep the head upright, for instance, the muscles of the neck must act upon the head. If, however, these muscles did this by forcibly contracting, the head would be pulled back and would put pressure on the spine and compromise the ability of the trunk to lengthen against gravity. This, as we can see in

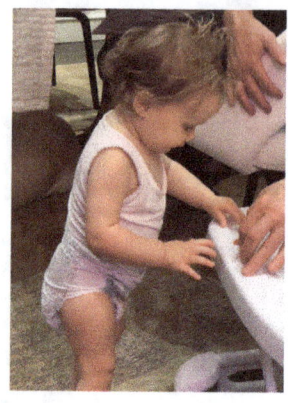

Fig. 2. Head balance in a toddler, showing how the neck muscles lengthen.

a young child, is not what happens. Instead, the head balances forward and, in doing so, counterbalances the action of the neck muscles (*Fig. 2*). In this way, the neck muscles maintain the support of the head, but in the context of a dynamic state in which the head acts on the neck muscles, which remain lengthened, allowing both the neck and spine to remain lengthened.

This same principle can be observed everywhere in the body. The spine, for instance, is an inert bony structure and requires muscular support. But the muscles of the spine don't simply pull on the spine by forcibly contracting; they are instead maintained in a lengthened state and, in this context, support the spine and trunk without actively contracting. Even the leg muscles, which stabilize the legs at the ankles, knees, and hips, do not simply shorten but are lengthened between bony attachments and, in this context, maintain the postural support of the body against gravity with a minimum of effort (*Fig. 3*).

But how is it possible for muscles to support the body by lengthening? Lengthening is not something a muscle can "do"—that is, muscles can only shorten or contract. Even if a muscle is

Fig. 3. Muscles lengthening everywhere in a child's body.

Fig. 4. A tent is a simple tensegrity structure.

passively lengthened (as when we forcibly stretch our hamstrings), it can not do anything positive in that state. How then is it possible for a lengthening muscle to contribute in any way to bodily support? The answer is that bones and muscles, working in partnership, create opposing forces that produce total support—an arrangement sometimes described as a tensegrity structure. To make this clear, think of what happens if you place a heavy pole on the ground and run guy wires from the ground to keep it from falling over. The guy wires support the pole but, at the same time, the pole keeps the guy wires lengthened. The pole, in this case, is doing a lot of the job of maintaining the support of the tent, but not entirely—in fact, much of the "load" is borne by the guy wires which, by resisting the tendency to be pulled apart, actually absorb the forces acting on the tent (*Fig. 4*).

Such a dynamic architectural arrangement was given the name "tensegrity" by Buckminster Fuller, an engineer and architect who explored non-traditional ways of using building materials (*Fig. 5*) [1]. Fuller noted that many living structures, including plants and animals, utilize tensegrity principles in their designs, which are far more

Fig. 5. A geodesic dome.

1 Fuller, Buckminster (1961). Tensegrity. *Portfolio and Art News Annual* (4): 112–127, 144, 148.

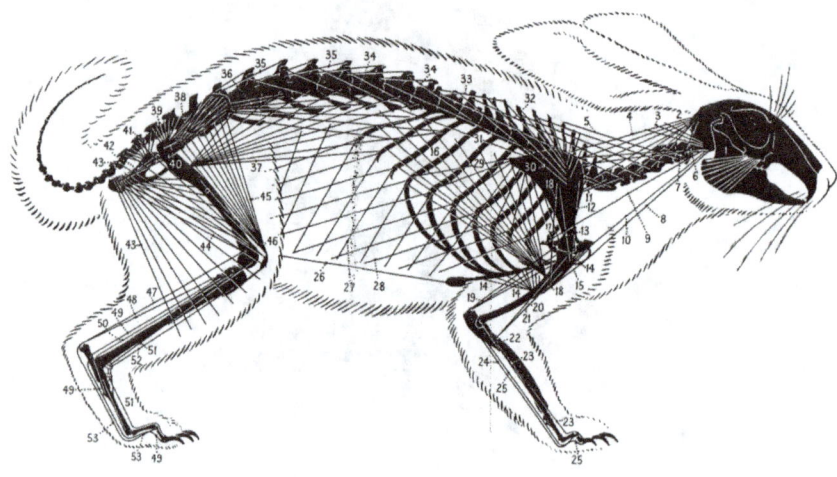

*Fig. 6. The tensegrity architecture
of the rabbit.*

efficient, mobile, and lightweight than compression structures. The same principle applies to muscles, which could not possibly do the work of maintaining postural support of the body simply by contracting, which is too costly and metabolically inefficient to be sustainable. Instead, nature found a much more efficient architectural principle in which muscles, connective tissues, and bones cooperate to form a pliable, mobile, lightweight structure such as we see in many vertebrates, with their lithe, lightweight, mobile designs (*Fig. 6*).

So how does this concept relate to muscles and bones, and to the design of the body as a whole? To maintain overall stability—that is, to maintain the postural support of the body as a whole—muscles, connective tissues, and bones work together as a total architectural arrangement in which muscles are lengthened between bones, and muscles act back upon bones to produce natural, automatic upright support of the body as a whole. Because this arrangement works

automatically in the infant, we think of it as hard-wired into the nervous system, functioning automatically as a kind of given. But it functions as a dynamic system that can be interfered with.

Muscle Tone

We have now seen that, to maintain bodily support, muscles do not crudely pull on bones but are lengthened between their bony attachments, working in partnership with bones to create an architectural framework, or tensegrity structure, consisting of muscles, tendons, fascia, and bones. But how do muscles provide support if they are not contracting but lengthening between their bony contacts? The answer is that muscles respond to length by firming or toning up—that is, they are designed in such a way that, when stretched or lengthened, they resist this outward force by pulling inward. Consider, for instance, what happens if you hold your breath. When

OVERLY-STRETCHED

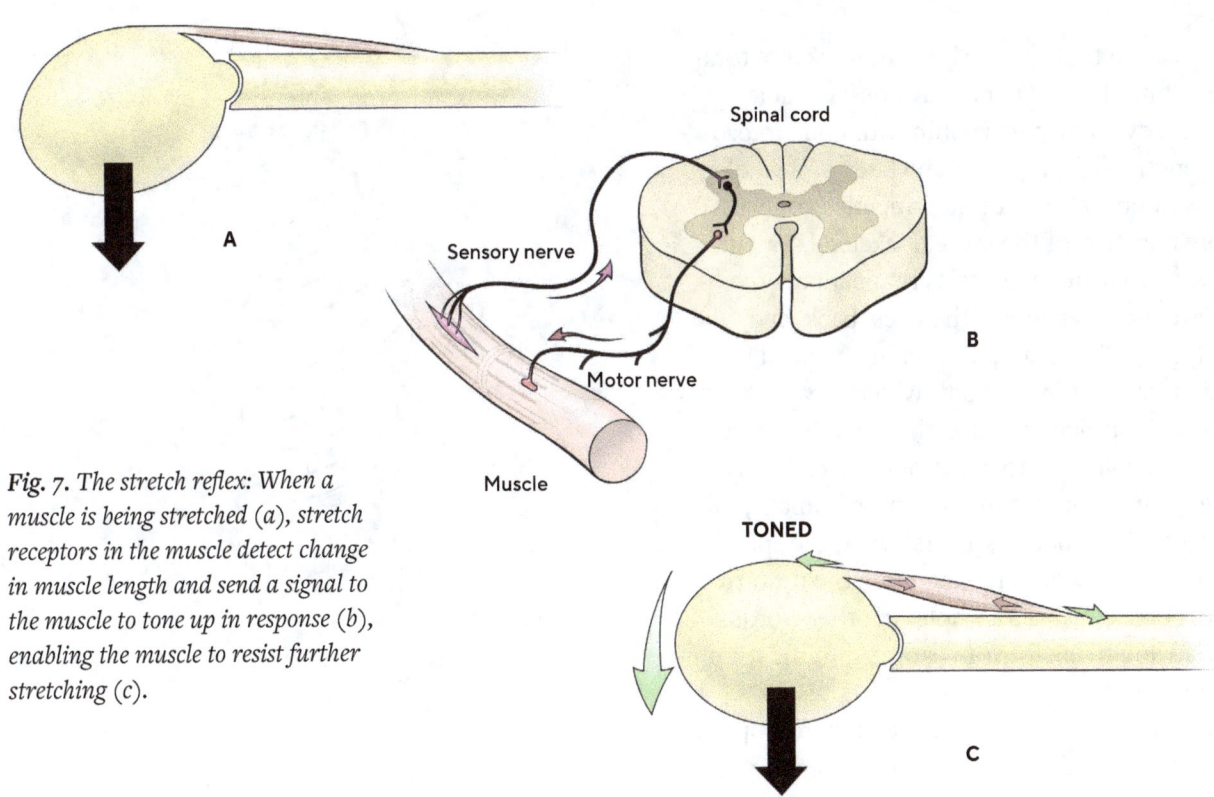

Fig. 7. The stretch reflex: When a muscle is being stretched (a), stretch receptors in the muscle detect change in muscle length and send a signal to the muscle to tone up in response (b), enabling the muscle to resist further stretching (c).

we take a deep breath, the ribs are raised, and all the connective tissues that open the rib cage are stretched. To let our breath out, we do not need to forcibly expel the air but only to allow these stretched tissues, which include fascia and tendons as well as muscles, to rebound to their resting length. The entire body is in some sense designed this way. When muscles—as well as all the connective tissues that run through muscles and that connect them to bones—are stretched or lengthened, these tissues store kinetic energy that, without any expenditure of energy, provides a rebound effect in which the connective tissues "pull back" against the forces pulling them apart.

But this is only part of the story. Muscles and connective tissues contain receptors that sense when the tissues are being stretched and signal to the muscles to tone up in response. In this way, sensory receptors and motor nerves form a feedback loop, known as a "stretch reflex," designed to maintain low-level activity, or tone, in muscles

(*Fig. 7*). When receiving these low-level signals, muscles are not actively contracting or performing work but are able to provide the background activity necessary to maintain support and movement on two feet with minimal effort.

This ability of muscles to resist lengthening and to firm up in response to forces that are pulling on them is built into the structure of muscle tissue itself. Researchers have discovered that, when muscles eccentrically contract—for instance, when we lower a weight, in which case the muscle is contracting but is being lengthened by the force of the weight—they seem to gain more contractile power. This is because, in addition to being able to contract, muscles possess spring-like qualities that contribute to their power. In this way, muscles provide effortless support, paradoxically producing greater effect with less work. Muscles all over the body function in this way as part of a larger system that maintains support with minimal work.

The Head/Trunk Relationship

We have seen that, for the body to work as a total
system, muscles and connective tissues must
work in a dynamic partnership with bone to produce lengthened support of the body as a whole.
Let's look now at how these principles apply to
the organization of the musculoskeletal system
as a whole. The main muscles that support the
body are the extensors of the neck, back, and
legs (*Fig. 8*). Sitting atop the spine, the head is
the highest point in the body, which means that,
to maintain upright posture, the head must not
be pulled down but (for want of a better word)
"moving" in an upward direction. In humans, the
head "leads" the body as a whole, and the spine,
in turn, has to lengthen to maintain the upward
support of the body as a whole. In other words,
the head and trunk form an essential foundation
for movement.

This central role of the head and trunk applies
even to the use of the limbs. If, for instance, you
reach with your arm to pick something up, you
must engage specific muscles of the shoulder and
upper limb. But the muscles of the shoulder and
arm never work in isolation from the head and
trunk, which must be supported and stabilized
as the basis for using the arms. Even when we
use the limbs, the muscles supporting the head
and trunk form the essential foundation for the
use of the limbs and are, in this sense, central to
all other movement. The system now lengthens
upward against gravity and not in the direction
of movement; but all action—even when this
involves sitting and using the arms—is still organized around the head and trunk, which lengthen
upward as part of our vertically-arranged tensegrity design (*Fig. 9*).

We now have a picture of how the entire musculoskeletal system works. Muscles do not just
contract to produce movement but are elastically
stretched within the skeletal framework and work
in cooperation with bones to produce tensegrity
support. In the context of this elasticity, muscles automatically maintain tone, converting the
entire musculoskeletal system into a spring-like
framework. The body as a whole is organized

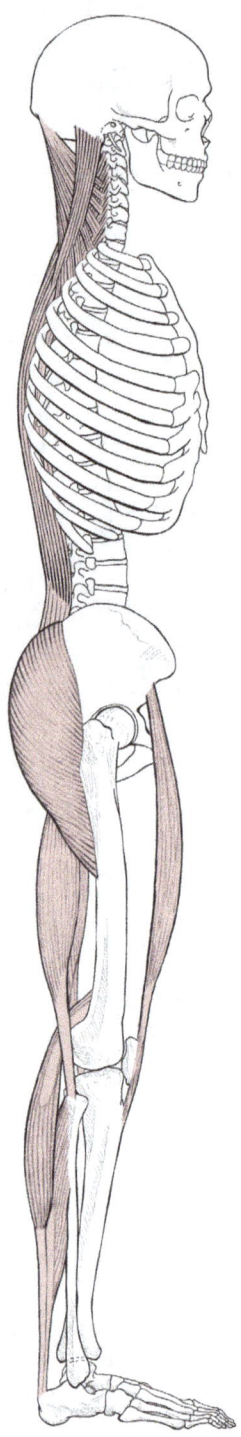

*Fig. 8. The extensors on the back of the body are essential
to postural support.*

to move through space with the head leading and the body lengthening, which in humans has become a vertically-poised, upright system. Based on these principles, the musculoskeletal system functions automatically as a working whole, or what I call the *PNR* (*postural neuromuscular reflex*) system.

To summarize:

A. Muscles are lengthened between bones to provide tensegrity support of the body as a whole against gravity.

B. Muscles and connective tissues are designed to respond to changes in length by toning up, converting the musculoskeletal system into a spring-like framework.

C. The relationship of the head to the trunk organizes the body to move as a whole in space.

D. All of these elements function at a largely automatic level to produce effortless, lengthened support against gravity.

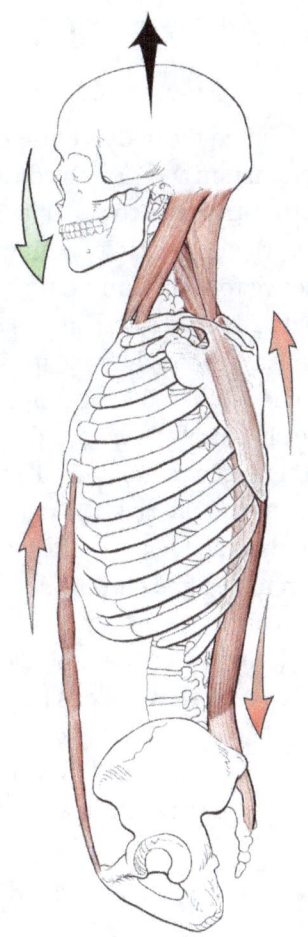

Fig. 9. With the head balanced forward and the trunk lengthening, the body as a whole lengthens upward against gravity.

Muscle Length: A New Principle in Muscle Function

We have now examined the body's tensegrity design and noted that, in addition to contracting, muscles work with bones to produce bodily support. Muscles, then, perform two functions. They produce active force by contracting, and they lengthen between bones and, in this context, maintain postural support. When the musculoskeletal system is interfered with, however, muscles become chronically contracted and thus cannot perform this second function. To understand what it means for muscles to lengthen, then, we must understand how muscles contract, what causes them to become chronically shortened so that they cannot assume their natural length, and what it means for them to release so that this length can be restored. Let's begin with the ability of muscle tissue to contract.

Muscles are made up of exceedingly thin, thread-like fibers that possess the special quality of being able to contract and so shorten in length. These fibers, which are wrapped together in bundles to form muscles, are attached to bones so that, when they shorten or contract, they pull upon the bones to stabilize parts of the body or to actively move them (*Fig. 10*). In highly specialized organs, like the eye, muscle fibers are a fraction of an inch long, and only a very few are sufficient for the job at hand; in other parts of the body, such as the thigh, these fibers can be up to two feet foot long, and many thousands are bundled together to form powerful, bulky muscles that make it possible to walk, jump, and run on two feet.

Within each muscle fiber are tiny, thread-like myofibrils, which are the contractile units within each muscle cell that make it possible for the muscle to perform work. Within each fibril are two types of molecular chains, the thin actin and the thick myosin chains. These two molecular strands interdigitate, giving the muscle the banded or striated pattern after which it is named (*Fig. 11a*). When the muscle fiber receives

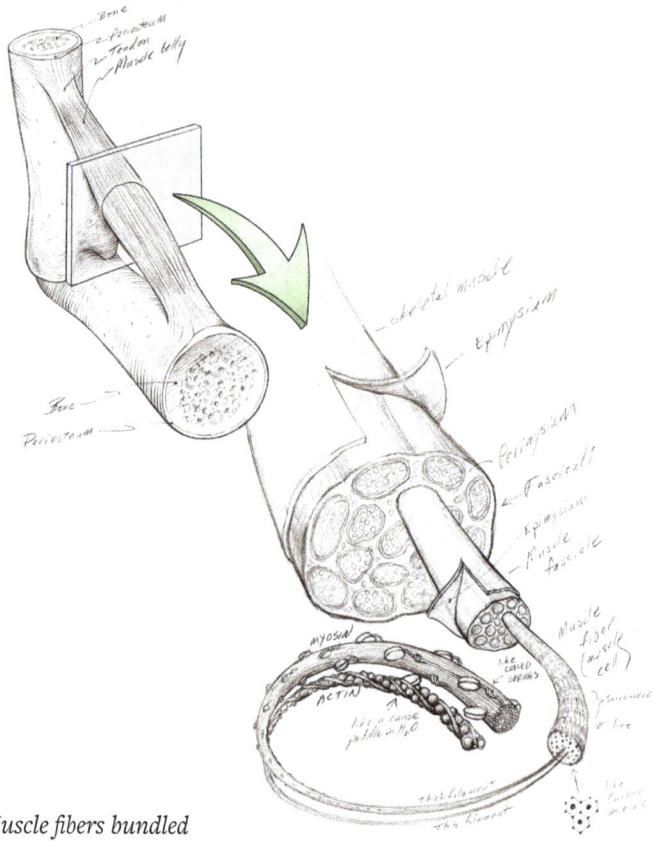

Fig. 10. Muscle fibers bundled together make up a muscle.

a signal from a motor nerve, cross-bridging takes place between the molecular strands. The thin actin chains begin to slide alongside the myosin chains, causing the muscle to telescope or shorten in length. This telescoping of the actin and myosin strands, which can be seen on an electron microscope as a narrowing of the striations in the muscle, causes the muscle fiber as a whole to shorten, or contract (*Fig. 11b*). The muscle fibers now produce force, acting upon the bones to which they attach. This happens every time we make a movement or deliberately tighten a muscle. This is a basic function of muscle tissue, whose main function is to produce force by contracting, or what is called "concentric contraction."

As we've seen, however, the ability of muscle to contract is not its only function. When a muscle is not actively contracting, it is able to lengthen between its bony attachments. This is not something that the muscle "does" but is the result of forces acting upon the muscle. When

this happens, the muscle tones up—that is, it gently resists the stretching forces, producing support without having to actively contract. This toning or stiffening of muscle in response to stretch is not incidental to how muscles function but represents a central function of muscle tissue, which is designed to maintain support with a minimum of effort.

This lengthening quality, it is important to point out, is not the same as eccentric contraction, in which case the muscle is being lengthened by forces acting upon it but is still actively contracting. This happens when, for instance, you have lifted a heavy weight and slowly lower it to the ground, in which case the muscle is contracting even though the contractile force of the muscle is being overcome by the sheer weight of the object. A muscle can also be lengthened by forcibly pulling on it, as when we stretch our hamstrings. The kind of lengthening we are speaking about here is a natural property of muscle tissue that enables it to lengthen between

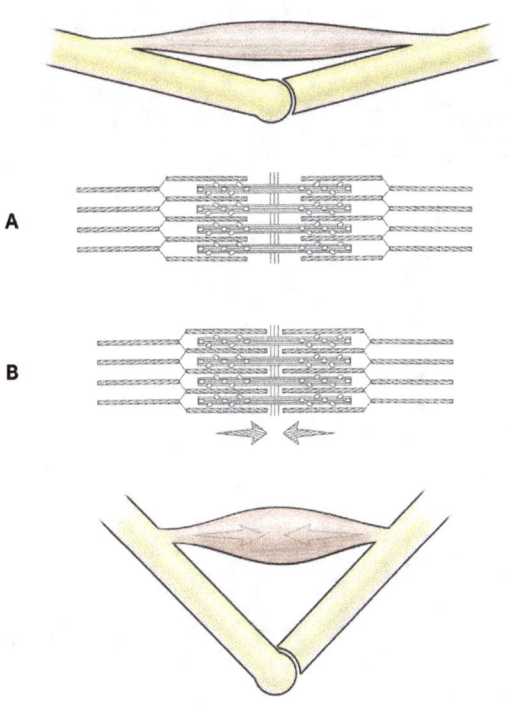

*Fig. 11a. The myofibrils within muscle fibers contain actin and myosin chains; **b.** When the actin chain moves along the myosin chain, the muscle contracts.*

CONTRACTED

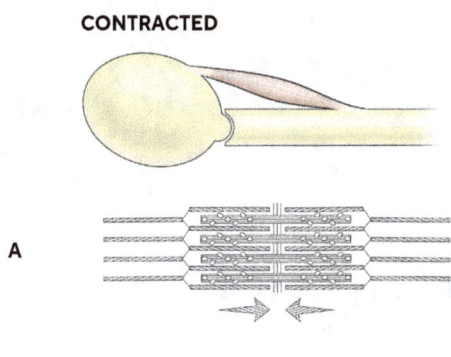

RELEASING INTO LENGTH

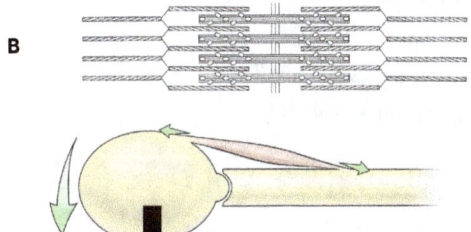

*Fig. 12a. When the actin and myosin strands are overlapping and cross-bridging takes place, the muscle is shortened and contracted; **b.** When the cross-bridging ceases, the contractile components can slide apart and the muscle releases and lengthens between its bony attachments.*

bony contacts, in which case it naturally tones up and resists further lengthening. For this to happen, active cross-bridging between the interdigitating molecular strands must cease, allowing the muscle to let go and release between its bony attachments (*Fig. 12*).

Consider, for instance, what happens when we slump in a chair and the head is pulled back by shortened neck muscles. In this posture, the extensor muscles of the back are inactive and, because the spine lacks the support needed to maintain its length, the trunk collapses into the slumped state. With the head pulled back in this way, the head is pressing down on the spine and the spine is unable to lengthen. To restore natural postural support, the head must stop pressing down upon the spine so that the trunk can come to its natural length. But restoring length is not simply a matter of making postural adjustments or stretching shortened muscles. In order to lengthen, the neck muscles must first

stop contracting, which in turn allows the head to move upward. When this happens, the muscles are able to assume their natural length in the context of their bony attachments, which allows them to tone up and to resist being lengthened further.

But how do muscles produce support if they are not actively contracting? The answer to this question lies deep within the structure of the muscle fiber itself. We've seen that each muscle fiber contains two types of molecular strands, the thin actin and the thick myosin chains, which are responsible for the contractile action of the muscle (*Fig. 13a*). Attached to the myosin chain is a third, less obvious molecular chain called "titin" (named for its huge size) (*Fig. 13b*). Titin is structured in such a way that, if it is stretched or pulled upon, it pulls back. That is exactly what happens when the actin and myosin strands slide apart from each other and the muscle lengthens between its bony contacts. In this case, the titin

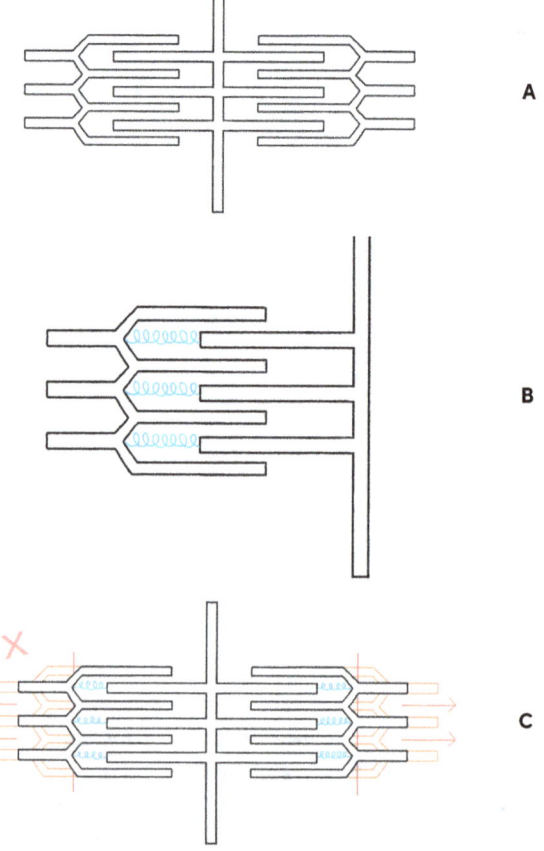

Fig. 13a. Myosin and actin strands form the contractile elements within a muscle fiber;
b. Titin: the hidden strand within the muscle fiber; c. When the muscle is lengthened and the myosin and actin strands slide apart, titin resists the pull, imparting a spring-like quality to the muscle.

Fig. 14. Child sitting effortlessly based on natural muscle length.

strand is stretched and, when this happens, it opposes this action, resisting the lengthening of the muscle and imparting a spring-like quality to the muscle (*Fig. 13c*). In this way, muscle tissue that is being actively lengthened resists this force, exerting a gentle oppositional force that enables the muscle to maintain spring-like support without actively contracting and without having to expend energy.[2]

None of this can happen, however, if the muscles have become chronically contracted and are unable to release naturally into length. To address the practical problem of muscle tension, then, we have to understand how to stop muscles from contracting so that the molecular strands can slide apart, allowing the muscle to lengthen between its bony attachments. For this to happen, the cross-bridging that takes place during contraction must cease so that the molecular strands are able to slide apart from each other (see *Fig. 12*), which in turn triggers the spring-like qualities in the muscle fibers, as well as tonic reflexes that maintain support without active contraction. Understanding this second function of muscles is an essential part of what it means for muscles to be healthy. Muscles that are chronically contracted are not only overworking but are also unable to perform the essential function of maintaining postural support with a minimum of

effort and strain. Producing this condition is not simply a matter of treating or stretching muscles; muscles lengthen naturally within their skeletal framework as the basis for maintaining effortless postural support, as we again see in this child (*Fig. 14*).

"Directing" Body Parts and Release of Tension:
The Key to Muscle Function

But what do we do when the system is generally interfered with, as it is when the neck, back, and leg muscles are shortened? Just as we can send motor messages by making the decision to do something, we can cease sending these messages, as when, for example, we are tightening our shoulders against the cold and make a conscious effort to relax our muscles. This process of consciously altering muscle activity is very clearly demonstrated in biofeedback techniques designed to give a subject greater control over specific muscles. John Basmajian, one of the early biofeedback researchers, attached very fine electrodes to muscle fibers so that motor nerve impulses to the muscles could be detected and displayed on an oscilloscope screen. When the subjects could observe the screen and therefore had feedback about what single motor units were doing, they could learn to consciously control individual motor units with only a few minutes of practice. Some subjects, after only a short time, could control the activity of specific motor units without the benefit of the oscilloscope by relying entirely on their kinesthetic feedback.[3]

But exactly which muscles need to let go, and how much? Trying to be aware of or to relax specific muscles is a haphazard process because we really do not know which muscles should relax, or how much. If, for instance, you lie flat on the floor with the limbs splayed, it may seem that this

---

2 Roberts, Thomas J (2016). Contribution of elastic tissues to the mechanics and energetics of muscle function during movement. *Journal of Experimental Biology* 219, 266-275.

3 Basmajian, John V., "Control of individual motor units," *American Journal of Physical Medicine*, February 1967, Vol. 46, Issue 1, pp 480-486.

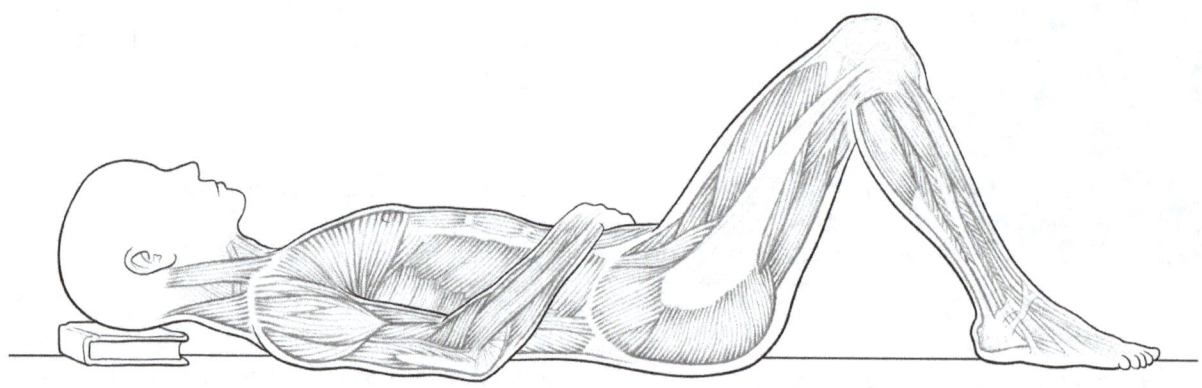

Fig. 15. The semi-supine position.

is an ideal position for relaxing muscles, since all the body parts are supported and the muscles do not have to perform work. But although this position may allow some degree of relaxation, it won't produce length and release in the muscles because in this position, the head will be thrown backward, the lower back arched, and the pelvis rotated the wrong way so that, instead of length-ening and releasing, the muscles of the lower back and neck actually shorten—exactly the opposite of what is needed.

How then do we encourage muscles to lengthen, if not by directly attempting to relax them? We saw that muscles are designed not simply to contract but to lengthen between skel-etal parts. This relationship of muscle to bone is the key to understanding how to restore muscles to their natural length. To function properly, mus-cles need to lengthen so that they can function with a minimum of effort—a condition that is much easier to achieve when body parts are sup-ported as in the semi-supine position (*Fig. 15*)[4].

In this position, the body parts are supported and, in this context, muscles can release into length. This leads, in turn, to a reorganization of the body parts, which can then work together in a more coordinated way. In this case, one does not need to try to be aware of tension directly, or to figure out exactly how much tension is required in spe-cific muscles, which let go naturally into length, without any manipulation or regulation, based on the body's inherent design.

The ability to use one's awareness and think-ing to bring about changes in the musculoskeletal system, as we'll see throughout this book, is a key part of a complete approach to kinesthetic awareness. When the musculoskeletal system is interfered with, muscles don't simply shorten; they do so as part of a larger design that is the key to how muscles work. When muscles are tight, or when imbalances are present, we must identify the interference based on the design of the body as a whole and learn to direct parts of the body so that balance can be naturally restored. Releasing,

---

4 The concept of influencing motor units indirectly by sending inhibitory messages to muscles in the context of skeletal attach-ments was first articulated by F. Matthias Alexander, who termed this process "direction." Alexander defines direction as "… the process involved in projecting messages from the brain to the mechanisms and in conducting the energy necessary to the use of these mechanisms." Alexander, F. Matthias, *The Use of the Self*. London: Victor Gollanz, 1996, p. 35.

stretching, and balancing muscles in the body can make specific improvements but, without an understanding of this design, cannot establish truly coordinated conditions. To be meaningful, an approach to kinesthetic awareness must be based on a clear knowledge of how the musculo-skeletal system works based on muscle length and coordination of body parts. We must also understand how contracted and shortened muscles can release into length as the basis for re-establishing their natural supportive function. Sending mental "directions" to muscles reestablishes the body's natural design, allowing the student, in turn, to become more kinesthetically discriminating. The process of directing, then, becomes a form of kinesthetic education and not simply a treatment, enabling the student to perform actions at a conscious level that can be applied in activity.

Tensegrity Design and Muscle Length: The Key to Functional Systems

In our account so far, we have seen that, far from being defective and requiring treatment, the body has a natural design that is essential to musculoskeletal health. Muscles and bones cooperate to form a tensegrity structure in which bones are supported by muscles, and muscles, in turn, lengthen between bony contacts, creating a pliable, movable structure that maintains support against gravity with a minimum of effort. Individual muscles contract to produce movement, but they do so within the context of a larger framework that forms a critical background for all specific movement.

Fig. 16. Child with naturally widening shoulders .

But what happens when specific parts of this system begin to fail, as when we experience chronic back pain or the shoulder muscles become chronically tense and painful? It is easy to assume that, because particular areas of the body have become strained, we must stretch, strengthen, or rehabilitate specific muscles or groups of muscles. But such an approach fails to explain why these systems work so efficiently to begin with. A typical three-year-old child can sit on the floor and use his or her arms for hours without any discernible strain in the muscles of the back and shoulders; in contrast, most adults cannot sit on the floor with their arms raised for even a few minutes without feeling strain and discomfort. The difference, as we can easily observe when we compare the two, is that when a child is sitting naturally, the shoulders are broadly and fully supported and, when working this efficiently, are completely free of strain (*Fig. 16*). This larger design is the key to specific tension in the shoulders, which naturally release when the upright support system is restored and the shoulders can function normally again. Understanding this design is far more effective than any form of treatment or exercise because, when we reinstate natural function, muscles naturally lengthen and the musculoskeletal system as a whole works without effort and strain.

The same principle applies to other key systems such as the muscles of the back. Back pain is arguably the most prevalent and costly health problem in the world. Thousands of people suffer from it and try to get relief by exercising, receiving chiropractic treatment, doing stretching exercises, or getting surgery. But the back musculature functions as part of the larger upright support system, and if this larger system is working well—as it usually is in young children such as the girl pictured in *Fig. 16*—the back muscles will be less prone to injury and, in addition, will be toned and supportive. This system functions optimally in young children but, precisely because it functions instinctively, once it stops working well, it cannot be recovered easily. When we understand how it works, however, the upright support system can be re-activated and, when it is, the back functions fully and supportively

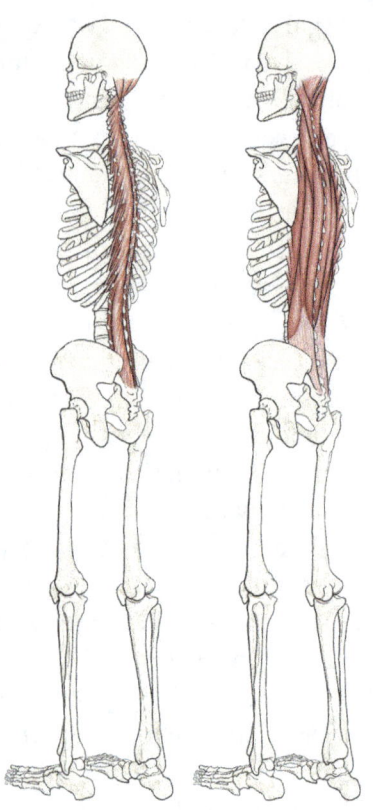

Fig. 17. The musculature of the back.

(*Fig. 17*). Each of the bodily systems, when looked at in the context of our larger design, can be clearly understood, and in such a way that we can learn to use them efficiently and naturally. In this book, we will examine some of these systems in depth—most notably the extensors of the back, the muscles involved in breathing, the shoulders and arms, and the hips and legs—understanding how they are designed, restoring natural function, and learning to use them more consciously. Readers who would like to know more about each of these systems are referred to *Anatomy in Action*, in which I describe each one in detail, including the various muscles involved and the key functional properties of the system.

Knowledge of the functional systems that make up the human body gives new meaning to kinesthetic awareness as an educational competency. Most kinesthetic approaches are open-ended and exploratory, focusing on specific areas of tension or muscle groups that are contracted and imbalanced as the basis for bringing about greater mobility and release. But without a clear understanding of how the musculoskeletal system works, such approaches lead nowhere and often produce a harmful state of relaxation and collapse. Here we have a clear structure—one that gives clarity to kinesthetic discrimination, affording the student a true educational language of kinesthesia. Many of the exercises in this course are built around knowledge of these systems, which gives clear direction and purpose in one's self-study, enabling the student to make progress on his or her own without relying on teachers and practitioners.

Educating the Kinesthetic Sense

Today the notion of a kinesthetic sense has become part of the popular lexicon. Dance, yoga, relaxation, meditation, bodywork—all refer to the role of kinesthetic awareness in learning to relax and become more mindful. But what exactly is kinesthesia, and what is its role in organizing posture and movement? In order to carry out tasks and to maintain body posture, the brain must not only tell muscles to contract but must also receive sensory feedback from muscles. Without this feedback, we would have no way to know how much to contract muscles or how to orchestrate the dozens of muscles involved in a simple act. This system for gathering information from our muscles, tendons, and joints in order to control what we are doing is the kinesthetic sense.

Since muscles accomplish their purpose through effort, and since we cannot perfect their use without a sense of how much effort is being used, this feedback from our muscles is crucial to their proper control. Whether handling tools, walking down the street, or singing a phrase of music, it enables us to constantly adjust our efforts to our desired goals. Sometimes called "muscle memory," this phenomenon forms the basis of all the actions that become part of the fabric of our everyday activity and learned skills. Whenever we master an activity, we have a sensation that accompanies our doing that enables us to perform the action fluidly, forming an incredibly rich array of sensations and feedback from our own bodies.

The notion, then, that we make movements simply by contracting or controlling specific muscles hardly does justice to the neural complexity of skilled movement. Movement involves constant feedback; without it, we would lack the most basic control, and action would be faltering and inefficient. If we are largely unaware of this kinesthetic feedback, and if it becomes unreliable, how do we educate it, and how do we restore normal function? One of the first prerequisites is that we need to reduce tension and re-establish length in muscles. Muscles do not function in a vacuum, and kinesthetic awareness is not a light that can be shined on muscles, as if they simply become tight and need to relax. Muscles function as part of a larger system, and we need to understand how the system works as the basis for heightening kinesthetic awareness. Restoring muscle length heightens proprioceptive awareness and thus the ability to perceive if we unnecessarily tighten muscles when we move. Through the study of action, it is possible to become more kinesthetically discriminating, to educate the kinesthetic sense, and to become more intelligent in action.

A New Principle In Action

In our account so far, we've seen that the body does not work in parts but as a coordinated whole and that, when something is wrong, the parts must reorganize in such a way that the different parts work together. When this happens, shortened muscles become more lengthened, gaining tone and performing their supportive function without effort. The body as a whole becomes more lightly supported, and we can sit and stand with less effort.

But how do we apply this improved function to action? When, for instance, we lie down in a supported position to bring about a more lengthened condition in muscles that are habitually shortened, this will feel new and unfamiliar, making it difficult to apply to standing or sitting. Here we come up against a new and different

kind of problem—that of learning how to pay attention not just to the body but to the process of performing actions in a new way. When we have performed an action for a long period, our way of doing it comes to feel right, even if it is harmful and inefficient. If the shortened muscles begin to release so that the body is now working more efficiently, we will nevertheless find it difficult to perform the action in this new way, for the simple reason that it will feel unfamiliar and different. When we do things, we do what feels right and, even if we want to change our habits, don't want to do it the new way because we rely on the feeling of what is right and the new way feels wrong. To solve this problem, we have to explore the process of performing the action in a new and unfamiliar way. We have to pay attention to the steps involved in performing an action, not worrying about the end and focusing entirely on the means.

The ability to perform actions in a coordinated way, and to identify in the process what we are doing to interfere with this larger system, is an essential part of the process of learning to be aware. Yet in spite of the importance of preventing our harmful habits in activity, this process is almost completely ignored by the various awareness and somatic methods, which treat the problem of muscle tension as physical and almost entirely neglect the study of how we do things. The ability to observe what we are doing in activity and, on this basis, to prevent harmful tension, is essential to a model of awareness based not on treatment and exercise but on real knowledge of how the body works. In this book, we will examine this problem in some detail, breaking actions down so that we learn to perform them consciously, and learning how to stop as the basis for performing actions in a new way.

Learning how to perform actions consciously, as we will see in this book, is an essential stage in the process of becoming aware. When we suffer from a specific problem, we almost always assume that something is physically wrong and must be fixed or treated; it almost never occurs to us that the problem may be caused by our harmful and unconscious ways of doing things. When we restore our natural coordination and observe closely what we are doing in activity, however, we can clearly observe how we are actively interfering with the body and must ultimately figure out how to prevent this. Learning to do this—and in so doing to perform actions in a new and balanced way—is a higher form of awareness that goes far beyond simply making physical changes and leads, ultimately, to mastery of action, the ability to perform actions in a mindful way, and a greater degree of awareness and control in everything we do.

How to Use This Book

We have seen that, to be complete, a method of kinesthetic learning must be educational in the fullest sense, requiring a theoretical foundation in how the motor system works, how to restore it, and how to heighten awareness in the performance of actions based on this knowledge. In the following chapters, we will outline some of the steps involved in learning this.

How the Book Is Structured

The book is in four parts:

Part Two begins with the basic observation of movement patterns; learning to send messages to muscles; an introduction to the basic positions ("positions of mechanical advantage") that help to bring about an improved coordination of parts; and a look at the anatomical features that are essential to kinesthetic awareness.

Part Three describes how particular systems work (e.g., shoulders, legs, breathing, and so on) and how to direct these systems in order to bring about a more coordinated working of these systems.

Part Four examines basic activities such as sitting and standing, breathing and vocalizing, and walking.

Part Five describes more advanced procedures, as well as the key elements of paying attention that are a necessary part of kinesthetic awareness.

How Much Should I Practice?

The curriculum presented in this book is not a form of treatment or bodywork but a series of competencies that take time to learn. In order to make real progress, it is necessary to practice consistently, which means nearly every day. If you take a day off, it is useful to at least spend a few minutes lying down in the semi-supine position, which brings about beneficial changes over time.

Here There Are No "Rights" or "Wrongs"—Only a Process

In the following chapters, you will be asked to perform certain movements as the basis for making changes and heightening your kinesthetic awareness. These exercises, however, are not meant to be performed in a rote fashion, or with the idea that you are simply repeating movements or strengthening some part of the body. The goal is not to learn to do something in the usual sense but to learn how to think more clearly about how we use our bodies when we do things.

This same idea applies to postures and positions. Many of us have been taught how to correct bad posture by tucking the pelvis, sitting up straight, or adjusting the position of the rib cage and other parts of the body. But how can such corrections produce real change if, in the process, we assume a fixed posture and thus prevent further changes from happening? Such an attitude presupposes that, if something is wrong, we know what the problem is and what to do about it. The truth is that, in our misguided attempts to correct the problem, the cure is often worse than the sickness! To make real progress, we must put aside the notion of right postures and corrective movements and seek instead the new and unfamiliar experiences that will allow real change to take place over time. This is what we're after: a process that will lead to beneficial changes, not a series of correct postures or poses.

Confronting the Unfamiliar

Many of the movements outlined here, such as bending your knees or raising your arms at the elbows, are part of our everyday movement repertoire and in this sense seem simple enough to carry out. When you are asked to do them here, however, they may seem strangely unfamiliar—especially if you are given instructions for doing them in a new or different way. There are two reasons for this. First, we perform movements like bending our knees all the time, but we do so as part of actions that we are performing—picking something up off the floor, sitting in a chair, walking down the street. We may choose consciously to perform the action, but how we do it, for most of us, is almost entirely unconscious—until we start to pay attention to what we are doing, in which case the movement will all of sudden feel rather strange and unfamiliar. Do not worry about this; facing the unfamiliarity of simple movements is part of the process of learning to be more conscious of what we are doing, and will yield distinct benefits. With time,

the new way of performing the movements will become easier and more comfortable, and you will find that you are able to perform them more easily and efficiently.

The second reason is that even simple physical movements like bending your knees have a feeling attached to them, and how we move or perform the movement is guided, not so much by the control of specific muscles but by the feeling we associate with that particular movement. If we are asked to perform the movement in a new way, that familiar feeling is gone and, without feeling as a guide, we feel unsure of what we are doing and can even become confused. Again, do not be concerned or worried about this. Performing actions—and experiencing the new and unfamiliar feelings that accompany them—are a necessary part of the learning process. Take your time, repeating and experimenting with the movements until they become more familiar. With time, you will discover new things about how your body works, and gain increasing awareness and control over actions that were once quite unconsciously and harmfully performed.

Going Beyond Movements to the "Thinking" Behind the Movement

There is another reason why it is important to give yourself time to repeat —and become familiar with—the movements outlined here. If you learn, say, to bend your knees in a new way, this is a good starting point for performing a number of related actions in an improved way—but only a starting point. The goal in performing such movements is not simply to move but to think in a new way, and we need to become familiar enough with the movement that we can focus on the thinking behind it. The actions we are learning here, in other words, are not ends-in-themselves but a means to a further end, and you will have trouble discovering these further ends if you're stuck on the basics. This is why it is useful to give yourself time to repeat the actions until they become familiar and comfortable. When that happens, you will be able to go beyond the movements themselves and learn to think and direct parts in new ways and, at the same time, to notice the changes that happen when you do this.

Change Takes Time

When we receive treatments, stretch muscles, or exercise, we quite naturally expect improvements within a short time. The goal of the course of study laid out in the book, however, is not simply to provide relief or to treat muscles but to restore natural conditions that are part of a coordinated whole, and to gain an understanding of this coordinated system as the basis for becoming more conscious in action. Bringing about such changes takes time. Don't be discouraged if, after working for a period of days, nothing happens. Various changes will happen and, when they do, will be well worth the wait!

The Body In Action: A New Field

If you have suffered from a particular musculoskeletal difficulty and have sought help, very likely you have been shown particular exercises aimed at strengthening or relaxing specific muscles. Many of these exercises are based on the notion that, because particular muscles are overworked and tight, we need to contract opposing muscles in order to restore balance or correct posture. Other exercises are designed to stretch or release muscular tension, and still others are aimed at strengthening weak muscles.

We've seen, however, that in order to make sense of a complex field, we need to understand, not simply how to correct what we think is wrong, but how the body works in a positive sense. The shoulders, for instance, are intimately linked with upright posture. If your shoulders are tight, you must address not only the tension in the shoulders but the interference in upright posture as well. At the same time, the harmful tensions in the trunk and shoulder are linked with misdirected actions that must ultimately be identified. That is what this book is intended to

offer. If, for instance, your shoulders are tight, it isn't enough simply to stretch or release muscles but to understand, in a positive sense, how the shoulders are actually designed to work, to restore natural function, and to raise this process to a more conscious level.

In transforming a field that has, until now, been dominated by corrective methods, exercise systems, and therapeutic techniques, there is both good news and bad news. The bad news is that, unlike corrective methods, which produce immediate but superficial results, kinesthetic awareness takes time and work. The good news is that, in taking the time to study the body in action, you will acquire real knowledge about how your body works, the ability to perform actions skillfully, and the self-knowledge that comes from learning to be aware as a new and emergent stage in human development.

The Roadmap: The Stages of Learning

There is another advantage in articulating this subject as a field. When we learn to play violin or take up a martial art, we have a very good idea of exactly what we are learning. We expect to get better over time, and we know that our efforts will yield identifiable results. In karate, the mastery of movements is measured in terms of belts; in learning an instrument, one overcomes technical difficulties and learns to play increasingly difficult pieces. Not so with our current subject. Here we are not acquiring a skill, nor learning to do something in the usual sense of the word but identifying how we interfere with efficient action, using our kinesthetic sense to become aware of unnecessary muscle tension and becoming more generally conscious in activity. None of these skills—if they can be called skills at all—is easy to measure and, when learned, do not add up to recognizable competencies.

It does not follow, however, that the elements outlined in this book are vague and amorphous. We've seen that the body has an orderly design and, based on this, that we can approach this subject in an orderly fashion. Doing this is not a form of relaxation or an open-ended exploration but involves clear and concrete stages of learning and mastery. Based on real observation and knowledge of the body, we can go beyond mere exercises and gain real understanding about the body. This makes it possible to outline, in definable stages, the skills and competencies leading to improved coordination, balance, movement and skill. Here are some of the elements involved in the process:

1 Identify how we interfere with the PNR system

2 Learning how the PNR system is organized

3 Directing, non-doing, and support

4 Positions of mechanical advantage in activity

5 Restoring the PNR system

6 Understanding elements of the PNR system

7 Identification of habit and heightening of awareness in activity

8 Applying direction and inhibition in structured activities

9 Conscious prevention and control

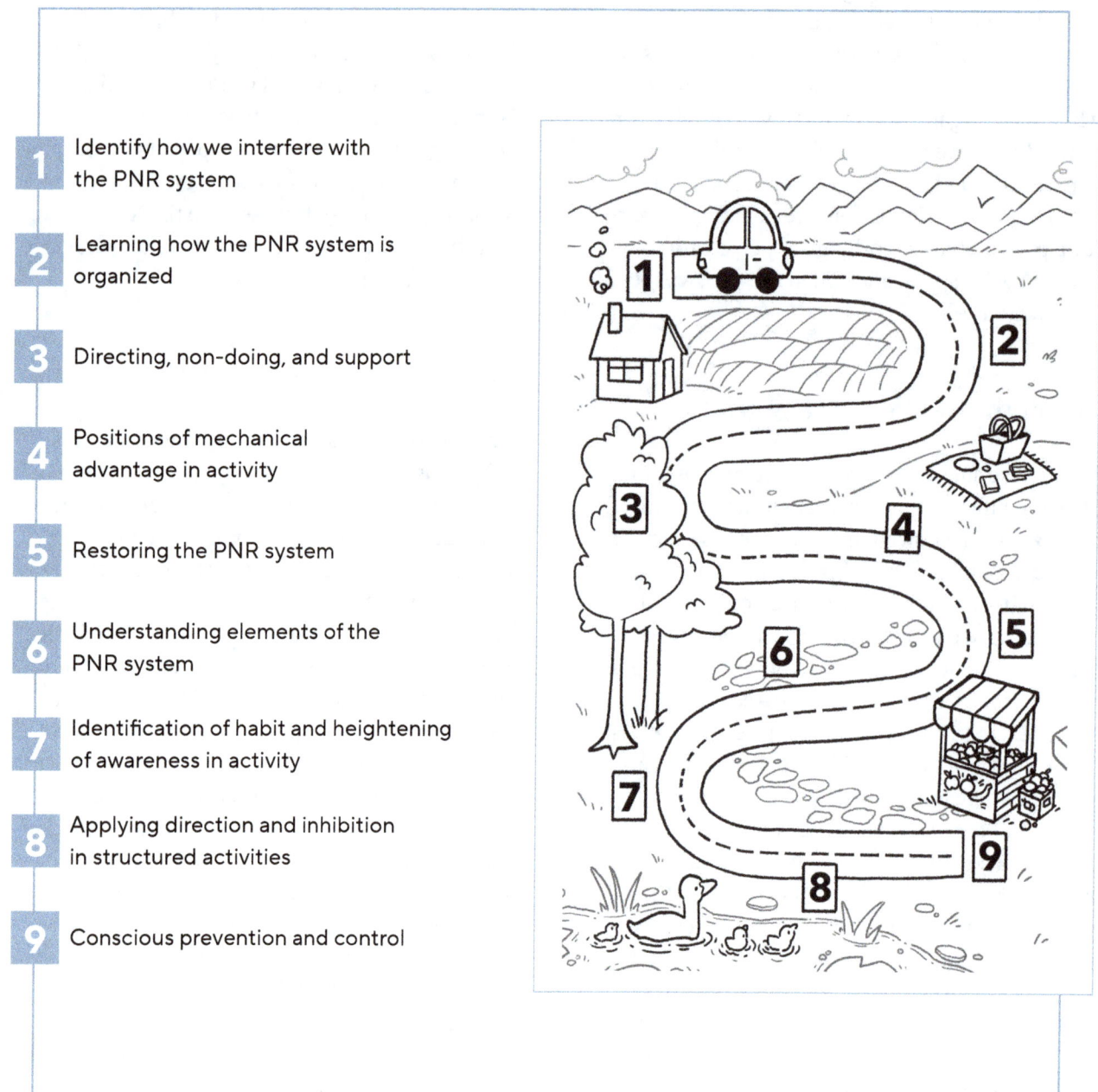

Fig. 1. Roadmap

The mastery of these steps involves both theoretical knowledge and practical know-how, as shown in the following:

Knowledge

- An understanding of the PNR system and how it works
- The PNR system, tensegrity, and muscle length
- Anatomical design of the PNR system
- The functional subsystems and how they work
- What it means to send conscious messages to muscles
- Positions of mechanical advantage
- The role of inhibition in activity
- The means-whereby principle in activity
- Mastery of actions (e.g., sit-to-stand, vocalizing, use of the arms, and walking)
- Conscious performance of action

Practices and skills (cognitive and kinesthetic)

- Observation
- The practice of non-doing
- Kinesthetic thinking and awareness
- The ability to sustain attention
- Explicit memory and the directive function of speech in carrying out procedures in sequence

Practices and skills (kinesthetic competencies)

- Self-observation of movement patterns
- How to identify and prevent habitual patterns of interference
- Development of kinesthetic thinking or "directing"
- Working with functional systems
- How to re-construct actions and perform actions intelligently
- How to apply this principle to motor skills

- Directing in positions of mechanical advantage to restore muscle length
- Identifying sub-systems (shoulder girdle, throat, extensors), how they are interfered with, and how to restore them

Resources

Because the procedures in the book represent skills that take time to master, a teacher with real knowledge and expertise in this field is an invaluable aid. The Dimon Institute offers in-person and online instruction in Sensorimotor Awareness (SMA); this includes guided work, discussion, and Q&A sessions. Our Instagram account also provides demonstrations and discussions. For more information, visit us at: www.dimoninstitute.org

Course calendar

This book provides the material for a year-long course of study, but the subject matter is presented topically and not in the order in which one actually learns. For a sample of the actual course curriculum, see the online courses offered on the Dimon Institute website (www.dimoninstitute.org).

Readings and Bibliography

In the book, we explore specific musculoskeletal systems that I have written about elsewhere in more depth. References to these books will be listed throughout, but here is the full list:

Alexander, F. Matthias. *The Use of the Self.* London: E. P. Dutton, 1942.

Dimon, Theodore. *Breathing and the Voice.* New York: Day Street Press, 1997.

Dimon, Theodore. *The Body in Motion.* Berkeley, CA: North Atlantic Books, 2011.

Dimon, Theodore. *Your Body, Your Voice.* Berkeley, CA: North Atlantic Books, 2014.

Dimon, Theodore. *Neurodynamics: The Art of Mindfulness in Action.* Berkeley, CA: North Atlantic Books, 2015.

Dimon, Theodore. *Anatomy in Action.* Berkeley, CA: North Atlantic Books, 2021.

The Basics

Observing the Pattern of Use

How the Body Works:
Observing How We Shorten In Stature

In this chapter we're going to begin, not by introducing procedures for being aware or reducing tension, but by observing how we move. Our ability to move is a remarkable feature of our upright human design. We are capable of a vast array of skilled actions and can control the body in incredibly precise ways. Perhaps because of this, few of us, if we begin to experience physical problems, question whether anything is wrong with how we are doing things but focus instead on what has gone wrong with the body and how to fix it.

As we will soon see, however, how we move is central to understanding how the body functions and how to be aware of ourselves in activity.

We come to this subject, all of us, with various preconceived ideas about muscles, about tension, about how the body works, and about how to go about gaining control over these things. If, for instance, we are experiencing back pain, many of us will attempt to relax our back muscles or to perform other exercises designed to reduce strain or to strengthen the back. But how do know which muscles are tight, and how much to relax them? How do we even know where the problem lies, if we have not actually observed what is happening with the musculoskeletal system and therefore lack the means of making some kind of diagnosis? The truth is that, when we suffer from physical problems, we are so focused on what we *think* the problem is that we forget to determine what the problem *actually* is.

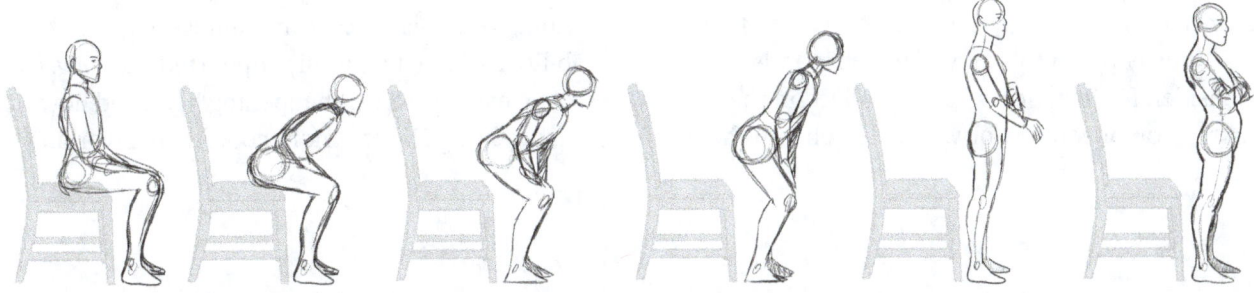

Fig. 1. *The pattern of use: sit-to-stand.*

This is where the study of movement comes in. When we observe movement—provided we know what to observe and how to observe—we can see that the body never works in parts but as a whole, and that what we think is specifically wrong is connected with the much larger question of how we interfere with this whole and how it can function naturally if we stop interfering with it. This last part—how the body is designed to function naturally as an organized whole—is critical because, without understanding something of this natural design, we cannot hope to understand the problem, or how to address it in a meaningful way. These are all crucial issues that must be addressed, at least in part, before we can hope to make real progress in understanding the question of how to become more aware in action.

Observing How We Move

The first movement I want to look at is the act of standing up from a sitting position, which we can see in Figure 1. In the sequence shown here we see a series of actions, but the act of standing from a sitting position can be broken down into two key actions: (a) coming forward in the chair in order to bring the trunk over our feet (*Fig. 2a*); (b) straightening the legs to stand fully upright (*Fig. 2b*). You can easily identify these two actions if you are sitting and take a moment to incline forward in the chair (that's the first action), and then come over your feet and straighten your legs to stand (that's the second action).

Because we sit and stand all day long, these actions will appear unremarkable, and we are likely to assume that there is nothing wrong with how we perform them. When we examine them more closely, however, it becomes apparent that few of us perform this movement efficiently. Consider, for instance, what is involved in the first action of coming forward in the chair. When

we are sitting, the trunk is naturally hinged at the hips so that, to come forward, all we need to do is to incline forward in the chair. In doing this, the head and trunk should move as one piece, and there is no reason that the head should change position in relation to the trunk, or that the shape of the trunk and spine should be altered in any way (*Fig. 2a*). But that is not what most of us do when we perform this movement. As we come forward in the chair, we retract the head, arching our back and tightening in the legs, using far more tension than is required to perform this action, and constricting the entire spine (*Fig. 3*).

Now look what happens at the second part of the movement. To finish standing, the only movement we need to make is to straighten our legs and bring our trunk to the upright position (*Fig. 2b*). But again, this is not what happens. As we straighten our legs to stand upright, most of us throw the rib cage and upper back backwards, going well past the vertical to the point that we are actually collapsing our rib cage and shortening in stature, pushing our hips forward and sinking into our legs (*Fig. 4*).

The second movement I want to look at is the reverse of the first one: sitting down from standing. Here again we must make two large-scale movements: lowering the trunk by bending at the hips, knees, and ankles (*Fig. 5a*) and then, when the trunk reaches the chair, coming backward from the hips to sit upright (*Fig. 5b*). But again this is not all that happens. To initiate the act of sitting down, our subject begins by pulling his head back and arching his back, shortening his spine and trunk. When he contacts the chair and begins to come back from the hips in order to sit fully upright, he throws his ribs back, again going further than is necessary so that he shortens his trunk, fixing his rib cage and interfering with his ability to sit in a naturally supported way (*Fig. 6*).

So exactly what is happening here, and how can we bring about a more coordinated working

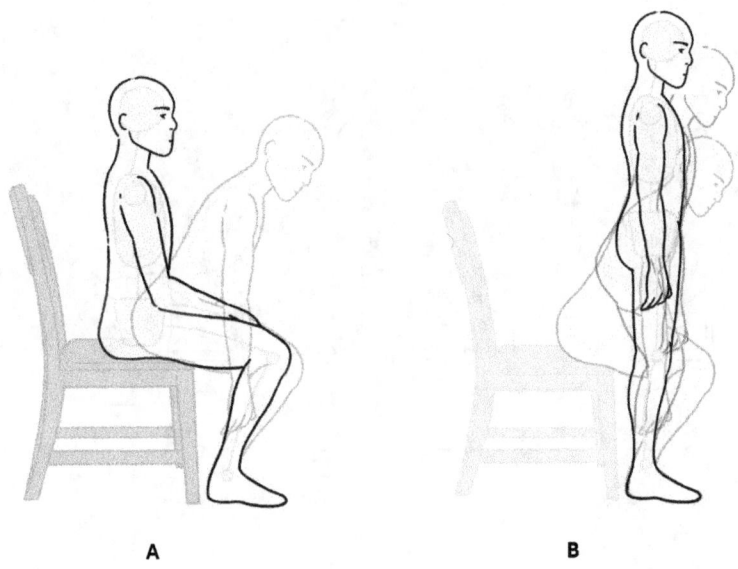

A   B

*Fig. 2a. Coming forward in chair by hinging at the hips; **b**. Straightening the legs to stand fully upright.*

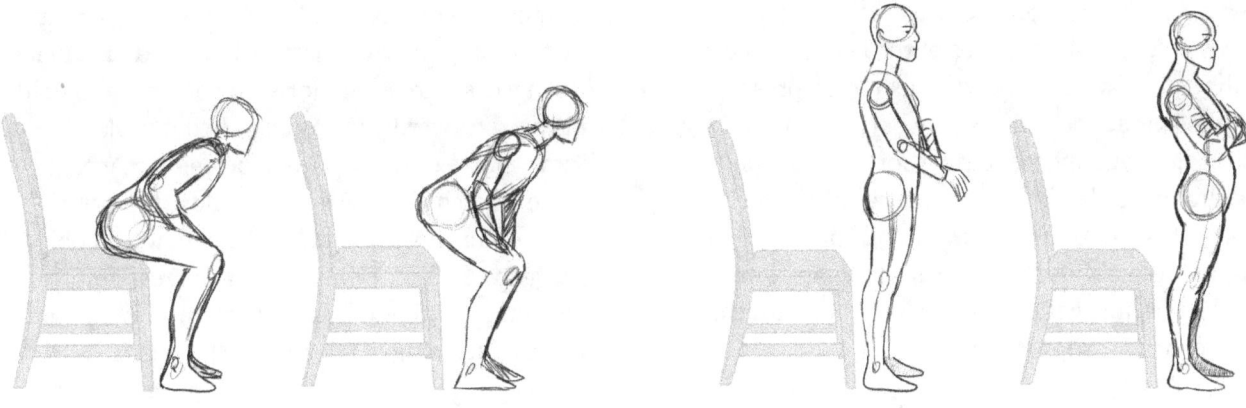

Fig. 3. Shortening in stature when beginning to stand from the sitting position.

Fig. 4. Shortening in stature when coming to fully upright standing.

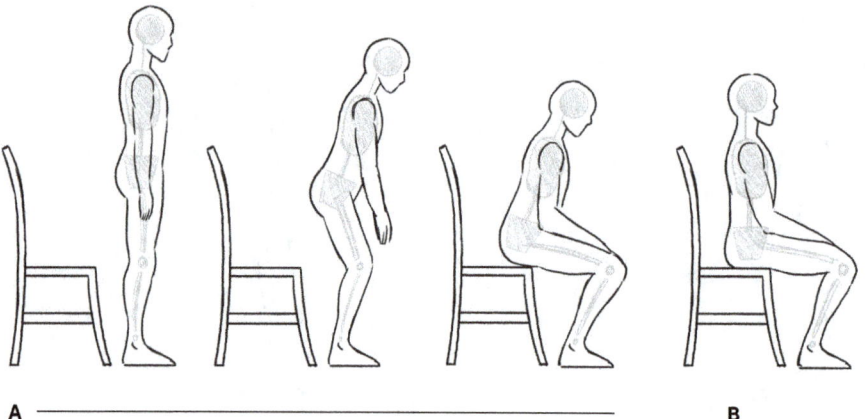

Fig. 5. Sitting from standing by (a) lowering the trunk to sit, and (b) coming back from the hips to fully upright sitting.

A ——————————————————————— B

of the body in action? The first thing we can say is that the pattern of shortening we are observing here is harmful in ways that are hard to appreciate. If you pull your head back by shortening the muscles of your neck, this in itself is not particularly harmful. If you do this habitually over many years, you will create chronic shortening that will not only cause the muscles of the neck to become habitually shortened but will also place pressure on the spine. The same is true of the spine and rib cage. If you momentarily shorten your spine by slumping, this in itself is not harmful. But doing this habitually will eventually place a huge amount of strain on the bones and joints, interfering not only with the spine itself but with the entire upright support system.

The second point to make is that the actions we are observing here are quite habitual and unconscious and are not easily changed. If, for instance, you pointed out these tendencies to someone and asked him to stop doing it, he would simply try to hold his head forward while continuing to pull it back. The result would be that, instead of improving matters he would only make them worse, creating more tension trying to hold his head forward even as he pulled it back. The same is true of the overall shortening that takes place when he stands up: he could attempt to improve his posture but, in the end, would only exaggerate what he was doing and create more tension by trying to hold himself in a better state while continuing to shorten in stature.

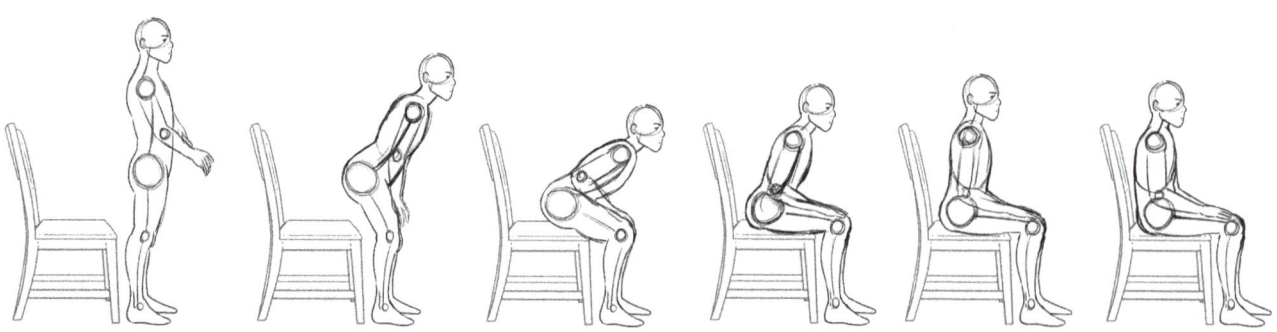

Fig. 6. Shortening in stature to sit in the chair.

The Primary Control of Use

How then do we improve this situation? To make sense of this, I want to focus on the first movement—that is, standing from the sitting position—because it is convenient for our purposes. The simple answer is that we must stop making the harmful movements that interfere with the body's natural function. If, for instance, we are able to stop pulling the head back when initiating the movement, the head will no longer press down upon the spine and the spine, in turn, can remain in a more lengthened state. It then becomes easier to incline at the hips because, instead of tightening and shortening to make this movement, the entire trunk will remain lengthened. The same principle applies to the final part of the movement. If, while coming to standing, we do not pull the head back or throw our ribs backward, we will remain more lengthened in stature with the head balanced nicely on the spine. In this more balanced state, there will be less pressure on the joints, a more lengthened posture, and less overall tension.

But these changes, simple as they are, are more than improvements in how we move and function. We saw in the introduction that, in order to raise an arm or perform some other movement, the developing child must first be able to support him or herself on two feet or while sitting. This upright posture is not simply a matter of holding the head up and balancing on the sit bones without falling over but requires muscle tone throughout the legs, hips, back, neck, and shoulders, functioning as a whole to maintain postural support. To perform any basic action, we do not simply engage muscles designated for that particular activity but, as a basic prerequisite, must first maintain support against gravity as a coordinated whole, as the basis for whatever specific actions are performed. This overall support is organized by the relationship of the head to the trunk, sometimes referred to as "the primary control," in which the trunk maintains lengthened support with the head balanced forward at the top vertebra of the spine (*Fig. 7*).

This organizing principle in movement was originally identified and described by F. Matthias Alexander, an actor who made a detailed study of his voice in order to overcome the tendency to become hoarse when he recited. Observing himself in front of a mirror to see what he was doing that might be causing his problem, he noticed that, when he vocalized, he pulled his head back, depressed his larynx, and gasped for breath.[5] He discovered that these tendencies were connected with a larger pattern of shortening in stature that involved not just his head and neck but his entire body and, after exploring ways of preventing this, concluded that, to use his voice properly, he needed "to maintain a lengthening of the stature" and that the head should go "forward and up"—a relationship of parts he called "the primary control" of using himself. Based on this discovery, Alexander developed a hands-on method, known today as the Alexander Technique, for bringing

---

5 Alexander, F. Matthias. *The Use of the Self*. London: Victor. Gollanz, 1996.

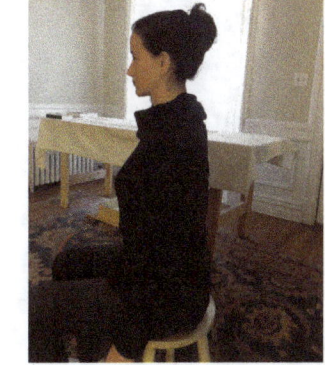

Fig. 7. The organization of the neck, head, and trunk: "the primary control of use."

about more efficient posture and for facilitating movement based on the relationship of the head and trunk.

But there is much more to Alexander's discovery of a "primary control" than a means of improving posture and facilitating movement. As we saw in Chapter 1, the body is designed to function automatically and, over time, becomes interfered with. The harmful tensions we have observed are not simply a harmful pattern that interferes with posture and movement but represent a disturbance in how the body is designed to function. Simply improving movement patterns will not restore this system if, as a result of chronic misuse, it has become interfered with. This is why, although we are observing the movement of sitting down in a chair, our goal here is not simply to improve upon this particular movement but to understand in a more general way how we interfere with the musculoskeletal system and how it is designed to function in a coordinated manner. We saw in the introduction that the way muscles function, and how they act upon bones to maintain posture and produce movement, play a crucial role in the study of movement and motor science. As we can see from our initial observations, however, we don't use muscles singularly but as a whole, and the subject of movement—and the various methods for improving muscular and movement patterns—have suffered from a lack of understanding of how the body functions as a whole in movement. The observations we have made here demonstrate very clearly that the body does not work in parts but as a coordinated whole and that, if we want to stop tightening particular muscles, we need to address the larger pattern of which this tightening is a part. Understanding how this larger system is designed to work naturally so that the parts function well, as we'll see throughout this book, is essential to a method of awareness that makes it possible to use this larger system efficiently, to stop interfering with it, and to become more generally aware of what we are doing in activity.

OBSERVING HOW WE SHORTEN IN STATURE

The purpose of the following exercises is to explore this subject in the spirit of a laboratory experiment. The goal here is not to simply carry out procedures or movements, as in a yoga or movement class, but to observe and see for ourselves how we do things. We are accustomed to learning procedures without knowing what they're for, or told how to perform particular actions, and corrected over and over again until the teacher determines that we are doing them correctly. But such mechanical procedures cannot produce real understanding, or give us real insight into the nature of movement. The goal here is make our own observations and draw our own conclusions, learning about how we function and making our own discoveries in the process.

Sit-to-stand: observing the act of getting out of a chair

Let's begin by observing what happens just as you begin to stand from the sitting position.

1. Sitting normally in the chair, notice how your head is balanced on top of your spine.

2. To come out of the chair, you must bring your entire head and trunk forward, so it will of course be necessary for the head to move in space (see *Fig. 2a*). But can you see what happens to your head in relation to your trunk as you move?

3. Sitting normally in the chair, stand up once more and observe what happens in your trunk. Do you begin to arch your back, tighten your ribs or collapse as you prepare to stand?

4. Finally, do you tighten your legs in preparation to stand up, even before you have actually come onto your feet?

Observing these actions in ourselves is not easy, especially if you are doing this for the first time. Remember that, at this early stage, it is not necessary to arrive at any definite conclusions but only to make some initial observations, to gain experience in observing yourself, and to begin to appreciate that different body parts must coordinate, or work together, to produce efficient action.

Exercise 2

Observing shortening in stature by using the wall

In this exercise, we will use the wall as a reference point for identifying what happens to parts of the body when we stand in our habitual way.

1. Stand with your back to a wall, with your heels 3 or 4 inches from the wall (*Fig. 8a*). Gently fall backward so that you are leaning against the wall, noticing what part of your body makes contact with the wall. If your upper back contacts the wall first, this means that your hips are forward of your upper back, which you have thrown backwards as you leaned against the wall.

2. Start over, but this time, see to it that your pelvis comes back so that, as you fall back against the wall, your upper back and pelvis are able to make contact with the wall at the same time (*Fig. 8b*).

3. Let your knees go so that you lower your weight, keeping your pelvis and back in contact with the wall (*Fig. 8c*).

4. Without altering the relative position of your upper back and pelvis, gently push yourself forward from the wall so that you are no longer leaning against the wall but balanced over your feet with your knees bent (*Fig. 8d*).

5. Come up very slowly from this position, taking care not to alter the position of your pelvis or trunk (*Fig. 8e*).

6. Now go into your habitual way of standing but, as you do so, observe very closely what happens in your trunk (*Fig. 8f*). Can you detect what happens when you go back to your habitual way of standing?

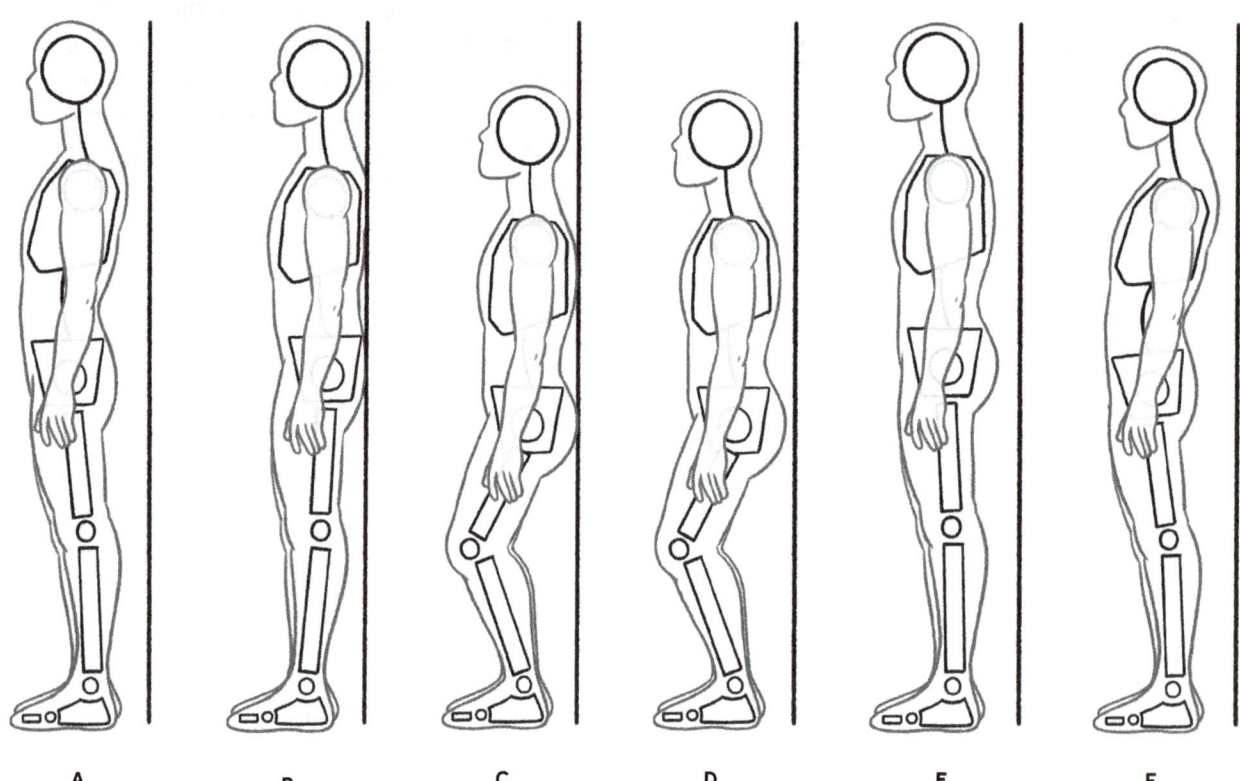

A   B   C   D   E   F

Fig. 8. Observing shortening in stature by using the wall: a. Standing; b. Falling back against wall; c. Bending knees to lower weight; d. Coming away from wall; e. Straightening legs; f. Returning to habitual way of standing.

Exercise 3

Identifying specific elements of shortening

In the previous exercise, we observed the general tendency to shorten in stature as we come to the fully erect standing position. In this exercise, we focus on specific regions as a way of seeing more clearly what this involves.

1. Repeat steps 8a through 8e above.

2. Go back to your habitual way of standing, and this time see if you can you notice any of the following:

   a. Do you stiffen your neck or pull your head back (top arrow)?

   b. Do you throw your upper back backwards or raise your chest slightly (middle arrow)?

   c. Do you throw your hips forward (lower arrow)?

   d. Do you sink into or brace your legs?

Although most of us tend to shorten in stature when we are standing or performing other actions, we are largely unaware that we are doing so. By observing ourselves more closely, we can begin to see that, in even the simplest actions, we tend to interfere with bodily movement.

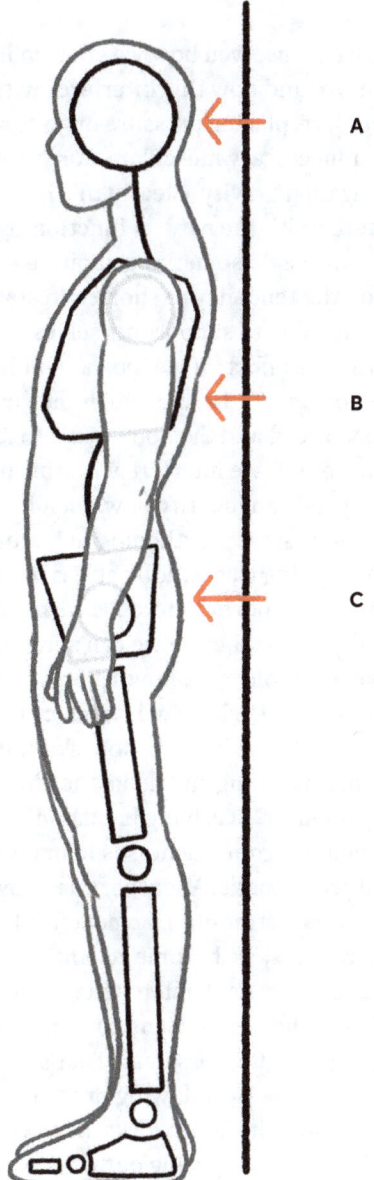

Fig. 9. Identifying specific elements of shortening.

LENGTHENING IN STATURE

So far, we have observed how we shorten in stature when we move and how this interferes with our natural support, placing pressure on joints and requiring unnecessary muscular effort to support ourselves against gravity. Clearly this is harmful and interferes with the natural functioning of the body. But can we do something about it—that is, can we stop the tendency to shorten in stature so that we are able to support ourselves against gravity with less effort? If we look at children, their bodies are long and lithe and, when they move, the head leads upward and the body tends to lengthen and not shorten. If we interfere with this natural lengthening and can identify how, then it must also be possible to restore lengthening in stature, which is what we're going to now look at. Trying this out for ourselves is important because we must first identify the problem before we can solve it. Doing what we've been told, or following prescribed procedures that we believe will produce beneficial results, is of little use if we do not take responsibility for what is wrong and make the effort to do something about it. Receiving hands-on or therapeutic guidance from teachers is in many ways even more problematic. A teacher can show us how things can work better or make beneficial changes but, in the process, we become reliant on their guidance and, in the end, fail to take responsibility for identifying the problem and for making the necessary changes for ourselves. That's why we're beginning here, not by following procedures but by observing how the body works, how we interfere with it, and then figuring out what we can do about it.

Exercise 1

"Forward and up" of the head

We've seen that, when we sit down in a chair or perform other actions, we tend to pull the head back and down. In this exercise, we will explore what it means for the head to go "forward and up."

1. Stand normally, and gently nod your head up and down. When we pull the head back, the chin goes up; when we put the head forward, the chin goes down. See if you can nod the head forward so that the head is not pulled back but is tending to go forward.

2. Again nod your head up and down. Now nod your head forward and keep nodding it in this direction. Do you notice that, at a certain point, the head will begin to go downward? Taken too far, in other words, the forward nodding takes the head down.

3. See if you can now put the head forward but, at the same time, allow it to come up in space. You are now putting your head forward and up.

Can you distinguish between pulling your head back and putting it forward? Can you tell that, when you nod your head forward, it can also go upward, taking pressure off the spine and allowing the trunk to lengthen?

Exercise 2

Lengthening in stature: the pelvis

When we shorten in stature, we put the hips forward and sink into the legs. A good way to identify these tendencies is to lean back against the wall so that, with the pelvis and upper back in contact with the wall, your trunk and hips will be in the same vertical alignment and you will be able to identify when you put the hips forward and sink into the legs.

1. Standing with your back to a wall, fall back so that both your upper back and pelvis make contact with the wall. Do not force your head to touch the wall; it should remain somewhat forward of the wall.

2. Allow your knees to bend so that you lower yourself in space, keeping your upper back and pelvis in contact with the wall.

3. Push off from the wall without disturbing the relative position of your head and trunk, and then gently straighten your legs. You will now be standing with your trunk poised over your pelvis.

4. Taking particular notice of your pelvis, go into your habitual standing position. Did you notice that, to stand "normally," you brought your pelvis forward and sank into your legs? Can you see that, when you sink into the legs, the legs become braced and stiffened?

5. Try the exercise one more time, falling against the wall, bending your knees, coming forward and standing. Begin to go into your habitual standing posture but, this time, stop and allow your pelvis to stay back. You will now see that, to stand, there is no need to bring the pelvis forward and that, with the pelvis remaining back, you are more lengthened in stature.

When we bring the pelvis forward and sink into the legs, the legs become braced and shortened. If you can identify this as it begins to happen and prevent it, you may notice that you are no longer bracing your legs, which in turn allows your legs to work more freely and to support the trunk with less effort.

Exercise 3

Lengthening in stature: the rib cage

A key component of shortening in stature is to throw the ribs backwards and to raise the chest. When we observe this in real time, we can identify and prevent it, which produces a more lengthened state.

1. Repeat steps 1-3 in Exercise 2 above.

2. Taking particular notice of your rib cage, go into your habitual standing position. Can you see that, to stand "normally," you bring your upper torso backward and slightly raise your chest?

3. Now start over, but this time, notice when you begin to do this and, instead, allow your rib cage to remain more balanced or poised over your pelvis. Can you see that you are now more lengthened in stature?

The Primary Control of Use

We have now identified some of the key elements involved in shortening in stature, which involves pulling the head back and down, throwing the rib cage backward, and sinking into the hips and legs. By identifying and preventing each of these movements, we can bring about a more lengthened state, which is a positive condition that represents a more natural and coordinated working of the body as a whole. This, as we saw earlier, is not something you can "do" but comes about as the indirect result of identifying how you shorten in stature and preventing this.

It is easy to assume that the harmful actions we have observed here apply only to upright posture and large movements such as bending and sitting down in a chair. But you have only to observe what happens when you raise your arms to type at a computer while sitting in a chair, or when you take a breath and speak a few words, to see that this harmful pattern is present in any action we perform, and constitutes a misuse of the musculoskeletal system.

Learning to observe, as we have begun doing here, is a necessary first step in gaining control over our actions, but it is only the beginning. Because most of us have interfered with the musculoskeletal system, it is critical to understand how the body is designed to work, to identify what we are doing to interfere with it, and to take time to reinstate this system, as we will do in the following chapters. In the process, we will gain a greater command over the body, becoming more kinesthetically aware so that we can learn to perform actions in a more conscious way.

The Organization of Awareness

All of us, at one time or another, have experienced tight and constricted muscles. Perhaps because we are able to relax specific muscles, and because we can stretch or treat them directly, it is easy to assume that we can solve the problem of muscle tension by practicing forms of awareness, stretching, or massage designed to directly alleviate muscle tension. However, such concepts are insufficient and misguided for at least two reasons. First, a muscle that is tense and constricted is not simply "tight" but, during everyday activities, is receiving a continuous stream of messages from the nervous system to contract, which is why the muscle will continue to tighten up once we have stopped relaxing or stretching it. To address this, we have to do more than simply treat the muscle; we must learn to stop sending these messages so that the muscle can stop contracting and return to its naturally lengthened state— a process we referred to in Chapter 1 as "directing." And we must learn to do this not only when we are still but during activity. All of this requires, not simply that we relax or stretch muscles but that we learn to heighten our kinesthetic awareness as the basis for using our muscles at a more conscious level.

Second, muscles function within a larger whole and are designed to lengthen in the context of this larger whole. If, for instance, you are shortening the muscles of your neck, it is no use trying to relax these muscles as long as you are sitting in a collapsed posture with the head pulled back, in which case the collapsed position of the head and trunk will make it all but impossible for the neck muscles to work properly. If, in contrast, the head and trunk are in a supported or lengthened state, the muscles of the neck will have a chance to let go between the parts to which they connect. In short, the only way to restore natural muscle function is to provide the kind of support muscles and connective tissues need in order to let go.

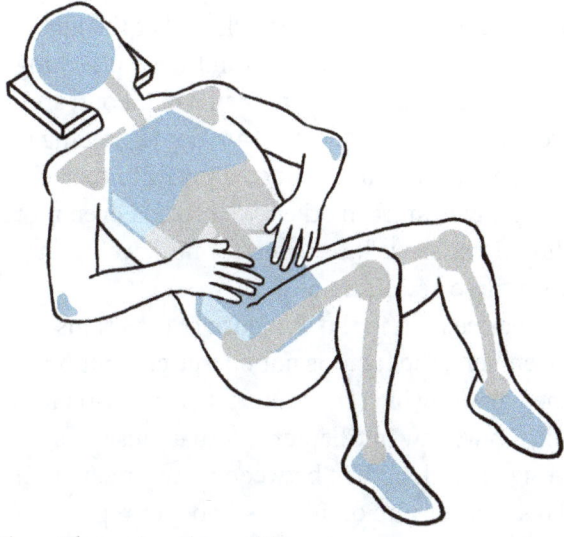

Fig. 1. The semi-supine position.

The Semi-Supine Position

One of the most useful things we can do to bring about the natural working of the muscular system is to place the body in a position that will provide optimal advantage for muscles to let go and for the system to begin to work properly as a whole. The simplest and most basic way to do this is to lie down in the semi-supine position, which provides almost complete body support while giving the neck, back, shoulders, and leg muscles a chance to lengthen and release (*Figs. 1 and 2*). It is important to be clear that lying down in this way must not be used as a relaxation exercise but as a way of bringing about tone and release in muscles that are habitually contracted. This requires energy and not collapse and, although it results in a lowered state of nervous energy, it must also be associated with a heightened state of alertness, muscle tone, and vitality. A corollary of this principle is that you must not lie on a cushy mattress or foam mat (which encourages collapse), but on a fairly hard surface such as a carpeted floor which supports the body properly.

Five key areas of the body bear weight in the semi-supine position: the occiput, or back of the skull, the upper back, the back of the pelvis, and the feet (*Fig. 1, blue sections*). The support of these key areas will allow the muscles of the neck, back, trunk and limbs to let go. For this to happen, we have to direct the parts in such a way that the muscles let go so that the parts go away from each other. In particular, we want to see to it that we are not tightening the neck so that the head can go forward and out; we want to stop arching the back so that it can lengthen and fill out; and we want to see to it that we are not tightening the legs so that the knees can go away from the pelvis and away from each other. We can add even more directions, as we'll see later; for now, we'll start with these key directions.

Notice that, in the sequence of directions given here, the focus is not on muscles but on the parts to which they connect. The reason for this, as we saw in Chapter 1, is that muscles are designed to lengthen between bony attachments. This relationship of muscles to bones represents a central organizing principle of muscular

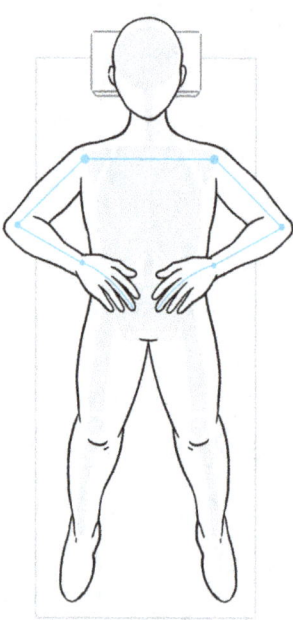

Fig. 2. The semi-supine position.

function. Muscles become chronically contracted, but simply trying to relax them will do little to rectify the situation if we do not understand, to begin with, how muscles and bones function together as an organized whole—that is, with the head going forward and up out of a lengthening trunk, and with the legs letting go into length. Thinking of the key segments of the body and how they relate to each other provides a framework for knowing what we are actually trying to accomplish when we are trying to be aware of muscles, and for thinking constructively about how to achieve this goal.

Although the semi-supine position provides almost complete body support, there is one exception to this—namely the legs, which will tend to flop outwards when we let go in the thigh muscles. To counter this, we have to think of sending the knees up to the ceiling so that, when the thigh muscles release, the legs let go into length instead of falling to the sides. How this can happen may not be immediately obvious and will take time, but as the other directions work, this will become clearer. The point is that all the directions begin to work together so that muscular release in different parts of the body become integrated into a whole, which in turn informs the parts.

The Principle of Non-Doing

Although many of us believe we can address tension by stretching or actively trying to relax our muscles, it is essential to recognize at the outset that we cannot establish proper muscle length by performing actions, correcting what we think is wrong, assuming postures or positions, or by forcing the body in any way. We must learn to be quiet and to stop doing anything so that the body can naturally right itself, which it is designed to do if we give the muscles a chance to lengthen. This requires an attitude of non-doing.

But what is non-doing? Sometimes people speak of non-doing as if it is a form of relaxation, which of course is true to the extent that we are stopping and giving ourselves time to do nothing. But the goal of practicing non-doing is not simply to relax or quiet down but to give muscles a chance to release into length, which is quite different from relaxation because it requires a certain kind of energy, a toning up of muscles that cannot be achieved through relaxation.

Another reason why it is crucial to practice non-doing is that, unless we stop the habitual tightening of muscles, they cannot release. We think that when we are relaxing or doing nothing, our muscles are inactive when in fact they are often contracting unconsciously. The only way to prevent this is by coming to a full stop and, by lying or sitting in a supportive position, to remain quietly alert, and to make sure we are doing nothing, so that this muscular activity can cease.

This cessation of activity, however, cannot happen immediately but takes time. When we lie down, at first it will seem as if nothing is happening because muscles that are chronically shortened do not want to let go. It is only when we have been lying quietly for some days, patiently asking for things to happen, that muscles will begin to release; when this happens, we begin to realize that we are actively tightening muscles and that our job is to stop doing this. This requires an attentive attitude because whenever we become distracted, our muscles will begin to tighten again, and our job is to notice this and to remind them to let go.

Anyone who has engaged in this practice knows that non-doing is a subtle art that runs counter to all forms of doing, bodywork, and exercise. Even when we try to relax muscles, we aren't really stopping. We may get release of some kind, we may produce changes that make us feel better, but the underlying chronic activity that keeps muscles from truly releasing, from letting go into length and from allowing the postural system to work as a reflex system, will persist. To overcome this chronic, unconscious activity, we have to make sure that we stop worrying, holding, and tightening in muscles. For many of us, this is a difficult step to take because we want to change things, to work at things, to do something to make things better, whereas non-doing requires that we stop trying to change things and, instead, allow things to work entirely by themselves. This is a practice that takes time; if we don't do it every day and with real clarity of purpose, we can't expect to command the working of the postural system as the foundation upon which this work is based.

Why the Semi-Supine Position?

We have seen that, when we lie down in the semi-supine position, the support provided by the ground encourages muscles to let go into length. But why lie in the semi-supine and not fully supine position, and why it is necessary to place books under the head? When the legs are fully extended, they tend to pull on the pelvis, which exaggerates the lumbar curve of the spine. At the same time, the head is thrown back, which causes the neck muscles to shorten. This is why it is important to put the knees up and to place a pile of books under your head. Putting the knees up reduces the lumbar curve of the spine, and supporting the head with books helps the neck muscles to lengthen and prevents the pulling back of the head. The books should be high enough to prevent the neck muscles from being shortened and the head from being pulled back, but not so high that the throat is pinched or the neck over-stretched. Both of these things encourage lengthening and release of the muscles of the neck, trunk, shoulders, and legs. As mentioned earlier, it is also best, when practicing the semi-supine exercise, to lie on a carpet or firm mat because this type of surface will provide good support for your head, your upper back, and your pelvis.

Exercise 1

Directing the parts

1. Lying in the semi-supine position, take a moment to be quiet. Don't try to change anything; take a moment to look at the ceiling without trying to do or change anything.

2. Take a moment now to notice the parts of your body that are supported on the ground, as shown in *Fig. 1*. This includes your feet, your pelvis, your upper back, your head, and your elbows.

3. See to it that you are not tightening the muscles at the back of your neck. It helps if you think of allowing the books to support your head so that you are not pulling your head onto the books. Also, make sure you are not holding your head off the books, so that you are allowing the books to fully support your head.

4. Think of allowing your head to come out of your back so that your back can lengthen and fill out. Do not try to move or position your head; as you release your neck muscles, it may feel as if your head is starting to come out of your back. At the same time, your back will tend to fill out on the floor.

5. See to it that you are not tightening in your hips and thighs so that your knees can come out of your hips and back. If your legs tend to flop outwards, think instead of your knees pointing up to the ceiling and let them go in this direction, or into length. As the other parts of the body work better, the thighs will let go as a continuation of the lengthening of the back so that the upward direction of the knees will become part of a total pattern.

You have now organized your awareness to include the body as a whole. When we suffer from discomfort in a particular area of the body, we often think we know what the problem is. But we must organize our awareness not according to our idea of what we think the problem is but according to how the body is actually designed to work as a whole.

It is important to remember that lying down in the semi-supine position is not a relaxation exercise—that is, it is not meant to bring about a state of complete relaxation but a toned, lengthened condition of the muscles. To this end, one must remain alert throughout the process. If you find you are getting sleepy, take a rest, but do not confuse resting with the process of giving directions, which is a discipline that requires an alert, aware state of mind. The semi-supine exercise is essentially a mindfulness practice, but one with a very definite physiological goal.

When you have spent some time in the semi-supine position and are ready to resume normal activity, do not get up suddenly by doing a sit-up and tightening the flexors on the front of the body, which will defeat the entire purpose of the exercise. Instead, roll gently onto your side, taking your time and using the books to support your head like a pillow so that you will now be lying comfortably on your side. Begin to face down to the ground and get your arms beneath you so that, instead of using your abdominal muscles and tightening in your ribs to get up, you can gently push yourself up into a sitting or crawling position. Then rise slowly onto your feet.

When you are standing, take a moment to come to your full stature. Notice your breathing, your legs, your back, your neck and shoulders. Do you feel different? Can you notice any changes in your body? Are you more calm?

"DIRECTING" IS A FORM OF THINKING

We've seen that muscles are designed not simply to contract but to lengthen between skeletal parts and therefore to contract in the context of length. This relationship of muscle to bone is key not only to understanding how muscles are designed to function but also how we can influence them with our awareness. In the same way that we can "tell" a muscle to contract, we can tell the muscle to stop contracting, provided we understand how it can lengthen between its bony contacts.

To give an example of this, consider the flexor muscles of the forearm, which flex the fingers and hand. These muscles can become quite contracted and shortened because we do so much gripping with the fingers and thumb. This is easy to see if you contrast the hand of an adult to that of a young child: the child's hand will be open and relaxed because the muscles of the forearm have not become chronically shortened; in contrast, the fingers and thumb of the average adult tend to be tightened and shortened because the forearm muscles have become chronically tense.

Given this situation, how would you get these muscles to release? The following exercise will serve as an introduction to the kind of work that will be presented throughout this course:

Exercise 2

Direction and support

1. Sit in front of a table and place your right elbow on the table so that your hand is at roughly eye height. Straighten your fingers so that they are pointing upwards.

2. Now, think about relaxing your fingers. You'll see that, once you relax your fingers, they will curl up. This is because muscle tissue, left to itself, will tend to shorten—a fact that is well known to nurses who care for convalescing patients, whose muscles will shorten and atrophy when they are sedentary for long periods, and who must be periodically moved.

3. Now rest your entire forearm on the table surface with your palm facing down, and gently extend your fingers so that your palm and fingers are in contact with the table. Because your fingers are now being supported by the surface of the table, they cannot curl up but, instead, are gently stretched. If you now think of the fingers "pointing" or extending gently, the muscles of the forearm will begin to let go or to lengthen between the elbows and fingers. The supported position of the fingers and hand not only prevents the forearm muscles from shortening but actually helps them to lengthen.

As we can see in this exercise, the key to releasing the muscles of the forearm is not to focus directly on muscles but to give them a chance to lengthen in the context of bodily support. To accomplish this, the hand and fingers must be supported in relation to the forearm, which prevents the muscles from shortening. This gives the muscles a much better chance of lengthening between their bony attachments—a change that can be felt as an increased liveliness and tone in the muscles, joints, and connective tissues. For this to happen, we must focus not on the muscles but on the parts to which they connect, directing the parts in such a way that the muscles can lengthen and release. This is the meaning of the word "direction" as we use it in this book: to consciously project messages to muscles by thinking of the body parts to which they connect, while being sure not to manipulate or control specific muscles or body parts.

As we'll see throughout this book, two key principles must be kept in mind when we direct parts of the body. The first is that, because muscles are constantly receiving messages to contract, we must come to a full stop in order to give them a chance to stop contracting. It is no use expecting something new to happen if we have not stopped doing what we have always done. The second is that, to restore natural muscle length, we must stop trying to relax or control muscles directly and instead allow the parts to which the muscles contract to move away from each other, which indirectly allows the muscles to work properly. When we direct the various parts of the body in this way, we are organizing our awareness in a constructive way that will restoring healthy muscle tone. Knowing how to put these principles into practice is more than a kinesthetic method for relieving muscle strain but represents a new approach to the problem of muscle function based on knowledge of how muscles work and the role of kinesthesia in restoring normal function.

Positions of Mechanical Advantage

A position of mechanical advantage is a skeletal configuration that encourages lengthening in stature and a corresponding release of muscles into length. For muscles to lengthen, we must learn to direct, or to send messages to muscles telling them to let go. But doing this in a haphazard way will not work; we must give ourselves as much mechanical help and support as possible. If, for instance, you are slumped in your chair, it is no use trying to bring about release in muscles by giving your directions because your trunk will be heavy and collapsed and cannot let go into length. To lengthen, we must provide ourselves with support so that, when we direct muscles, they have a chance of letting go. A position of mechanical advantage is a skeletal configuration that helps this to happen.

In the last chapter we saw that, when we direct, we want to provide the optimal conditions for muscles to lengthen. This means, in a very general way, that the spine must be lengthened and not unduly curved and the back supported and not collapsed, as when we lie in the semi-supine position. This position not only encourages length in the muscles but also gives us points of reference so that, when we direct, we can be very specific about what body parts to direct and where we want them to go. This allows muscles to release and lengthen between their bony attachments, so that they can perform their function in the context of length.

We have to remember, though, that the purpose of directing and restoring muscle length is not simply to produce healthier, more lengthened muscles but to establish a more balanced use of the system in activity. The following positions of mechanical advantage do exactly that: they allow us to begin to use the system, with our muscles lengthening and the parts well coordinated, in a very active and dynamic way. In the inclined monkey position, for instance, we are not only lengthening muscles; we are lengthening them in a way that can be used for all kinds of actions: sitting and standing, bending, throwing and swinging, lifting weight, and so on. In this position, then, we not only release muscles and restore the working of the PNR system; we release muscles so that they can function properly in activity.

In this chapter, we will explore two positions of mechanical advantage; later in the book, we'll explore ways of utilizing these positions in basic activities such as sitting, standing, and using our arms.

THE VERTICAL STANCE

One of the simplest positions of mechanical advantage is the vertical stance, the basic position used in the martial arts in which we lower our center of gravity by bending at the knees. When standing normally, most of us shorten in stature and sink into the hips and legs. In the vertical stance, the knees are bent in such a way that, instead of shortening, the trunk and spine tend to lengthen with the head going forward and up, and the hips, instead of sinking into the legs, tend to work with the back. To learn this position, let's look first at how we assume the position; then we'll look at the thinking process behind the position.

Exercise 1

Going into vertical stance

1. Place your feet about shoulder width apart so that you will be able to bend at your knees without jamming your hips. Be aware of your feet on the ground and, without lifting your chest, come up to your full stature (*Fig. 1a*).

2. Think of releasing the knees to bend forward so that you lower your trunk (*Fig. 1b*).

3. If you have controlled your legs and lowered yourself slowly, come up again and let your knees go the same distance but a bit more quickly so that you are now releasing your knees away to lower your weight rather than controlling the movement and lowering yourself slowly.

4. Notice if you have brought your pelvis forward or if you have put too much pressure on your knees (*see Fig. 2 on opposite page for more details*). If you have, it means that you are sinking into your hips and legs and the leg muscles will not be able to lengthen. Come up to normal standing and perform the exercise again but with an added step, as follows:

5. Come back slightly onto your heels, letting your pelvis come back slightly. You should now be balanced over your feet. You may also notice that you are no longer sinking into your legs. The different parts of your body should now be working in a more oppositional way, so that your knees are tending to go away from your hips, your hips from your knees, and your trunk is lengthened.

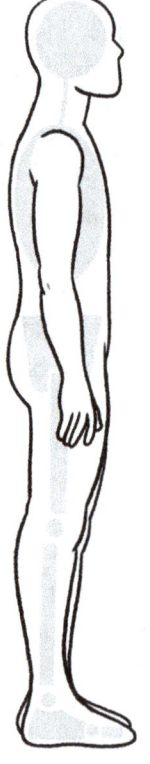

A   B

Fig. 1a-b. The vertical stance.

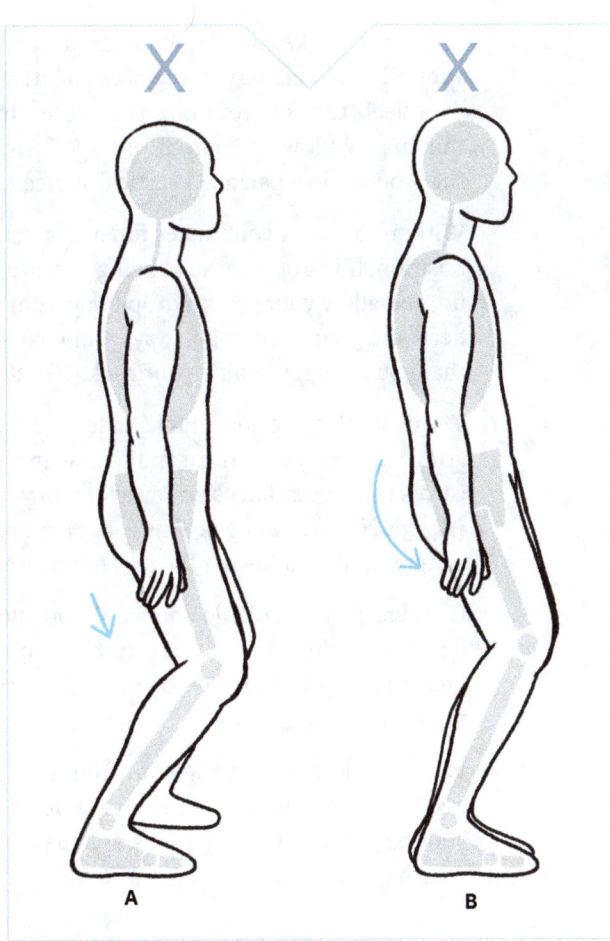

Fig. 2. *Going into vertical stance: **a.** Notice if you have dropped into your knees and, if so, come back up and see if you can let your knees go without putting pressure on them; **b.** Notice if you have brought your pelvis forward and, if so, see if you can let your knees go forward without bringing your pelvis with them; **c.** Balanced vertical stance.*

Exercise 2

Directing in vertical stance

Once you are in a balanced position, you are ready to give your directions, as follows:

1. Think of allowing your head to go forward and up and, without tucking your pelvis, allow your buttocks to drop away from your head so that you are allowing your back to lengthen (*Fig. 3b*).

You should now feel the length of your back from the base of your head right down to your sacrum and buttocks. This means that you are allowing the muscles of the lower back to release slightly, and that the muscles of your neck and back are tending to lengthen. Performing this movement, then, isn't simply about posture or body mechanics; it is intended to bring about muscle length through the opposition of body parts, as a basic principle governing body support.

Exercise 3

Vertical stance with added directions

When you have spent time directing in the vertical stance try adding the following directions:

1. With your feet slightly apart, come to your full stature. Take time to allow length between your hips and head (*Fig. 3a*).

2. See to it that you are not tightening in the buttocks, thighs, behind your knees, and your ankles. Allow your knees to release forward so that you go into the vertical stance. Again, do not go slowly by controlling your legs but let your knees go

all at once. Make sure you have not dropped into your hips; if necessary, come back slightly onto your heels to allow your hips to release while still thinking of allowing your knees to go forward so that you are in a balanced vertical stance (*Fig. 3b*).

3. Without bending your knees further or changing position, think of your head going forward and up, and allow your seat to drop away from your head and your head to go away from your seat so that you are lengthening your back (*Fig. 3b*).

4. Think of releasing your thighs to let your knees go "away" from your hips, and release in your calves to let your knees go "away" from your heels (*Fig. 3c, blue lines in legs*). This is not a movement; simply think of allowing the legs to release.

5. Come back to your head and trunk and allow your buttocks to drop away from your head and your head to go up and forward by not tightening in the back of your neck.

6. With your knees releasing away from your hips and heels, you may feel some extra release in your back, so that your back as a whole feels more lengthened.

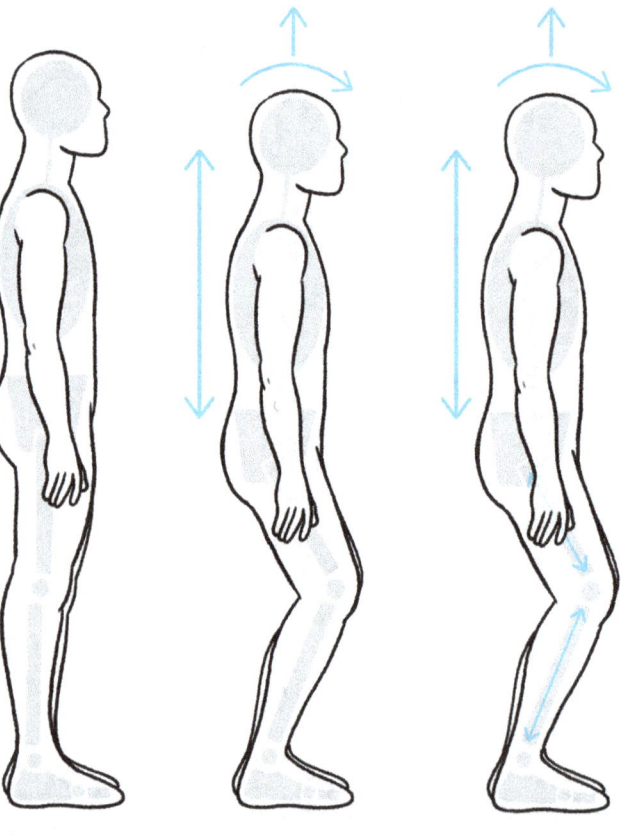

Fig. 3a-c. Vertical stance with directions.

A   B   C

POINTERS

It is important to remember that the directions are not voluntary movements but thoughts, and that release happens in response to your thinking. If you "do" the directions by making movements, then you are doing just that: making overt movements. If, for instance, you "do" the direction for the knees by actually moving the knees forward, the hips will move with the knees and you won't get any release, just an overall movement of the knees and hips. You must not "do" but only "think" the directions, so that there is an internal release of the thigh muscles between the hips at one end and the knees at the other, not an actual movement of either part in space.

Also, do not lose one direction when giving another. For instance, it is easy, when directing the knees from the hips, to think first of allowing the knees to go forward and, a moment later, to let the hips move back. Again, try not to "do" the directions and, keeping still, simply allow release to happen internally by thinking of letting go between the two points.

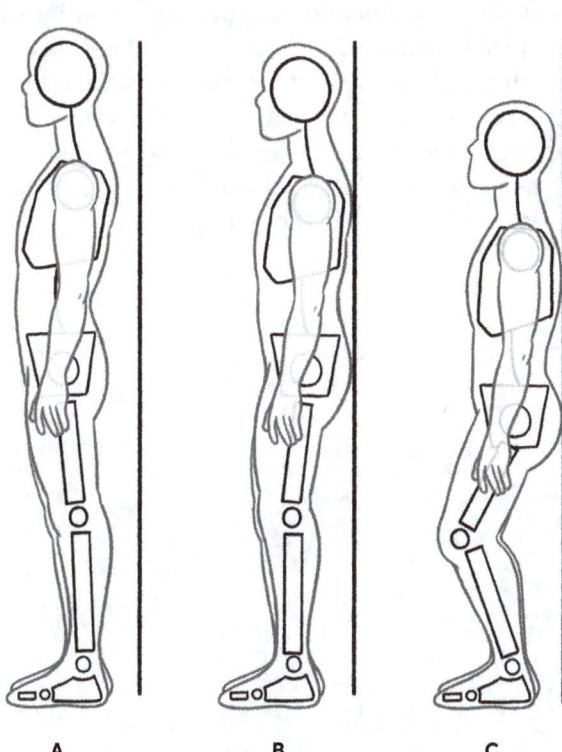

A   B   C

Fig. 4a-c. Vertical stance with your back against the wall.

Exercise 4

Going into vertical stance with your back against the wall

In this exercise, you will go into the vertical stance using the wall as a reference point, which provides a way of monitoring what you are doing with the trunk. The position and directions are more or less the same as Figure 1 above, except that your pelvis and upper back will be in contact with the wall. Note that your head should not be leaning back against the wall.

1. Stand with your back to a wall; place your feet near the wall so that your heels are three or four inches from the wall (*Fig. 4a*).

2. Fall gently back against the wall, but in such a way that both your pelvis and your upper back are in contact with the wall. Let the wall support you so that you are lengthening in your legs and are not tightening in the buttocks, thighs, behind your knees, and your ankles (*Fig. 4b*).

3. Allow your knees to release forward so that you go into the vertical stance (*Fig. 4c*). With both your upper back and pelvis in contact with the wall and your knees going away, see if you can you feel the length of your back. The object is not to flatten your back or spine against the wall but simply to use the contact of your back against the wall to increase your awareness of where your back is.

4. Without bending your knees or changing the position you're in, think of releasing in your calves from your heels to behind your knees so that your knees go "away" from your heels. This is not an actual movement but a release. Think of allowing your buttocks to drop away from your head. With your knees releasing away from your heels and the contact of your back against the wall, you should feel some release in your lower back, so that your back as a whole feels more lengthened.

5. Now gently come up, without stiffening in the legs or pressing your back against the wall. You may notice that, by using the wall, you can let go in the legs; this means that the legs are not bracing and can support you with less tension and effort. This is part of how the muscular system as a whole creates support against gravity.

THE INCLINED "MONKEY POSITION"

Another very useful position of mechanical advantage is the so-called "monkey position," which is identical to the vertical stance except that the trunk is inclined forward at the hips. As with the vertical stance, the knees are bent but, because the trunk is inclined forward, there is a greater opposition between the head, hips, and knees, which encourages more lengthening and release in the back muscles, the thighs and legs, and the trunk as a whole.

The monkey position, as you will see when you try out the following procedures, also places an increased demand on the extensor muscles of the back. When we are standing fully upright, the muscles of the back don't have to work very hard because all the body parts are stacked on top of one another. Because we habitually shorten and interfere with ourselves, many of the key supporting muscles in the body become too lax, forcing us to rely on ligaments when we are slumping, and then to overcompensate by tightening the wrong muscles when we need to sit up. When we are in the monkey position with the trunk inclined forward, the back muscles have to work quite hard to keep the trunk from toppling forward. In this situation, one of two things can happen. The first is that, to maintain this position, we can tighten, shorten, and strain the back muscles, particularly in the lower back region. That is of course what most people will do when bending. The second is that, by encouraging release and opening out, the back can become more elastic and released, so that the work load is distributed over the whole of the back, the supporting muscles become more toned and elastic, and we begin to restore the supporting function of the back muscles. By encouraging the antagonistic or lengthening action of the muscles of the neck, back, and legs, we produce a healthy, toned, elastic state of the musculature.

This elastic state of the muscles is a physical condition, but it is brought about as the result of a thought process, without which the monkey position is useless. When we are able to direct effectively in this way, we bring about a state of release in the muscles of the neck, back, and legs, allowing them to function more efficiently and helping to restore the proper working of the muscles that support upright posture.

Before sending directions to muscles in the monkey position, however, we have to think about how to go into the monkey position. Because we tend to collapse and shorten the body when we bend, it is easy to go into this position by pulling ourselves downward in front and losing length in the trunk. This defeats the purpose of the exercise, since we want to prevent shortening, to maintain lightness, and to achieve as much opposition of body parts as possible. As a first step, then, we must think carefully about how to go into the position. If we are able to maintain freedom in the joints and length in the body as a whole, we will have a much better chance of bringing about further release as we proceed. We'll look first at going into the monkey position; then we'll look at the process of directing once we're in the position.

Exercise 1

Going into the inclined monkey position

When we go into the monkey position, there are two tendencies we must avoid. The first is folding or bending in the hips; instead of deliberately folding ourselves into position, we must think of releasing to allow the body to incline forward at the hips. In this way, the bending happens as a result of hinging at the joints and not because we are pulling ourselves into position.

The second tendency is to drop or pull down in front, collapsing in front and sinking into the legs. You want instead to come to your full stature and then, when you initiate the movement, to think of letting your head lead as you "fall" upwards to incline forward. Again, you do not want to think of bending and instead want to maintain a sense of length while releasing in your joints as the basis for moving.

1. Stand with your feet apart and come up to your full stature (*Fig. 5a*).

2. Free your neck to allow your head to tip forward, but in such a way that the head goes up. The movement of going into monkey will then be initiated by this forward and up movement of the head.

3. Take a moment to identify your ankle, knee, and hip joints.

4. Think of releasing the fronts of your ankles, the backs of your knees, and the front of your hip joints and, with your head leading, let your knees go to "fall" into the inclined monkey position (*Fig. 5b*).

5. Come back onto your heels so that you are balanced nicely over your feet.

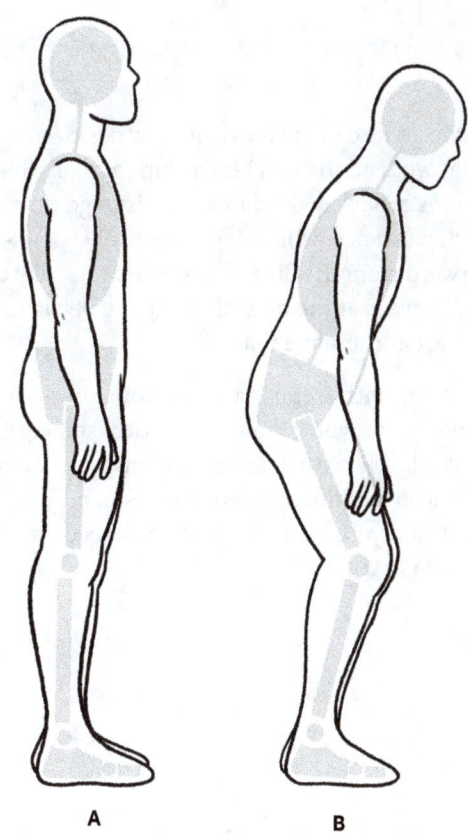

A   B

Fig.5a-b. Going into the inclined monkey position.

Exercise 2

Going into the inclined monkey position using the vertical stance

When we go into an inclined monkey position, we saw that we tend to "fold" at the hips and lose length in front. A good way to address this is to go first into the vertical stance, which does not involve bending forward from the hips. From there, it is easy to incline forward at the hips, allowing the pelvis to come back at the same time.

1. Standing with feet apart, allow your knees to bend so that you go into the vertical stance. Come back slightly onto your heels so that you are in a balanced position with your knees bent, your hips back, and your head and trunk balanced over your feet (*Fig. 6a*).

2. Think of allowing your head to nod forward, your back to lengthen from head to hips, and your knees to go away from hips and heels (*Fig. 6b*).

3. Place your fingers at your hips, just below your hip bones. This will make it possible, as you incline forward at the hips, to take your hips backwards.

4. Go ahead now and incline forward as you gently take your hips back, at the same time allowing your knees to bend as you "fall" into the inclined monkey position (*Fig. 6c*).

5. Come back onto your heels so that you are balanced nicely over your feet.

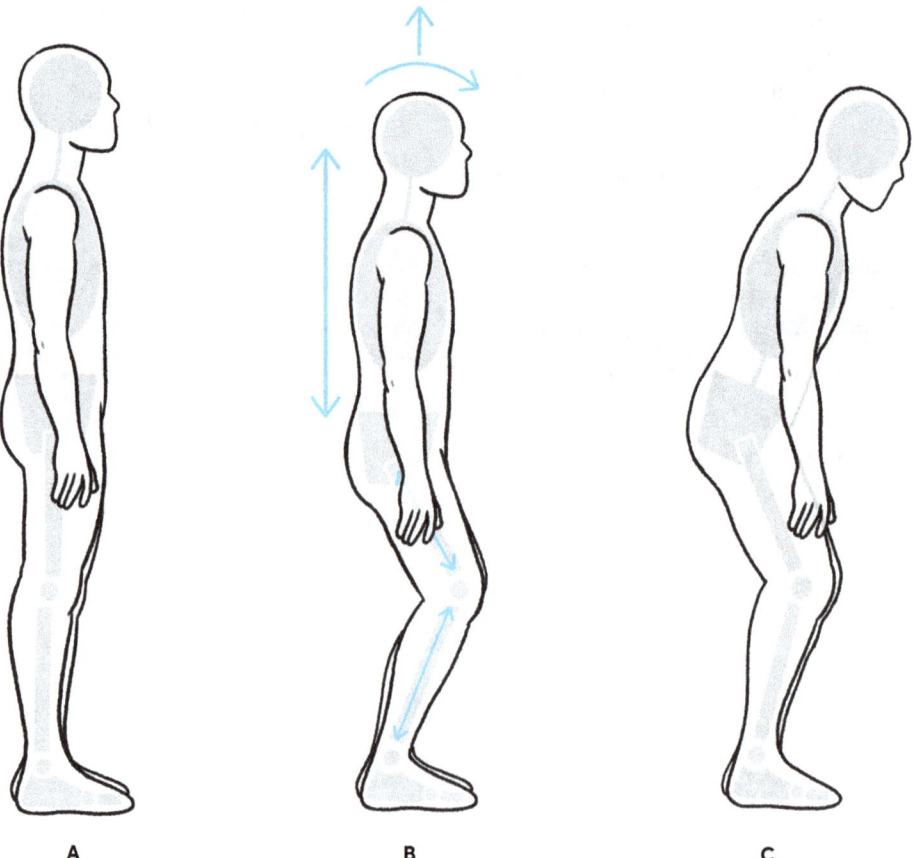

A   B   C

Fig. 6a-c. Going into the inclined monkey position using the vertical stance.

Exercise 3

"Directing" in the inclined monkey position

Once you are in a balanced "monkey" position, you are ready to give your directions, as follows (*Fig. 7*):

1. Think of releasing at the back of your neck to let your head go forward and out of your back.

2. Think of lengthening your back by allowing your head to go away from your hips and your hips to go away from your head.

3. Think of allowing your knees to go away from your hips by releasing your thighs. Think also of releasing in your calf muscles by letting your knees go away from your heels.

It is important to reiterate here that the directions are thoughts that bring about release, not actual movements that we are trying to deliberately make. This means that there must be no attempt to "do" the directions but only to "think" them, which will bring about an internal release of the muscles of the neck, back, and legs.

Do not worry if, at first, the inclined monkey position seems awkward or difficult. At this early stage, the goal is simply to identify what it is and to try it out. As we proceed, this procedure—and the reasons for doing it—will become clearer.

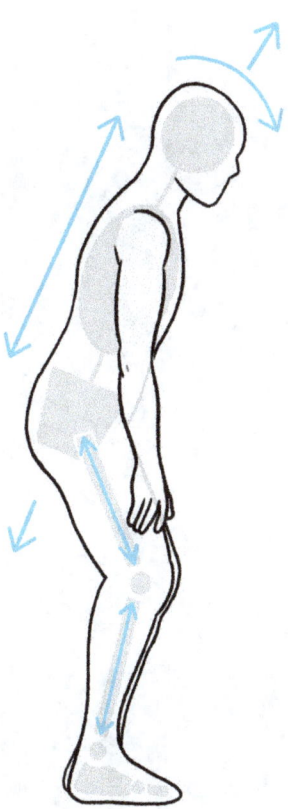

Fig. 7. *Directing in the inclined monkey position.*

6

The Anatomy of Directing

So far in this course, we've focused on the process of directing, or sending messages to muscles, as a way of reinstating the natural functioning of the body. By placing the body in a supported position, directing the head, trunk, and limbs, and allowing the parts to reorganize, muscles that are chronically contracted will let go so that they are restored to their natural length and the body as a whole can begin to work more efficiently.

Even when we have some idea of how to direct, however, we will not be successful if we have a muddled idea of exactly what is being directed. When, for instance, you think of allowing your head to go up in space, what exactly do you mean by "head"? Does the head include the jaw and parts of the neck, and where does the neck end and the skull begin? Furthermore, when you think of the head going forward and up, what does this mean? Does it go up in space or is this just a thought? To direct effectively, it is necessary to be clear not only about how to direct but about what parts of the body are being directed and how they move. That's what we're going to explore in this chapter beginning with the forward and up direction of the head.

The Head

The head rests on the top vertebra of the spine (C1), known as the atlas because, like the Greek titan supporting the universe on his shoulders, it supports the globe of the head. The base of the skull, or occiput, is the part of the skull that sits on the atlas, the two bones forming the atlanto-occipital or AO joint.

The most prominent feature of the occiput is the large hole, called the *foramen magnum*, through which the spinal cord emerges. On either side of the foramen magnum are two rounded bumps, the occipital condyles, that fit like rockers into two depressions on the atlas, making it possible to nod the head up and down, or extend and flex the head (*Fig. 1a and b*).

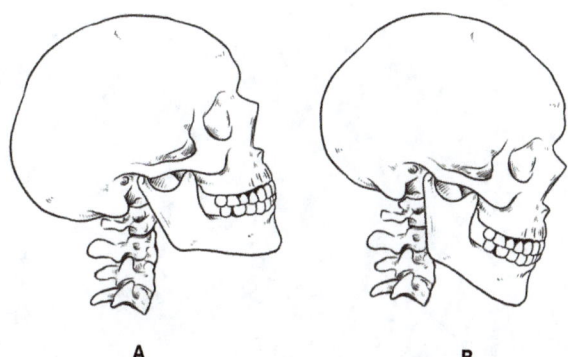

A   B

Fig. 1a-b. Nodding movement of the head on the atlas.

Nodding the head is not the only movement we can make in this region. The atlas sits on the second vertebrae (called the axis) and, with the head sitting on it, can rotate around the axis, making it possible to turn the head. So the AO joint is one part of a two-joint complex that makes it possible to both nod and rotate the head. For our purposes, however, we're concerned mainly with the movements at the AO joint alone, or the nodding up and down of the head.

Seeing that the AO joint is formed by the junction of the base of the skull with the atlas, it is easy to assume that we know where this junction is actually located. But seeing pictures of this joint and being able to locate it on our own person are two different things. When asked to demonstrate where the joint is in themselves, most people point to the back of the neck, indicating a spot much lower than the actual joint. One reason for this misconception is that, because we think of the head in terms of the face and jaw, we assume that the base of the skull is about level with the jaw. If we observe an actual skull, however, we can see that the jaw is not part of the main sphere of the skull but hangs down below the base of the skull, which is much higher than the jaw, just about between the ears (*Fig. 2*). If you remove the jaw entirely (as you can do with an anatomical model), you can see that the skull is actually elliptical or egg-shaped, and that the bottom of the egg sits on the atlas at this point just about between the ears (*Fig. 3*).

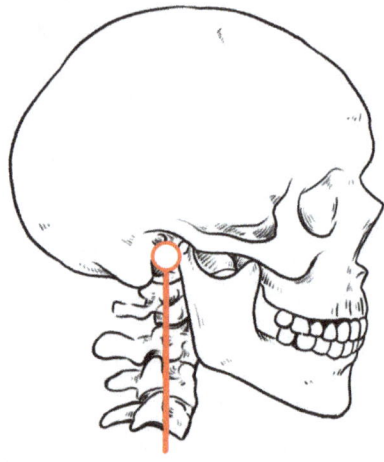

Fig. 2. The base of the skull is higher than we think and well above the line of the jaw.

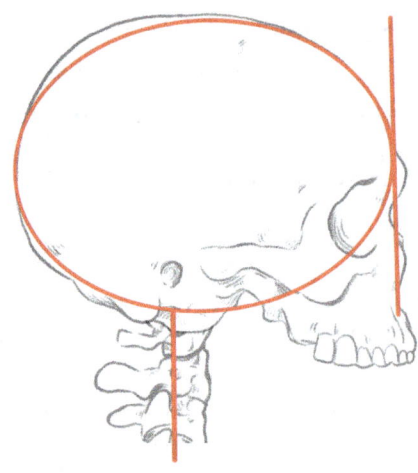

Fig. 3. The skull sitting on the atlas, with jaw removed, is like an egg sitting on its side.

What Is "Forward"?

Let's now look at what we mean by "forward." When we observe someone getting out of a chair, one of the key movements we see is a tendency to pull the head back. But what exactly does it mean to pull one's head back, and what does it mean to put it forward? We saw that the movement we can make at the AO joint consists of nodding the head up and down. We are all familiar with this movement, which we make when nodding in assent, or when we lift our head to look at something above us. But we make these movements rather unconsciously and, unless we take the time to observe what we are actually doing, we will not be fully aware of what it means to nod the head.

Put simply, nodding is rocking the head up and down at the AO joint. If you imagine the head sitting on the atlas like a seesaw that goes up and down at each end, the nodding movement becomes clear (*Fig. 4a-c*). When we shorten the muscles at the back of the neck and pull the head back, it's the seesaw going down in back— otherwise known as extension of the head (*Fig. 5*). If we do the opposite and put the head forward, we are flexing the head (*Fig. 6a and b*). The pulling back of the head is the seesaw going down in back; putting it forward is the seesaw going the other way, or down in front. That second movement— the seesaw going down in front— is what the "forward" refers to: letting the head nod so that it tilts forward and not backward at the AO joint.

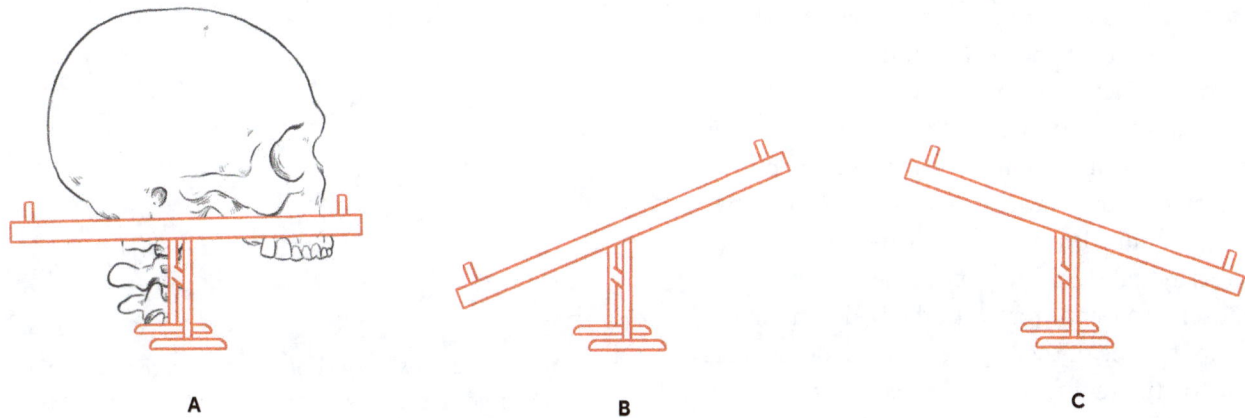

A   **B**   **C**

Fig. 4a-c. The head sits on the atlas and pivots like a see-saw going up and down.

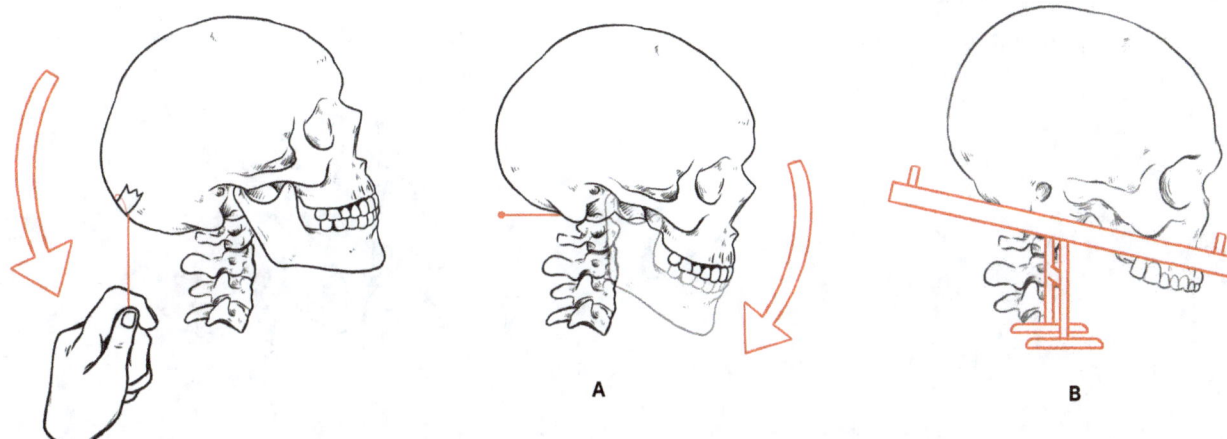

A   **B**

Fig. 5. The head being pulled back and down is like the seesaw going down in back.

Fig. 6a-b. Putting the head forward is the seesaw going down in front.

Why Forward?

But why do we pull the head back to begin with, and why should we want it to go forward? One of the main functions of the neck muscles is to maintain the support of the head, which would otherwise fall forward. But, as we saw in Chapter 1, the neck muscles do not perform this function simply by contracting. The head rests on the atlas but is balanced forward of the point of support (*Fig. 7a*). This causes it to nod or fall forward (*Fig. 7b*), counterbalancing the pull of the neck muscles and keeping them stretched between the skull and the spine. In this way, the neck muscles maintain the support of the head while, at the same time, the forward balance of the head maintains length in the muscles (*Fig. 8*).

What happens in many of us, however, is that we begin to interfere with this dynamic arrangement, pulling the head back and shortening in stature. When this happens, we can no longer maintain the natural lengthened support of the head and trunk and must resort to actively trying to correct our posture by sitting up. To rectify this, we must learn to recognize—and prevent—the habitual shortening of the neck and back muscles that interfere with the body's natural support. One of the key elements in doing this is to stop tightening the neck muscles and to allow the head to naturally nod forward. This forward weight of the head on the atlas, which corresponds to the "forward" direction of the head, is how the head is naturally designed to counterbalance the force of the extensor muscles of the neck and to maintain postural support with a minimum of effort.

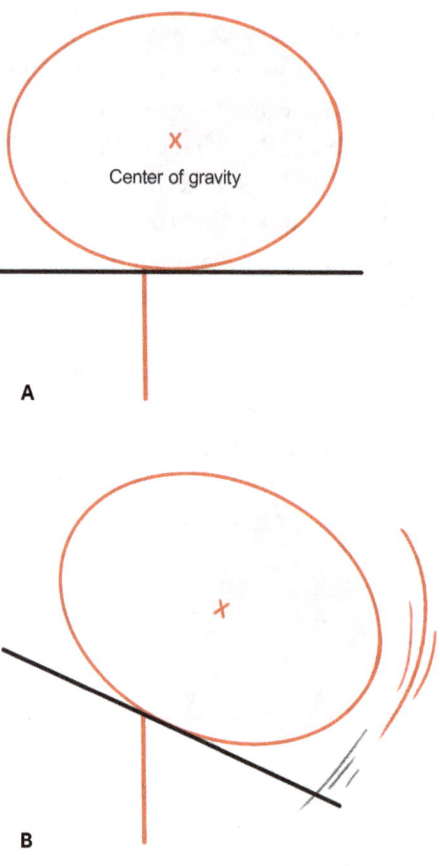

A

B

Fig. 7a. *The egg-shaped skull sits off-balance on the spine;*
b. *The head naturally tends to nod forward at the AO joint.*

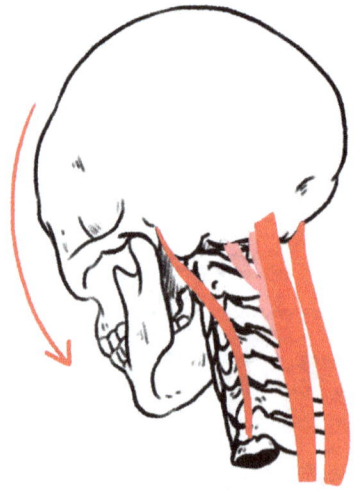

Fig. 8. *The forward balance of the skull*
maintains stretch on the neck muscles.

What Is "Up"?

So that gives us some idea of what the "forward" refers to. The head sits off-balance on top of the spine, which is how the system is designed to naturally counterbalance the pull of muscles in back. And because we habitually tighten the neck muscles and pull the head back, we have to stop this tightening to allow the head to nod forward at the AO joint, or what we call the forward direction of the head.

But what does the "up" refer to? Consider what happens if you are slumping in a chair or pulling your head back (*Fig. 9a*). In this case, the spine is markedly curved or shortened, which means that you are shortened in stature as a whole. If you then straighten up so that your spine is more lengthened, you will be gaining in overall stature and your head will move up in space. The head is clearly going up (*Fig. 9b*), but this movement is not happening at the AO joint; it is happening as a result of the lengthening action of the trunk and spine as a whole.

When we speak of the "up" direction of the head, then, we are not speaking of a movement of the head at the AO joint but of the overall lengthening of the trunk and spine. We habitually pull the head back at the AO joint and need to let it nod forward, but we must also allow the head to come up so that we lengthen in stature up to the AO joint. That's really what the two directions mean. The "forward" direction takes place at the AO joint; the "up" includes the length of the entire trunk right up to the base of the skull.

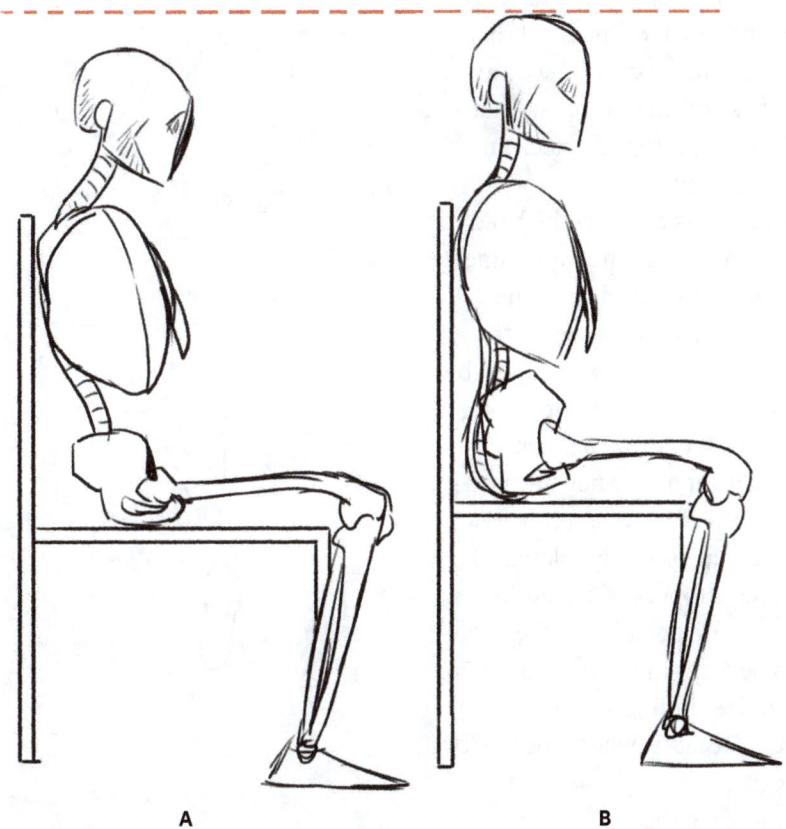

A   B

Fig. 9a. Slumping with the head pulled back; b. When coming out of a slump, the head goes up in space.

The Up Direction and Lengthening the Spine

Let's look now at how we can think about the spine as a way of directing the head up and not just forward. We saw earlier that, when asked to identify the AO joint, most people point to the back of the neck, indicating a spot much lower than the actual joint. One reason for this misconception is that, because we think of the head in terms of the face, we forget that the base of the skull is not the jaw (which is not part of the skull but a separate bone entirely!) and is situated higher up, near the level of the cheekbones. In practical terms this means that the upper spine is longer than we think, extending to a point almost between the ears (*Fig. 10*).

So why does this matter? If you think the neck ends at the level of the jaw, you will think that your head, for all intents and purposes, is part of your neck. Instead of freeing your neck to allow your head to go forward and up, you will instead fix the head and upper spine forward in space and prevent the trunk from lengthening fully. To stop the pulling back and down of the head that is associated with shortening in stature, we have to be clear where the base of the skull is so that, when we direct the head, we allow the neck and trunk to assume their full length.

One way to think of this is to allow the head to go forward at the AO joint, but at the same time to allow the head, AO joint included, to come up in space. In this way, you are thinking of the "forward" direction, but not at the expense of the "up." If you think of these two things happening simultaneously and give time for these mental directions to work, you'll get a very new idea of what "forward and up" refers to. When it works properly, you'll see that "up" is really related to restoring the lengthened support of the entire trunk and not just about the position of the head, which has no meaning except in relation to the system as a whole. Understanding where the AO joint is actually located—that is, where the neck ends and the skull begins—is thus a key part of getting these directions to work.

We now have two parts of the head direction. First, we allow the head to nod forward—that is

the "forward." This includes a clear conception of where the head sits on the atlas, or in other words where the base of the skull is at the level of the cheeks. This conception is also key for the second part—the "up." We must allow the spine and trunk to have their full length by thinking of the head going up in space in relation to the trunk as a whole. Once again, this can only happen if we have a clear conception of how long the cervical spine is, which extends above the jaw right up to the cheeks (*Fig. 11*).

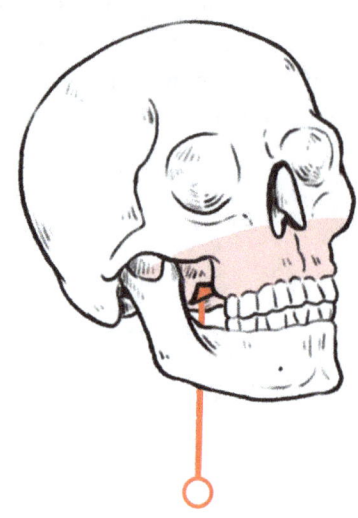

Fig. 10. The base of the skull is between the ears.

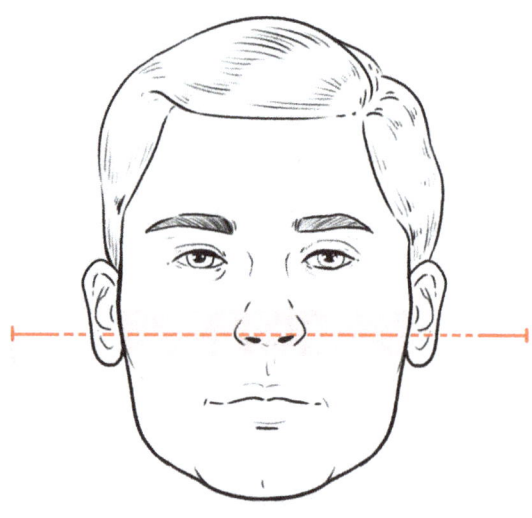

Fig. 11. The AO joint is higher than we think, almost at the level of the cheeks.

Exercise 1

Find your AO joint

To get a clearer idea of where the AO joint is, try the following exercise.

1. Place the tips of your thumbs in your ears with your fingers extending upwards (*Fig. 12a*).

2. Let your fingers touch, wrapping around your face so that your pinkies are just underneath your nose and your other fingers touch the bridge of your nose and your forehead (*Fig. 12b*).

3. Imagine that a pin has been inserted right between your thumbs and that your skull nods at the level of that pin. Your fingers are the skull itself. Use your thumbs and fingers to nod your head lightly at the level of the pin, where your thumbs are (*Fig. 12c*). This is your AO joint.

It is very useful to understand this because most of us have a shortened concept of the neck which corresponds to habitual shortening of the neck and pulling back of the head. Clarifying conceptually where the head sits and moves on the spine helps to establish a more accurate concept of how long the neck is, and enables us to gain more freedom and mobility in this region.

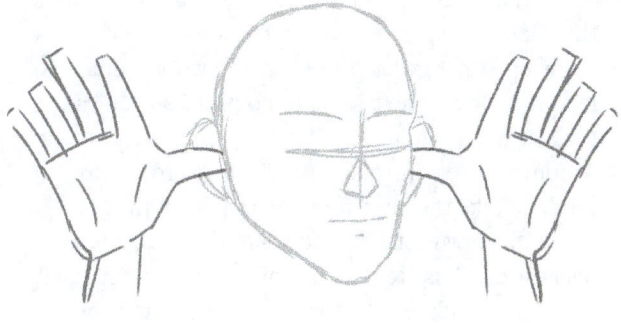

A

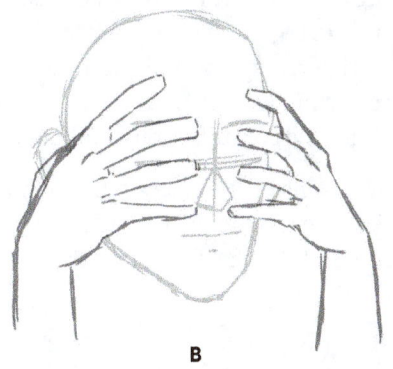

B

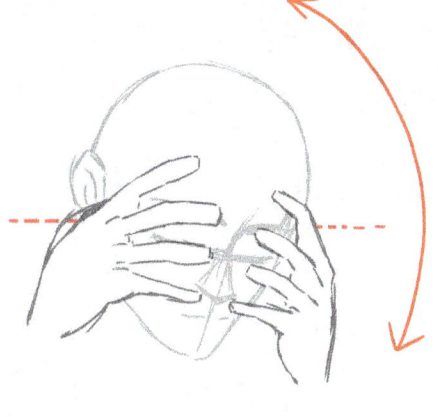

C

Fig. 12a-c. *Identifying the AO joint.*

Exercise 2

Directing the head two ways

Try actually putting your head forward. When you do this, does it start to come down? Now let your chin come up—that is, let your head as a whole come up in space. Does it now seem to go back? As you can see, the head can move in two ways, and they are in some sense contradictory. The forward motion tends to take the head forward and down in space, while the upward motion tends to throw the head backwards. This creates a bit of a dilemma, especially when you think of actively putting the head forward, which achieves the first of these—the forward—at the expense of the second—the up. The dilemma is resolved when you stop trying to position the head and, instead, let it go forward without putting it down, and let it go up without putting it back. This allows both directions to work at the same time. In any case, it's fun to explore the two directions by playing with the contradiction as follows:

1. Sit in a comfortable chair with your hips fairly far back in the chair and your back supported against the back of the chair.

2. Be aware of the full length of the front of your body from your hip joints right up to the base of your skull, at the level of your cheek bones.

3. Nod your head gently up and down.

4. Think of releasing your neck to let your head nod forward but, at the same time, allow your head to come up in space.

5. See if you can think each of these things, allowing one to check the other so that, if it goes down you let it come up, and if it goes up and back, you let it go forward.

6. Spend a few minutes thinking these two thoughts, and remind yourself where the base of your skull is so that you are clear about allowing your head to come up.

7. Notice the contact of your back against the chair, allowing your back to lengthen and widen and your head to go forward and up.

8. Think of your knees going away.

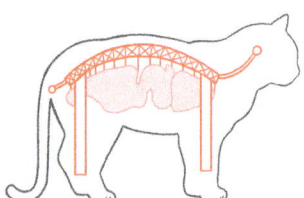

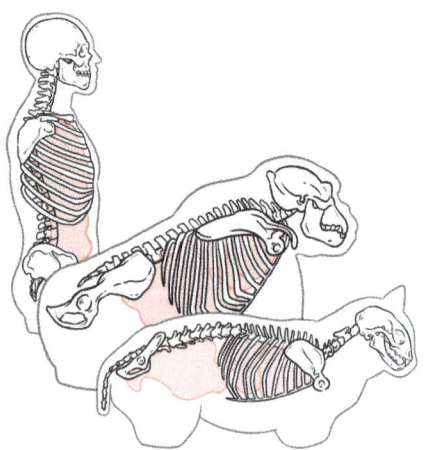

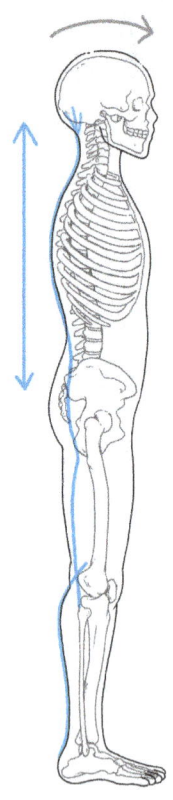

Fig. 13. *In a four-footed animal, the spine forms a bridge with the rib cage and gut hanging below it.*

Fig. 14. *In primates that stand on two feet, the rib cage and organs are now in front of the spine.*

Fig. 15.
The extensors and head balance.

Front Length

One of the most important features of our human anatomical design is our front length. In a four-footed animal, the spine serves as a kind of bridge between the fore and hind limbs, and the internal organs hang below the spine (*Fig. 13*). When the first hominids reared up on their hind limbs to become fully upright, everything suspended below the spine now hung out in front of the spine (*Fig. 14*). This means that we are unevenly balanced between the front and back because most of the weight of the body is in front and not in back. This places the onus of support on the extensors of the back, which can work properly only when the head is balanced on top of a lengthening spine (*Fig. 15*).

But what about the flexors in front of the body? In order to support upright posture, the structures in front of the body—the throat, rib cage, and gut—must hang freely from above, and they must do so in a way that does not compromise our front length (*Fig. 16*). This means they must be suspended from above and not drag down from below. This is why, when we direct, we must be aware not only of the neck, head, and back but also of the front of the body, which must have its full length in order for the entire system to work properly.

A simple way to think of front length is to trace the abdominal muscles from the pubic bone to the rib cage, continue up the sternum to the origin of the sternocleidomastoid muscles at the top of the sternum, and follow these to the mastoid processes on either side of the skull (*Fig. 17*). If you are not familiar with the mastoid processes, these are the large bumps on either side of your skull just behind your ears, which serve as key attachments for several muscles (*Fig. 18*). When we trace the flexor line on the front of the body, this gives us a much clearer conception of how long the body is in front and of the necessity of allowing the body to have its full length in front.

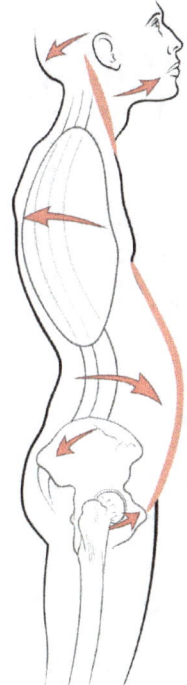

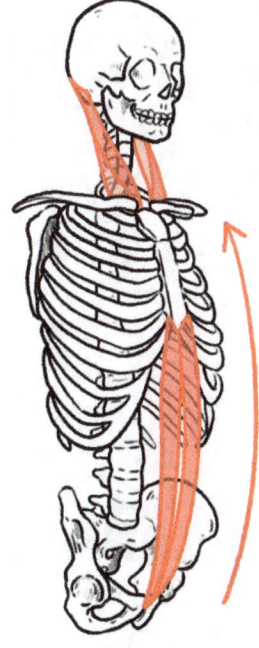

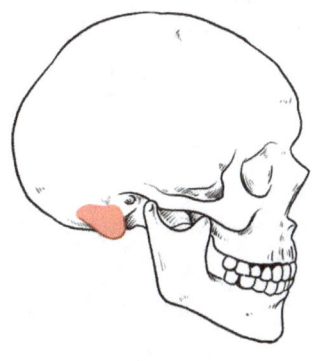

Fig. 16. In order to support upright posture, the structures in front must hang from above without shortening.

Fig. 17. A simple flexor line can be traced from the pubic bone right up to the base of the skull.

Fig. 18. The sternocleidomastoid muscle attaches to the mastoid process of the skull.

But how does front length relate to head balance and the forward and up direction of the head? The jaw and throat are suspended from the skull and tend to drag it down—that is, they flex the skull. We might attribute the same tendency to these key flexors on the front of the body, since the extensors retract the head and the flexors would appear to produce the opposite effect. But in fact it doesn't work this way. If you look closely at the sternocleidomastoid muscle, you'll see that its point of attachment at the mastoid process of the skull is slightly behind the atlanto-occipital joint, the point at which the skull balances on the spine. This means that, although the sterno-cleidomastoid muscle will tend to drag the neck or upper spine forward, it will actually pull the head back in relation to the spine (*Fig. 19*). This pull becomes even more accentuated when we collapse or draw ourselves down in front, which increases the drag upon the neck and upper spinal column (see *Fig. 16*). In order to counter this tendency and to maintain upward support, the head must balance forward at the AO joint so that, instead of dragging down upon the head, the rib cage and abdomen are suspended from above (*see Fig. 17*).

Once again we find that the balance of the head is a key organizing factor governing the working of the muscular system. The forward balance of the head is crucial to the lengthened working of the back muscles, but it is equally crucial to the length and support of the body in front. Because the front of the body is suspended from the head, the head must be balanced forward in order to maintain front length as well as length in back (*Fig. 20*).

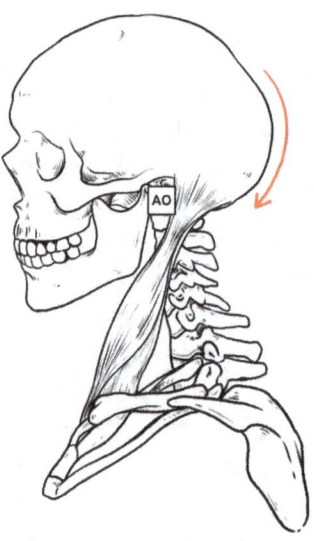

Fig. 19. *Although the sternocleidomastoid muscle is a flexor muscle at the front of the body and will tend to drag the neck or upper spine forward, it will actually pull the head back in relation to the spine.*

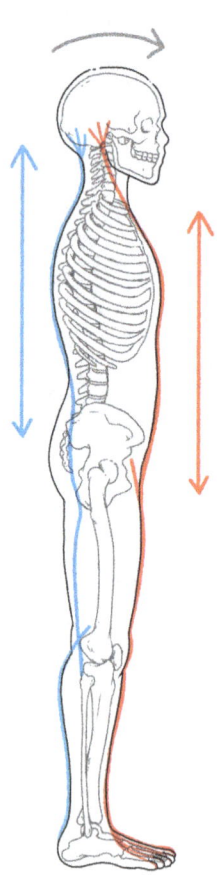

Fig. 20. *The forward balance of the head is crucial to the lengthened working of the back muscles, but it is equally crucial to the length and support of the body in front.*

FRONT LENGTH IN SEMI-SUPINE POSITION

The semi-supine position is ideal for restoring length along the front of the body because it gives the flexors and rib cage a chance to open up while the back muscles, instead of overworking, can lengthen and fill out as well.

Exercise 3

Directing in semi-supine

1. Lying in semi-supine, begin by noticing the air going in and out through your nostrils. Don't do anything except simply to notice this.

2. See to it that you're not tightening in your neck, so that your head can go out of your back.

3. Notice the length of your back from your occiput to your sacrum.

4. Take a moment and reiterate the thoughts for the neck to release and your head to go out, and your head to go out of your back as it lengthens and widens.

5. Notice your hips and thighs and see to it that you're not tightening them so that your knees can come out of your back.

6. Take a moment and reiterate these thoughts so that your thighs can let go and your knees can come out of your back.

7. You're now allowing your neck to be free to let your head come out of your back, your back to lengthen and widen and your legs to let go so that your knees come out of your back.

8. Think now of your front length from your hip joints right up to the base of your skull about where your cheeks are (*Fig. 21*).

9. Be aware now of the length of your back from your pelvis right up to the back of your neck and head, and the length of your body in front from your hip joints right up to the front of your neck and head. When you think of your head coming out of your trunk, it is now coming out of the entire length of your trunk in front as well as in back.

10. Finally, direct your knees to the ceiling so that your head is going out of a fully lengthening trunk, your knees are going out the other end, and your back is lengthening and widening in between your head and knees.

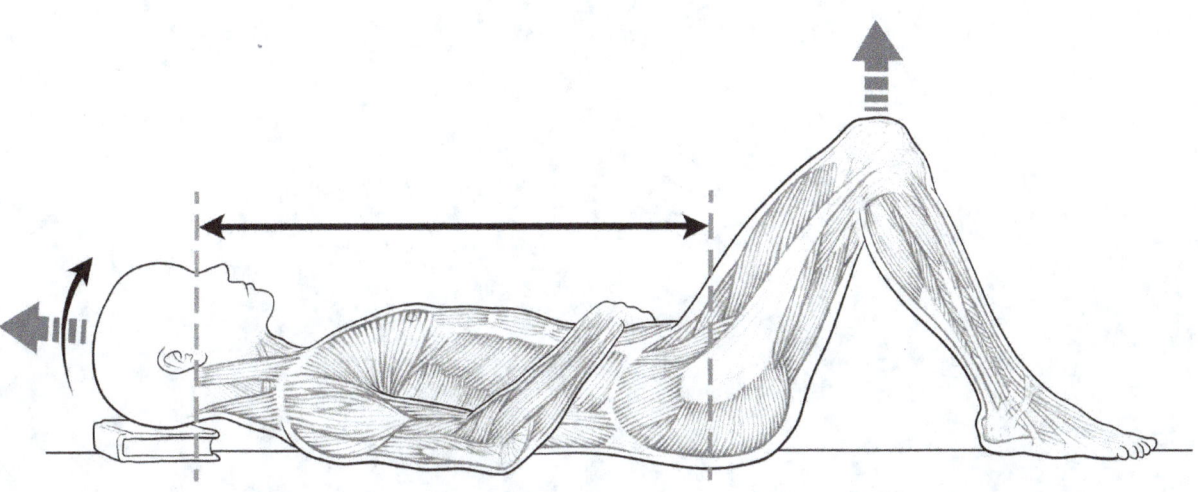

Fig. 21. When we direct the head, back, and knees in semi-supine position, we can include front length from the hip joints to the base of the skull.

PART THREE

The Head, Trunk, and Limbs

The Shoulder Girdle

As the support structure for the arms, the shoulders are a particularly important system in the human body. Every day we use our arms for many hours. If we do not engage the shoulder girdle efficiently to do so, the shoulders will not only overwork but will also interfere with the larger upright support system, which is why it is critical to understand the connection of the shoulders with the larger upright support system. When using their arms, most people badly narrow across the front of the shoulders, which become fixed and pulled forwards. Under these circumstances, it is impossible to use the arms efficiently, and attempts to relax or stretch muscles only makes things worse. The good news is that, by restoring a coordinated working of the shoulders, you can use the arms more efficiently and, at the same time, go a long way towards restoring the working of the system as a whole.

How the Shoulders Widen

In simple terms, the shoulder girdle is a system of levers that supports the arms. The arm itself is a system of levers for moving the hand, which is used to grasp and manipulate objects. The shoulder, in turn, is a movable crosspiece that supports the levers of the arms (*Fig. 1*).

As a system of levers, the arms and hands appear to work independently of the trunk. When we experience strain or weakness, our initial impulse is to stretch or strengthen particular muscle groups, or to try to release and mobilize the shoulder joint. We must remember, however, that the arms and shoulder girdle are part of the larger postural system and, as such, are part of the upright support system. We have only to lean on our elbows, or to pick a child up by the elbows, to see that, even in humans, the arms function as forelimbs that support the trunk and, in this sense, are intimately linked with it. Only

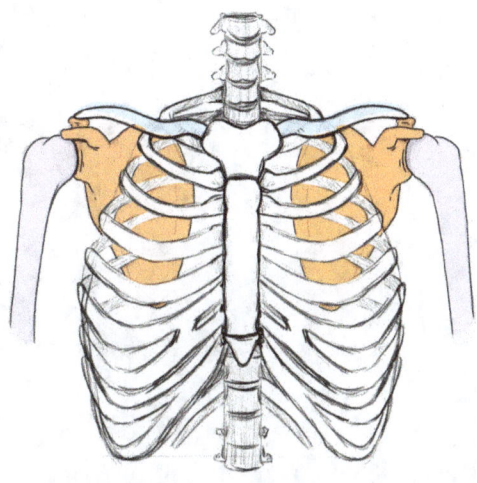

Fig. 1. *The shoulder girdle is a system of levers that supports the arms.*

Fig. 2. Young child with shoulders integrated into her back. Notice how her shoulder and arm joints are in the coronal plane of the trunk and are not pulled forward despite the fact that she is manipulating an object with her hands.

secondarily do they operate as a lever system for moving and positioning the prehensile hands.

If you look at a young child of, perhaps, two years old, this integrated working of the shoulders with the back is easy to see (*Fig. 2*). Most two-year-olds are physically active and have not yet begun to perform the kinds of complex fine-motor activities that engage the flexors of the shoulder and arm, such as using touch screens or drawing. As a result, there is little shortening or narrowing in the pectoral region of the shoulders and in the flexors of the arm and hand. In contrast, adults are almost continuously performing

activities that actively engage the flexors of the hand, forearm, and shoulders, with a corresponding narrowing or shortening across the front of the shoulders. Coupled with the tendency to slump while sitting (which further contributes to the tendency to both disengage and tighten the shoulders), the flexors of the shoulders and arms in most adults become habitually shortened, narrowing the shoulders and pulling them forwards and downwards. This imbalance cannot be corrected by stretching tight muscles or strengthening the opposing muscles, which will only further imbalance and disrupt the overall system.

To reverse this harmful state of affairs, two things must happen. First, it is necessary to release and undo the shortened flexor muscles that pull the shoulders forward and cause narrowing across the chest (*Fig. 3*). This cannot be accomplished simply by targeting or treating specific muscles but only by bringing about the natural, widened support of the shoulders. The shoulders can then integrate with the back, where they get most of their support (*Fig. 4*).

Second, the shoulders must widen apart as part of lengthening in stature. Release across the front of the shoulders is an essential part of this, but we must also restore the lengthened support

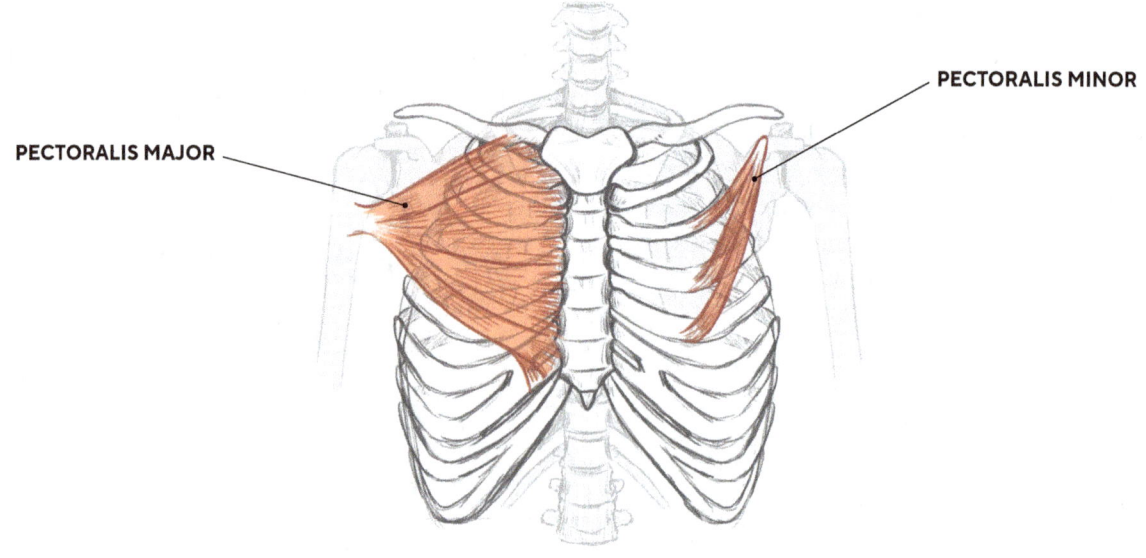

PECTORALIS MAJOR

PECTORALIS MINOR

Fig. 3. The two pectoralis muscles that pull the shoulders forward, pectoralis major and minor.

of the trunk itself. If this is lost and we are collapsed and shortened in front, the shoulders droop and are disengaged from the back. In order for the shoulders to work properly, the trunk must lengthen so that that shoulders can widen apart, connecting in back with the larger muscular network of which they are a part.

When both of these conditions are met, one of the first things that you will notice is that the muscles at the back of the shoulders become more elastic and toned. It might seem strange that releasing muscles on the front of the shoulder should so directly affect the back muscles, but we must remember that the shoulders actually get their support from the back so that, when the shoulders widen apart, the muscles in back, including the scapulae muscles, naturally regain tone. This allows the back muscles to work in a fuller and more supportive way, which in turn contributes to the widening support of the back as a whole. It also allows the ribs to move more freely, restoring the full capacity of the thorax in breathing and the flexibility and mobility of the ribs where they articulate with the spine in back. The shoulders are thus a crucial element in restoring the widened support of the back and the free and full movement of the ribs in breathing.

Another essential component of the shoulders is the rotator cuff, which is made up of four scapula muscles that support the humerus in its shallow socket, forming a "cuff" around the joint that gives this group of muscles its name (*Fig. 5*). When we use our shoulders in such a way that we narrow across the front of the chest, the rotator cuff muscles often become badly overworked, sometimes to the point that the joint becomes raised and "frozen" and completely loses mobility. When this narrowing is reduced, the rotator cuff muscles release, and it feels as if the joint softens and melts into the back. Flexibility and mobility return and the shoulders also become less raised so that they can float above the rib cage, but without being held or stiffened.

In all, at least four muscle groups are involved in the widening support of the shoulders: the flexors in front (including the serratus anterior and biceps brachii muscles), the scapulae muscles in back, the elevators above, and the rotator cuff supporting the joint itself, including the deltoid muscle wrapping over the shoulder in the same way that the gluteal muscles wrap over the hip joint. All these muscles contribute to the full and widened support of the back and trunk, from which the shoulder girdle gets its support.

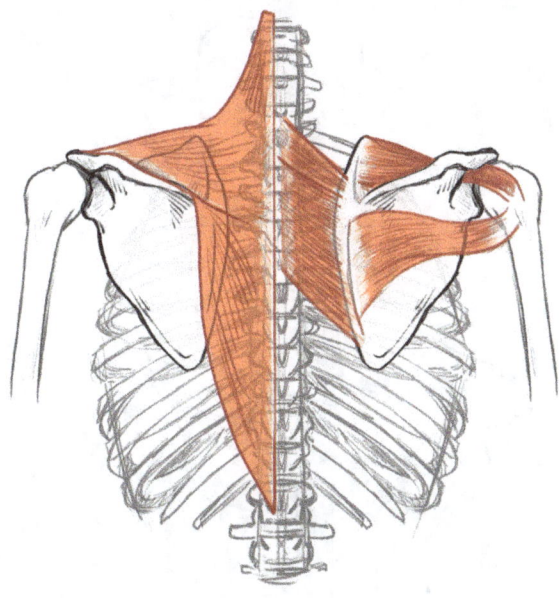

Fig. 4. The key muscles providing support for the shoulder are in back.

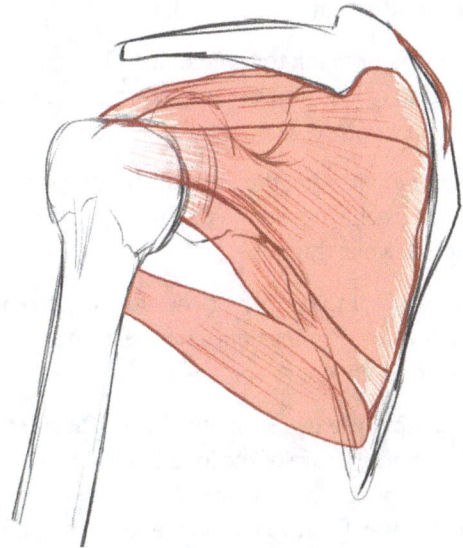

Fig. 5. The rotator cuff is comprised of four muscles that originate on the scapula and attach to the head of the humerus to support and move the humerus at the shoulder joint.

DIRECTING THE ARMS

In the following exercises, we will explore the shoulders and arms while sitting and lying down. Because it is difficult at first to make changes in the shoulders and arms, it is useful to begin by simply being aware of the segments of the arms and shoulders. In the sitting and semi-supine positions, the back and shoulders are nicely supported and we can take our take time identifying—and becoming aware of—the shoulders and each part of the arms. To do this first exercise, it is useful to spend a few minutes giving your primary directions before going through the following steps.

Exercise 1

Directing the arms in sitting position (Fig. 6)

In this exercise, we identify the hands, lower arm, upper arm, and shoulders, becoming aware of each piece and putting them together to form a whole (see blue lines). This exercise can be done while sitting in a supportive armchair with elbows and forearms resting on the arm of the chair. If you do not have an armchair, sit in a straight-back chair with your hands resting on your lap, close to your trunk so that your arms are not dragging your shoulders forward.

1. Sit in a chair with your feet flat on the floor, your back supported, and your hands resting on the arm of the chair or on your lap.

2. Allow your trunk to come to its full length, your head to balance forward and up, and your knees to go away from your hips.

3. Think of allowing the fingers of both hands to lengthen from your wrist, not forgetting to include your thumbs.

4. Be aware of the length of your forearm from your wrist to your funny bones on the inside or lower part of each elbow.

5. Link up these two segments in both arms so that you're aware of the length of each arm from fingertips to elbow. Think of your fingers lengthening away from your elbow, and your elbow lengthening away from your fingers.

6. Now be aware of your upper arm from your elbow to your shoulder joint, paying attention to this segment for a few moments until your upper arms come into your awareness.

7. Now link up hands and forearms with upper arms until you can feel the length of both of your arms from fingertips to elbow to shoulder as a continuous whole.

8. Turn your attention now to your shoulders and notice the distance or length between your left and right shoulder joints so that your right upper arm is going away from your left upper arm, and your left upper arm from your right upper arm.

9. Now think of linking up your left arm from fingertips to left shoulder, across your shoulders, down your right arm to your fingertips. You should now feel the entire length of your arms and shoulder girdle from the fingertips of the left arm to the left shoulder, across the chest, and right down to the fingertips of your right hand, as a continuous whole.

If you take some time to work with this exercise, you will find that your kinesthetic awareness of your upper limb, including your shoulders, will become heightened.

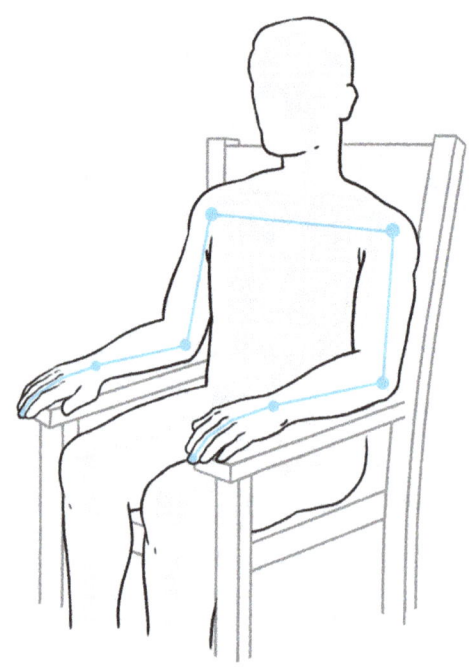

Fig. 6 . Directing arms and shoulders while sitting.

Exercise 2

Directing the arms in semi-supine (Fig. 7)

The semi-supine position is an ideal one for exploring the shoulders and arms. The head, trunk, and shoulders are fully supported, and the shoulders are fully in contact with the floor. This is also an ideal position from which to explore arm movements, which we will do in the next section/chapter.

1.   Lying in semi-supine with your hands on your abdomen, take a moment to be aware of the parts of your body that are supported on the ground: head on the books, upper back and pelvis supported on the floor.

2.   Be aware of the length of your forearm from your fingertips to your elbows. If you give this some time, you will begin to get a clearer sense of the length of your forearm, and you will also begin to feel your fingers lengthening out of your forearm.

3.   Be aware of the length of your upper arms from your elbows to your shoulders.

4.   Be aware of the breadth of your shoulders in front and in back.

5.   Link up the parts so that you feel the length from your fingertips to your elbows, elbows to shoulders, and across your shoulders. Take your time, repeating parts of this exercise as needed, until you can clearly feel the length of your arms and shoulders as a continuous whole.

After trying this exercise, notice if you feel more elasticity and release across your back, where the shoulder blades are supported by, and embedded in, a network of muscles. Notice also if you feel more room or widening across the front of your shoulders.

Exercise 3

Raising your arms at the elbow to direct your fingers in semi-supine position (Fig. 8)

When we use our hands to do something, we are usually focused on what we're doing and not on the arm and hand themselves. To perform fine motor movements, however, we must be able to precisely control the arm, which is under direct conscious control and which, once we begin to do something, will come very clearly into our awareness. By raising the arms at the elbows—that is, by performing a deliberate movement with the arms and placing them in an advantageous position—we become more aware of our arms and hands and can bring about beneficial changes. This exercise continues from the previous one.

1.   Repeat steps 1 to 6 in Exercise 2, then:

2.   Raise your hands from the elbows so that, with your elbows still on the ground, your fingers are pointing upward.

3.   Take a moment to think of your fingers and thumbs lengthening from your wrists and out of your forearms so that your fingers are pointing to the ceiling.

Notice if, after directing the fingers and arms in this position, you are more aware of the length between your fingers and elbows, between elbows and shoulders, and across your shoulders. In this position, the shoulder girdle as a whole can begin to widen.

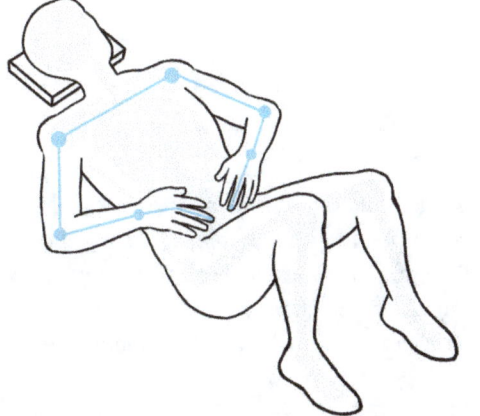

Fig. 7. Directing arms and shoulders in semi-supine position.

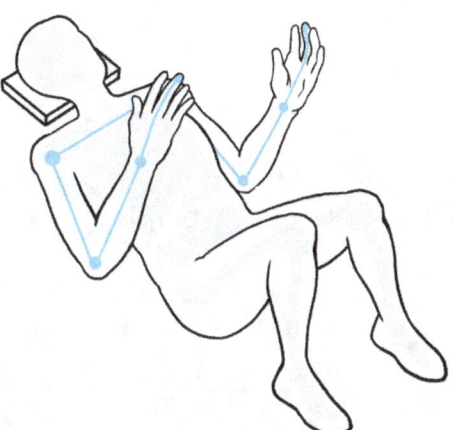

Fig. 8. Arms raised in the semi-supine position.

The Rotator Cuff

The shoulder joint, formed by the articulation of the head of the humerus with the glenoid cavity of the scapula, is the most mobile joint in the body (*Fig. 9*). The humerus is held in place and moved by the rotator cuff, which as we saw previously consists of a set of four muscles that attach to the head of the humerus, forming a cuff around the joint that gives this group of muscles its name (*Fig. 10*).

Each of the rotator cuff muscles attaches to a different part of the head of the humerus, stabilizing the humerus at the joint and moving it in different directions. Infraspinatus and teres minor attach to the back of the humerus; supraspinatus attaches at the top and subscapularis to the front. Subscapularis is particularly significant because, when it becomes chronically shortened, it rotates the head of the humerus forward and fixes it in place, contributing to the narrowing of the shoulders and interfering with the freedom of the joint.

When we use our arms in fine motor tasks for long periods, the rotator cuff muscles often become overworked and the resulting chronic muscular contraction causes the shoulder joint to lose mobility. The rotator cuff muscles are thus essential to the proper function and mobility of the shoulder joint and the shoulder girdle as a whole.

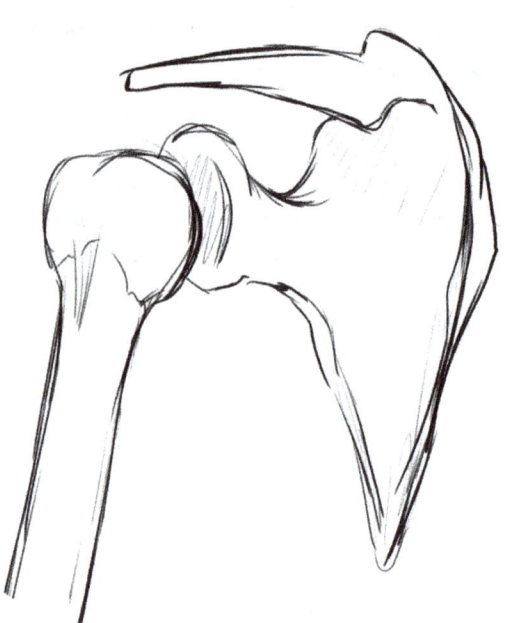

Fig. 9. The shoulder joint is shallow and highly mobile.

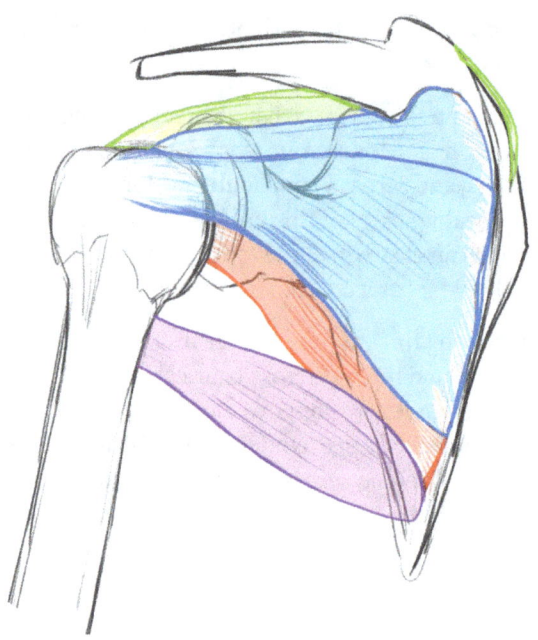

Fig. 10. The humerus is held in place by the rotator cuff muscles originating on the scapula. Three of the rotator cuff muscles are shown here: supraspinatus (green); subscapularis (blue); and teres minor (red); the purple muscle is teres major, which is not a rotator cuff muscle.

ROTATOR CUFF AND ARM MOVEMENTS

Exercise 4

Supporting the arms in semi-supine

In the last chapter, we gave attention to the different segments of the upper limb and shoulder. In this exercise, we use the support of the arms on the ground for a similar purpose: to heighten awareness of the arms and how they can lengthen out of the back and shoulders.

1. Lying in semi-supine position, take a few minutes to give your directions.

2. Take a moment to direct the segments of your arms.

3. Lower your arms onto the ground so that they are at or near your side (*Fig. 11a*).

4. Take a moment to notice the length of your arm and the contacts of the arm on the floor. In this position, you will feel the back of your upper arms, your elbows, part of your forearms, and parts of your hand and fingertips.

5. Gently extend your fingers so that you can feel them as extensions of the arm.

6. Slide your arms away from your body so that your shoulders open up slightly, and leave your arms there for a minute or two (*Fig. 11b*).

Lying in semi-supine position with your arms supported on the ground, are you more aware of your arms? Can you feel that your arms can unravel out of your back and shoulders? You may find that, as this happens, the muscles across your shoulders in back become more elastic and lengthened.

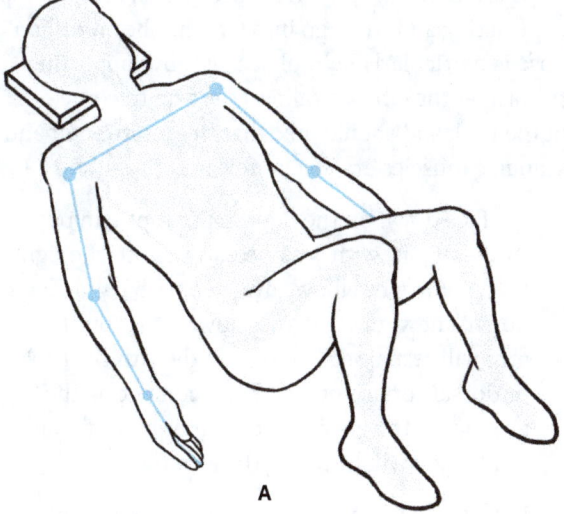

A

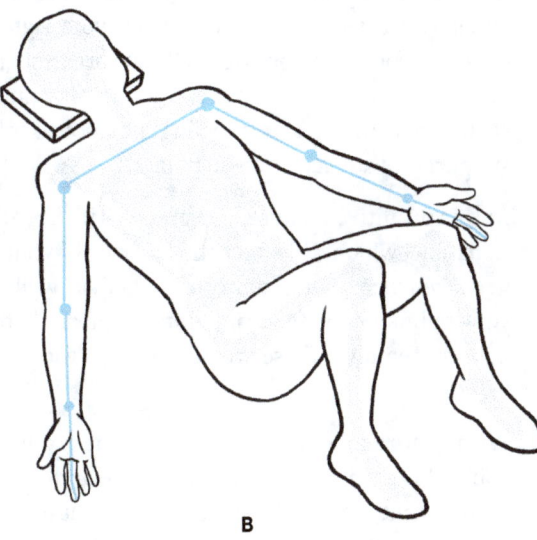

B

Fig. 11a. The arms get support from the ground; b. Directing fingers with arms supported on the ground.

Exercise 5

Reptilian pose and the rotator cuff (Fig. 12)

Lying on the floor in developmentally primitive postures is a useful way to give muscles a chance to stop contracting and to let go into length. The "reptilian" pose is particularly helpful because, by supporting the arm at the elbow, it allows the arm to come out of the back and shoulder so that the rotator cuff and scapulae muscles are able to release.

1. Lie face down on the floor in the reptilian posture—that is, with your head turned to the right side, your right elbow advanced with palm facing down, and your right knee advanced. Your left arm will rest alongside your body with the back or dorsal surface of your hand contacting the ground. In this position, the inner part of your right ankle will be facing the ground.

2. In this posture, notice which parts of your body are fully supported on the ground. This includes the left side of your head, parts of your ribcage and pelvis, the length of your left leg, your right knee and foot, and your right elbow, forearm, and palm. Take time to notice these points of contact, seeing to it that you are allowing the floor to fully support you at each of these points.

3. In this primitive posture, you are twisting to your right side, which will affect the muscles of your neck, which are being gently stretched, as well as your right shoulder and right hip. If you are habitually stiffening in these areas, this helps them to let go.

4. With your right elbow supported on the ground, you will find that your arm can release and "widen" out of your shoulder. Take a minute to notice this contact.

5. After lying in this posture for several minutes, switch to the other side.

After trying out this posture on both sides, do you notice a difference between the two sides? Do you notice changes in your neck, shoulder and arms, trunk and legs? Spending time every day lying in this primitive, fully-supported posture is a useful way to give muscles a chance to release, to regain flexibility, and to allow the nervous system to quiet down. In particular, the contact of the elbow on the floor makes it possible to let go in the shoulder muscles. The support of the head and limbs helps the neck and trunk to unwind or de-rotate, and the support of the arm also allows the back muscles to widen out. We'll use this posture again when we explore the flipper movements of the legs.

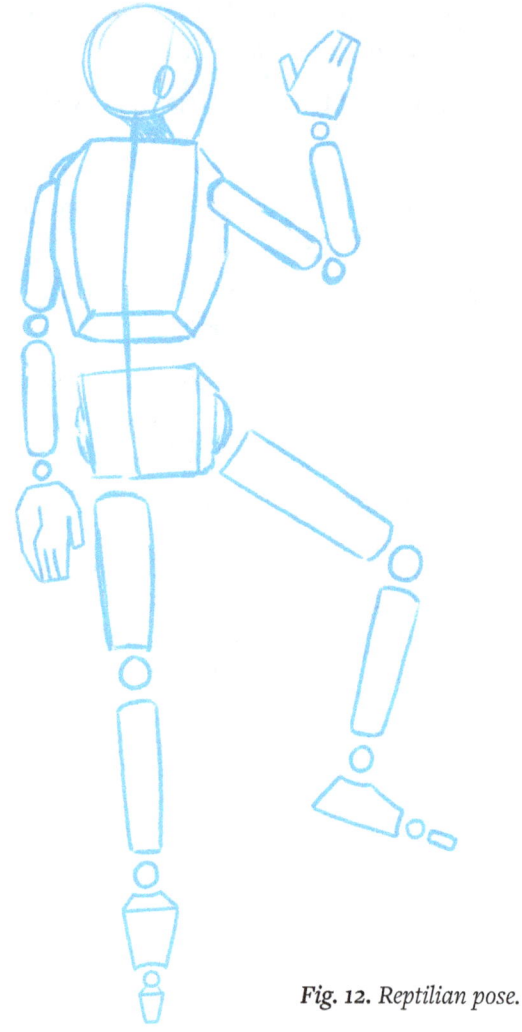

Fig. 12. Reptilian pose.

USING YOUR HANDS LIKE FEET

When we use our hands to do things, we must employ the flexor muscles of the arms and hands, which enable us to grasp and manipulate objects. But this is not the most basic function of the arms, which served, in our four-footed ancestors, as forelimbs that supported us above the ground by extending away from the trunk with the hands or paws opening onto the ground. Although we humans no longer use our arms primarily in this way, this function is still essential to the proper use of the arms, which are linked into, and gain their support from, the extensor muscles of the back and shoulders, which widen apart to support the arms in whatever we are doing. This balanced use of the shoulders and arms can easily be seen in young children, whose shoulders and backs are broadly expansive even when they are grasping and manipulating objects (see *Fig. 1* in previous chapter).

In adults, however, the flexor function tends to dominate and interfere with this extensor function, causing us to habitually shorten the back muscles, narrow across the shoulders, and overuse the flexors of the arms when using our hands and arms. To overcome this, we must restore the lengthened and expansive support of the trunk and shoulders. With the arms now being used in a supportive way, we can stop narrowing across the front of the shoulders and in the biceps, which in turn allows the shoulders to spread apart and the back to work

more fully. When this happens, we get a wonderful sense of widening across the chest and a completely different experience of using our arms.

Exercise 6

Placing hands on a table while in monkey position

To use our hands like feet, we must assume a developmentally primitive posture that makes it possible to support weight on the hands as well as the feet, which is why we begin here with the inclined monkey position. Because this procedure requires that you be able to comfortably place your palms face down on the table, it is important to make sure the table is high enough. If you are fairly tall, you may find that you have to straighten your arms to reach it. If this is the case, place a pile of books on the table for each hand, raising the contact height of the books so that you don't have to extend your arms when you place your hands on the books and they remain somewhat flexed at the elbow.

Part 1: Placing hands on a table

1. Stand in front of a table with your feet shoulder width apart. Give your directions to release your neck muscles to allow your head to nod forward; allow your back to lengthen, and see that you are not gripping in your gluteal muscles so that your seat can drop away from your head and your legs are not braced (*Fig. 13a*).

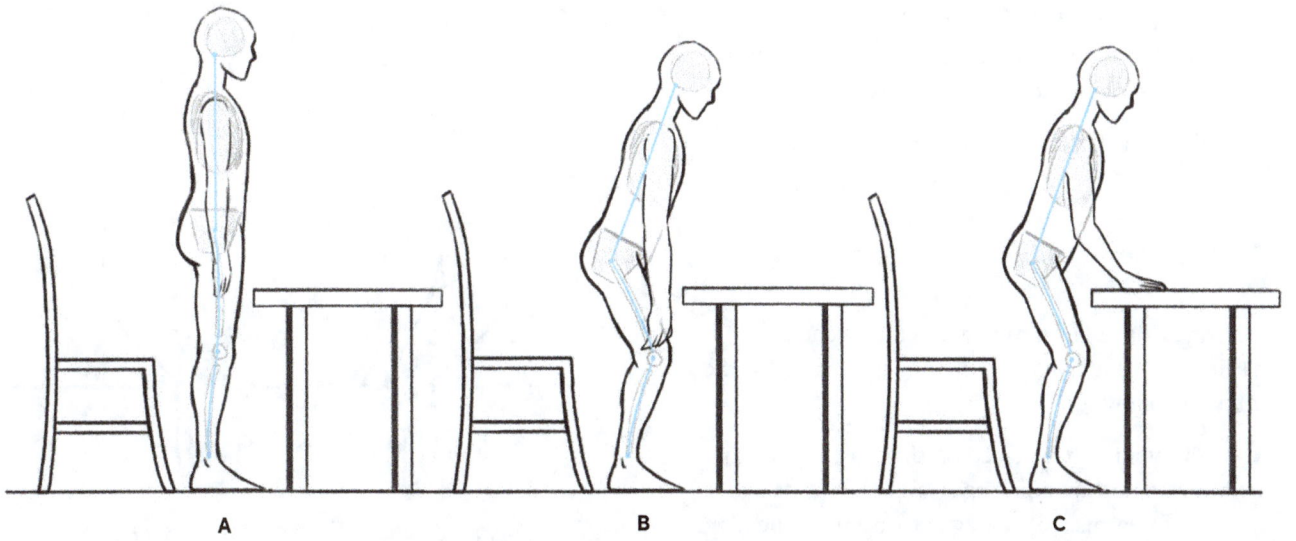

A   B   C

Fig. 13a-c. Placing hands on a table in monkey position.

2. Take yourself into a fully-inclined monkey position and carefully go through your directions, allowing your head to go away from your pelvis and your pelvis from your head so that your back can lengthen, and think of your knees going away from your pelvis and feet so that you are lengthening along the thighs and calves (*Fig. 13b*).

3. Place your hands on the table, palms facing down (*Fig. 13c*).

4. Repeat the directions, allowing your head to go away from your pelvis and your pelvis from your head so that your back can lengthen, and think of your knees going away from your pelvis and feet so that you are lengthening along the thighs and calves.

5. Take your hands off the table and come back to standing.

When you have become thoroughly familiar with this process, you can add several more directions, as follows:

6. Again standing in front of the table, take yourself into monkey position and carefully go through your directions (*Fig. 13b*).

7. Before raising your hands and placing them on the table, think of straightening your fingers to point to the ground. With your fingers straightened, raise your hands at the elbow and place your hands on the table (*Fig. 13c*).

8. Free your neck to allow your head to go forward and up and think of lengthening your back from your sacrum to the back of your skull.

9. Ask for length along your thighs between your gluteal muscles and the back of your knee, and from your heels to the backs of your knees.

10. Take your hands off the table and come back to standing.

Part 2: Directions for the arms and shoulders with hands on table

When you have taken time with Part 1, repeat the earlier steps and add the following directions for the arms, as follows:

1. With your palms placed on the table, notice that your fingers are pointing straight forwards and your forearms are angling outward from the hand (*Fig. 14*).

2. Think of your fingers lengthening from your wrists to your fingertips (*Fig. 14, blue lines on hand*).

3. Think of lengthening your forearms from your wrists to your elbows so that your elbows go away from your wrists (*Fig. 14, blue lines on forearm with arrows to the elbows*).

4. Finally, allow your upper arms to go away from each other so that the upper right arm is going away from the upper left arm and the upper left arm from the upper right arm. This allows the arms to widen apart at the point where the pectoralis major muscle on the front of the body and the latissimus muscle in back attach to the humerus (*Fig. 14, blue line across the shoulders*).

5. Take your hands off the table and come back to standing.

In this four-footed monkey position, your weight is mostly over your feet, which means that you are not actually supporting weight on your arms. With your hands on the table, however, your back is supported more fully than if your arms were hanging freely, allowing your shoulders to spread apart and your back to lengthen and widen as an integrated whole. You may also notice that, in this position, your arms can let go as your palms "open" onto the table surface, which in turn allows your pectoral muscles to undo to allow your shoulders to widen.

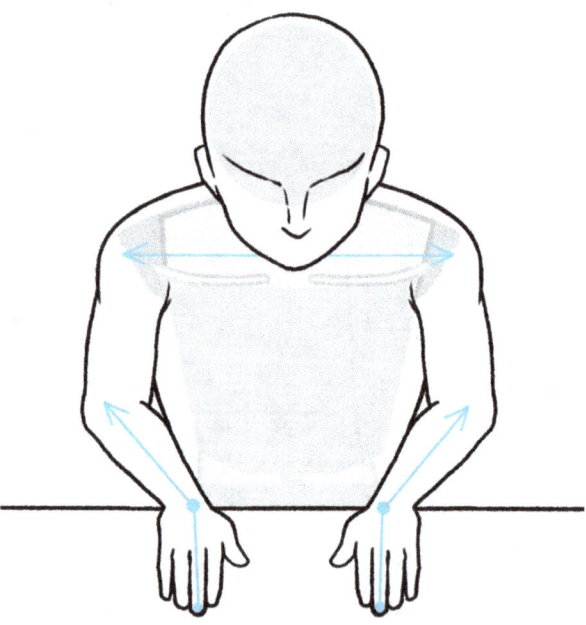

Fig. 14. Directions for the arms and shoulders with hands on table.

The Upper Limb

One of the key ideas we've explored in this book is the principle of muscle length. Muscles contract to produce movement, but they are also scaffolded within a bony framework and, in this context, maintain lengthened support of this framework with a minimum of effort. To be healthy, muscles need to be able to lengthen as well as contract. When we exercise muscles, we are focused on the contraction part of this equation, maintaining muscle mass and keeping muscles toned and healthy. When, in contrast, we passively move or position parts of the body, the muscles are scaffolded within bones, giving them a chance to release into length and allowing muscles that have become chronically short-ened to regain length. Because tight muscles can benefit from being stretched, we tend to assume that we can achieve this condition by relaxing and stretching muscles, but forcing muscles to lengthen does not restore their natural length. To do this, we must position the body parts in such a way that, by using our awareness and thinking process, we encourage muscles to stop contract-ing and to let go between their bony attachments.

In this chapter we will focus specifically on moving and positioning the arms and fingers in such a way that we can encourage lengthening and release in the muscles of the shoulder, rotator cuff, arm, and hand.

The Flexor and Extensor Lines of the Arms

The upper limb is comprised of two muscle groups: the flexors on the front of the upper arm and forearm, and the extensors on the back of the arm and forearm (*Fig. 1*). These muscle groups form the two main compartments of the arm, which we can see in a cross-section of the upper arm (*Fig. 2*).

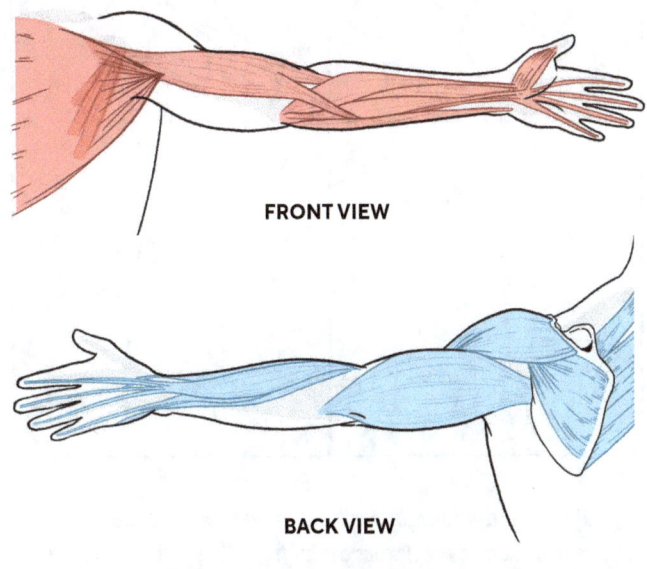

FRONT VIEW

BACK VIEW

Fig. 1a. The flexors (red) and b. Extensors (blue) of the arm.

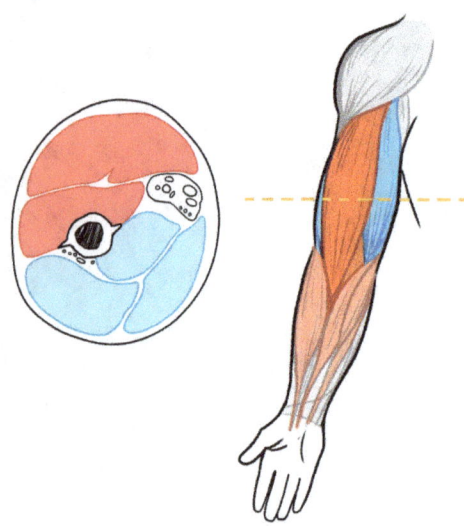

Fig. 2. The arm has two main compartments: the flexors (in red) and extensors (in blue).

In anatomical position—that is, with arms by your side and palms facing forward—the extensors (shown in blue) are on the back of the body and the flexors (shown in red) are in front (*Fig. 3, top row*). If you rotate your hands so that your palms face back, however, you can see that the extensors on the back of the upper arm spiral around to the forearm to face forward, and the flexors on the front of the upper arm spiral around at the forearm to face back (*Fig. 3, middle row*), forming a double-spiral that wraps around the arm (*Fig. 3, bottom row*).

To identify the spiral action of the arm, extend your right arm as if to push something away (*Fig. 4a*), and then raise your hand as if to bring something to your mouth (*Fig. 4b*). In the first action, you will pronate your forearm to face your palm downward, rotating your arm inwardly as you extend at the elbow; in the second action, you will supinate your forearm to turn your palm upward, rotating your arm outwardly as you flex at the elbow. These are the two spirals of the upper limb.

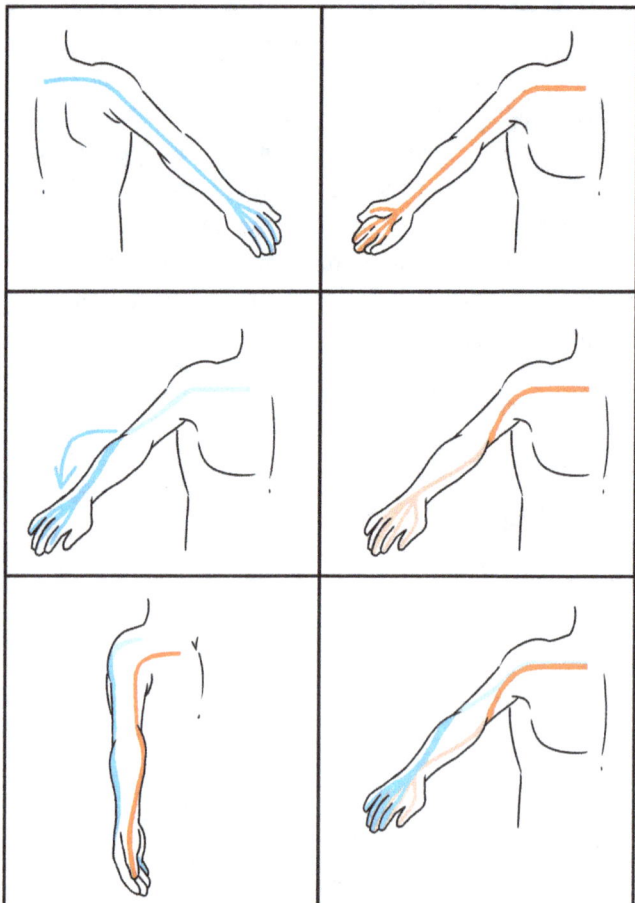

Fig. 3. In anatomical position, the extensors of the arm are in back and the flexors are in front, but when the hand is pronated, the flexors wrap around to the back and the extensors wrap around to the front, forming a double spiral.

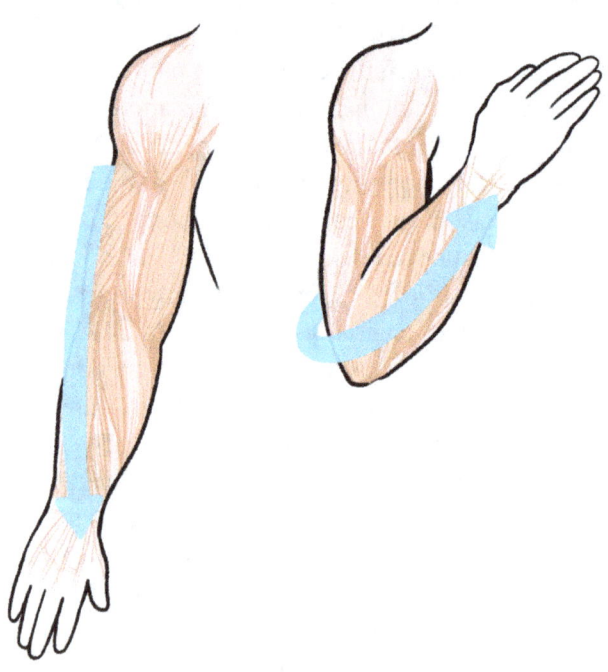

Fig. 4. The arm spirals inwardly when we extend the arm, and outwardly when we flex it.

SUPPORTING THE ARMS TO RELEASE THE EXTENSOR AND FLEXOR SPIRALS OF THE ARMS

When you move your arm, muscles that attach to bones contract to make movement happen. If, in contrast, you let your arm rest on the ground, the weight of the arm exerts gentle stretch on the muscles, which now have a chance to passively lengthen between their bony attachments. This is the idea behind the following exercises, which are designed to encourage lengthening and release of the flexors of the arm. Lying in the semi-supine position with arms and fingers extended is an ideal position for releasing the flexors and extensors of the shoulder and upper limb. In this position, with your palms facing upward, your hands may not fully contact the floor. If necessary, place a pillow under your arms and hands for support, as shown in the illustration (*Fig. 5*).

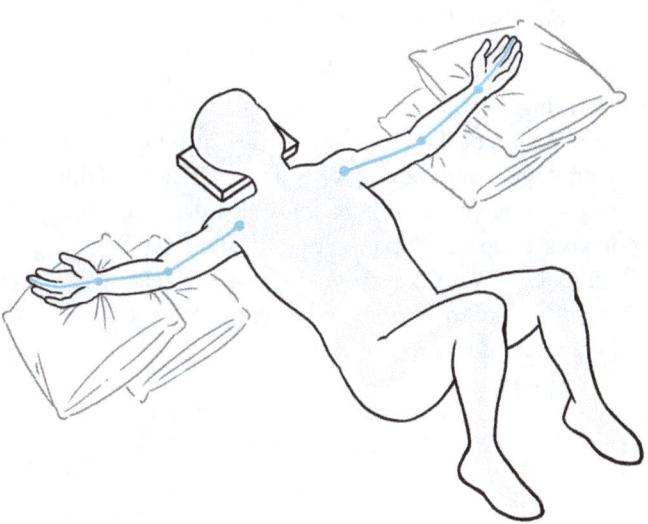

Fig. 5. Semi-supine position with arms extended.

Releasing the extensor spiral of the arm

The extensor line of the arm begins at the spine with the trapezius and rhomboid muscles. Lying in the semi-supine position with arms extended, you can trace a continuous line from the rhomboid and trapezius muscles to the deltoid, triceps, the dorsal surface of the forearms, and into the fingers and pinky side of the hand (see *Fig. 1b*). As you experiment with the following exercise, you will feel this extensor sheet more and more clearly, aided by the contact of your shoulders, arms, and hands on their supporting surfaces.

1. With your arms extended and palms facing upward, gently extend your fingers so that they are pointing away from you (*Fig. 6*).

2. After you have gone through the basic directions, take a moment to be aware of the length of your arms and the contact of your shoulders, arms, hands and fingers on the floor and pillows.

3. Think of your fingers lengthening out of your wrists, paying special attention to the pinky side of your hand.

4. Be aware of the length of your forearms from elbows to fingertips.

5. Be aware of the length of your arms from your shoulders in back to your elbows, and from your elbows to your fingertips.

6. Continue to be aware of your fingers pointing out of your forearm, upper arm, and shoulders.

Thinking of the arm and hand in this way will bring about release in the extensors of the hand and forearm, as well as the muscles at the back of the shoulders. This is coupled with an undoing of the entire shoulder girdle and a toning of the extensor muscles of the shoulder girdle and back.

Exercise 2

Releasing the flexor spiral of the arm

Wiith your arms in the same position, you can trace a continuous line in front from the pectoralis major muscle into the humerus, from the pectoralis minor muscle into its common insertion with biceps brachii at the corocoid process of the scapula, from the biceps muscle to its insertion into the flexors of the forearm, and from the flexors of the forearm into the fingers and thumb (*see Fig. 1a*).

1. Lying in semi-supine position with your arms extended, gently extend your fingers so that they are pointing away from you (*Fig. 6*).

2. Again notice the contact of your arms, hands and fingers on the floor and pillow.

3. Think of your fingers lengthening out of your wrists.

4. Be aware of the length of your forearms from elbows to fingertips.

5. Be aware of the length of your upper arms from the pectoral region of your chest and shoulders to your elbows, and from your elbows to your fingertips.

6. Now think of the length of your entire arm from chest to fingertips.

After you have spent time with your fingers in line with your forearm, deviate your hand so that your thumb is in a straight line with your forearm and continue the exercise as follows (*Fig. 7*):

7. Gently extend your thumbs so that they are "pointing" away from your wrists.

8. Again notice the contact of your arm, hand and fingers on the floor and pillow.

9. Think of your thumbs lengthening out of your wrists. As you do this, you will become more aware of the flexors of the thumb that make up the thenar eminence, the fleshy pad of the thumb.

10. Be aware of the length of your forearms from elbows to thumbs.

11. Be aware of the length of your upper arms from the pectoral region of your chest and shoulders to your elbows, and from your elbows to your thumbs.

12. Continue to think of your thumbs "pointing" out of your forearms, biceps, and pectoral region of your shoulders.

After taking time lying with your arms supported and your fingers and thumbs "pointing" out of the pectoral region of the shoulders, notice any changes in your fingers and right up to your shoulder. Thinking of your fingers may bring about release and opening in your hand, affecting right up to your shoulder. Thinking of your thumb will bring about release of the flexors of the thumb and forearm, as well as the biceps and pectoral muscles.

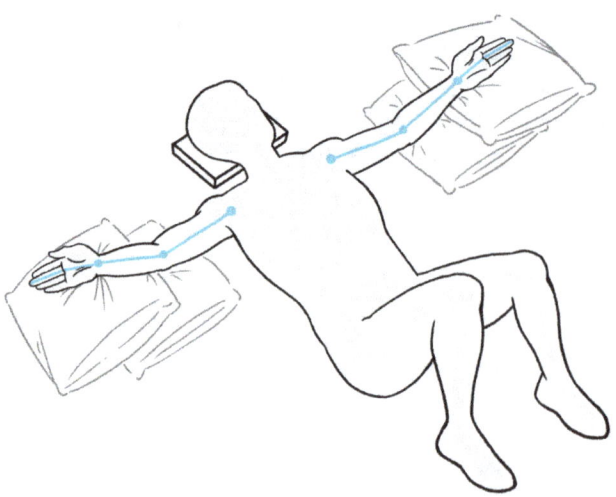

Fig. 6. Semi-supine position with fingers lengthening.

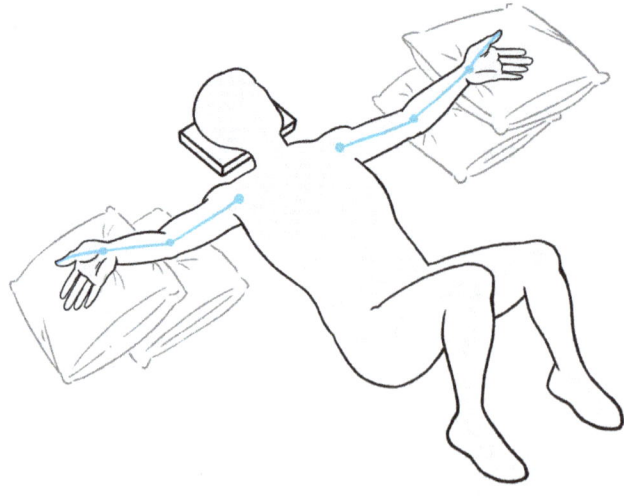

Fig. 7. Semi-supine position with thumbs pointing.

Exercise 3

Semi-supine position and directing your thumbs

In this exercise, we continue with lengthening thumbs and fingers from the arms in semi-supine position.

1. Lying in the semi-supine position, take a moment to be aware of the parts of your body that are supported on the ground.

2. Think of your neck, back, and legs.

3. Raise your hands from the elbows so that, with your elbows still on the ground, your fingers are pointing upward (*Fig. 8*).

4. Take a moment to think of your fingers and thumbs lengthening from your wrists and out of your forearms so that your fingers are pointing to the ceiling.

5. Face your palms toward your feet and lower your arms onto your midriff so that your thumbs are in contact your body and your fingers are pointing upward (*Fig. 9*).

6. Direct your thumbs toward each other.

This exercise uses the contact of the thumb on your body to heighten awareness and bring about release in the flexor spiral of the arm.

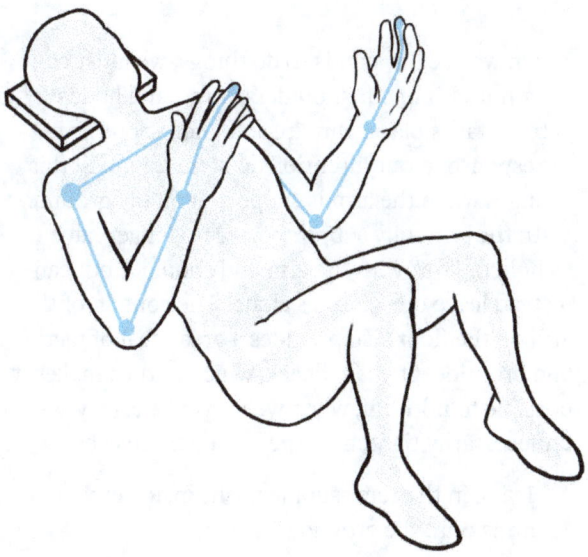

Fig. 8. Semi-supine position with arms raised.

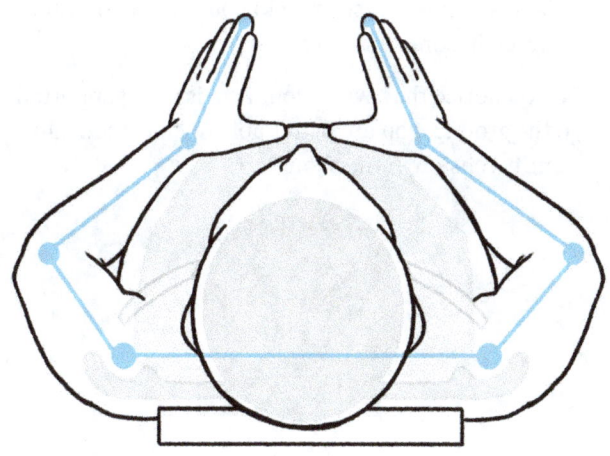

Fig. 9. Thumbs on midriff.

Exercise 4

Moving the arms from a position of support

When we use our hands to do things, we must contract muscles in our shoulders, arms, and hands. This activity takes place, at quite an unconscious level, in response to our intention do something. All this changes when the arm is supported on the ground. With the arm fully supported, we no longer have to hold or "do" with the arm and shoulder but can instead leave our muscles alone. The contact of the arm on the floor also provides a great deal of tactile and proprioceptive feedback, which in turn makes it possible to notice if, when we move the arm, we are unnecessarily tightening the shoulder muscles.

1. Lying in the semi-supine position, lower your arms onto the ground (*Fig. 10a*).

2. Take a moment to notice the length of your arm and the contact of the arm on the floor.

3. Now go ahead and slide your arm along the floor, stopping to notice if you have tightened your neck and shoulder muscles, held your breath, or interfered in some other way (*Fig. 10b*).

Do you notice that, when your arm is fully supported on the ground, you are better able to kinesthetically identify tension in the shoulder?

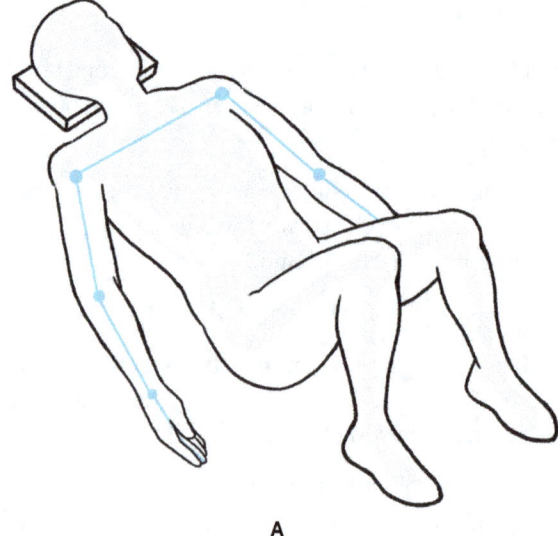

A

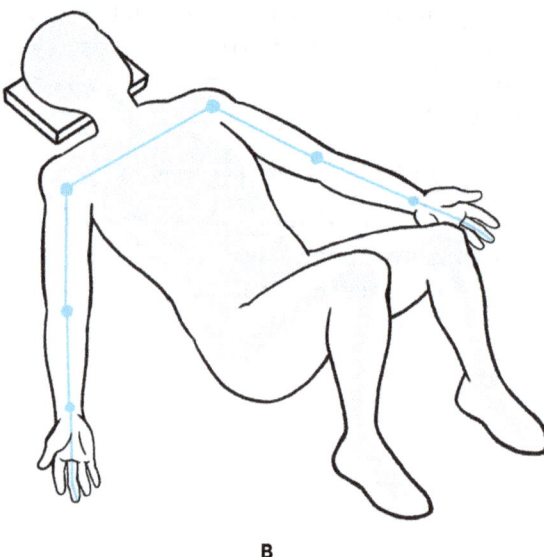

B

Fig. 10a. Arms supported on the ground; b. Moving the arm along the ground.

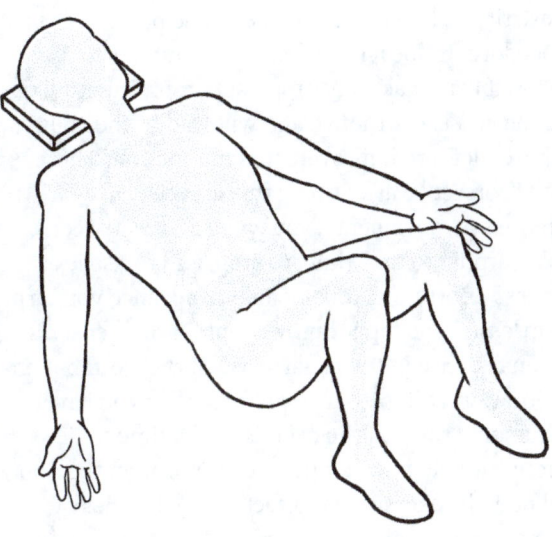

Fig. 11. Lying in semi-supine position with arms placed on the ground.

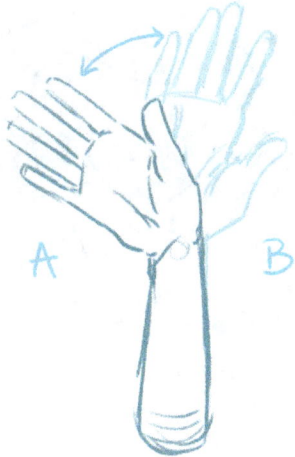

A   B

Fig. 12. Flipper movement of the hand at the wrist.

Exercise 5

Flipper movements of the arm in semi-supine

Before trying out the following procedure, it is useful to consider the reason why we use the hands (or feet) as flippers. When we move the arm along the floor, there is a very strong tendency to move the arm by tightening the shoulder muscles. If you wanted to advance the arm without tightening in this way, a simple way to do this would be to use your hand to move the arm so that the movement is initiated by the hand and not the shoulder. That's the purpose of this exercise: to lead the movement of the arm with the hand so that, instead of contracting shoulder muscles to move the arm, the arm is moved passively by the hand, giving the shoulder muscles a chance to let go. When advancing the arm in this way, you can begin to kinesthetically identify—and prevent—the tightening of the shoulder muscles. With repetition of these exercises, the back and shoulder muscles will become more elastic and the arms will seem to lengthen out of the back.

1. In semi-supine position, lower your arms onto the ground (*Fig. 11*).

2. Take a moment to notice the length of your arm and the contacts of the arm on the floor.

3. Explore the flipper movement of the hand by moving your hand sideways at the wrist (*Fig. 12*).

4. Using your hand as a flipper, see if you can advance your arm away from your body (abduction), without tightening at all in your shoulders (*Figs. 13 and 14*).

5. Stop for a moment and then, without moving your arm as a whole, simply flipper your hand at the wrist. It is this movement that, when your hand pivots on the floor, passively moves the arm. Normally we tighten the shoulder muscles to move the arm and hand; here you are using the hand to move the arm so that, instead of moving the arm from the shoulder, the movement of the arm affects the shoulder.

6. After trying this exercise with both arms, return to the normal semi-supine position and give the directions for neck, head, back, and limbs.

In trying out this exercise, you may find that the temptation to tighten the shoulder will be nearly irresistible. Noticing this is the whole point of the procedure. It does not matter if, at first, it seems impossible to make any progress; simply identifying the tension is instructive and will lead to the ability to make definite improvements in function. There is no "correct" way of doing this exercise. As you explore the movements, you will gain greater control, learning to take time, to stop, and to use less and less effort until you are able to advance your arm effortlessly. The flipper movement, in this sense, is not an exercise in the usual sense of the word but an exploration of how to use the arm. After you have spent some time on the exercise, take time to lie quietly, noticing the contact of your arm on the floor, and how the exercise has affected the muscles of your shoulder and trunk, helping them to let go and release into length.

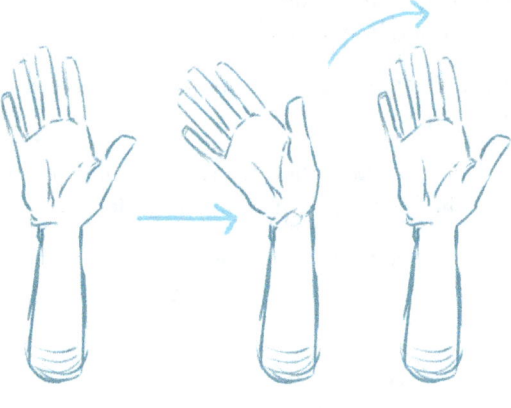

Fig. 13. Using the hand as a flipper, the arm can be advanced along the floor.

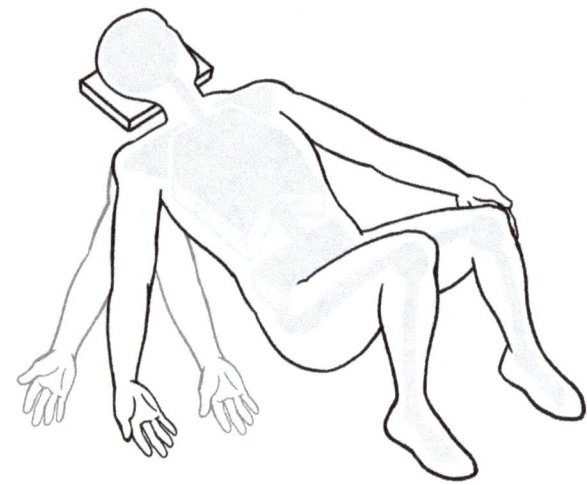

Fig. 14. Advancing the arm along the floor.

The Hand

The hand is a remarkable achievement of nature—what Jacob Bronowsky in *The Ascent of Man* called "the cutting edge of the mind." With it, we can touch and feel objects, use tools, play musical instruments, and create works of art. Comprised of no fewer than 27 bones, over 30 muscles, thousands of motor units and even more touch and pain receptors—all mapped out in fine detail on the sensory and motor cortices of the brain—the hand is both an extraordinarily sensitive sensory device and an equally subtle motor tool.

But how does the hand actually work? Perhaps because we have such direct control over our fingers and hand, most of us do not question how we use our hands or whether we need to learn more about the hand and how it works. Is the use of the hand related to the shoulders? How do we oppose the thumb to the fingers? Does constant flexion of the fingers affect how the hand works? How do we know if we are using the hand efficiently?

We have already seen that the use of the hand is based on our upright posture and, in particular, on the naturally widened support of the shoulder girdle. To use the hand properly, we must see to it that we do not overuse the flexors of the shoulder and arm so that, when we oppose the thumb to the fingers or perform other fine motor movements, the hand as a whole remains open and

flexion takes place with a minimum of effort. In the exercises that follow, we will look at the use of the hands in relation to the arms and shoulder, exploring ways of opening the hand as the basis for using them with a minimum of effort. We'll begin by exploring the forearm muscles that act on the hand and fingers, and progress from there to the hand itself.

Further reading:

Anatomy in Action,
Chapter 9. The Shoulder Girdle

Anatomy in Action, Chapter 10. The Arms

The Body in Motion,
Chapter 5. The Shoulder Girdle

The Body in Motion, Chapter 6. The Upper Limb

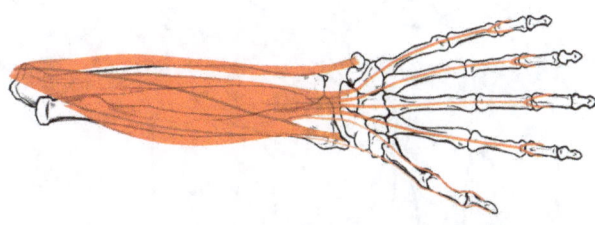

Fig. 1. The muscles of the forearm taper into tendons that move the hand and fingers (right hand with palm facing).

Opening the Hand

The main muscles that move the hand and fingers are on the forearm, not the hand itself (*Fig. 1*). Some of these muscles taper into tendons that attach to, and move the hand at, the wrist; the muscles that move the fingers taper into tendons that pass over the wrist and attach to the thumb and fingers. Because we spend so much time flexing the hand, these muscles tend to become shortened and overworked, making it difficult to fully extend the fingers and open the palm. Even when we actively extend our fingers, they will quickly curl up again, indicating that there is chronic tension in the forearm muscles and that we are not fully in control of the hand.

How then do we release these muscles and open the hand? Think what would happen if, instead of tightening and flexing your fingers, someone were to gently extend your fingers at the joints. We saw that, when the forearm muscles tighten, the tendons pull on the fingers, but here it's the other way around: when the fingers lengthen, they pull on the tendons and exert a gentle stretch on the muscles. That's how we can begin to open the hand. By extending and "directing" the fingers, the forearm muscles will begin to release, the fingers will start to lengthen out of the forearm and the palms will open up.

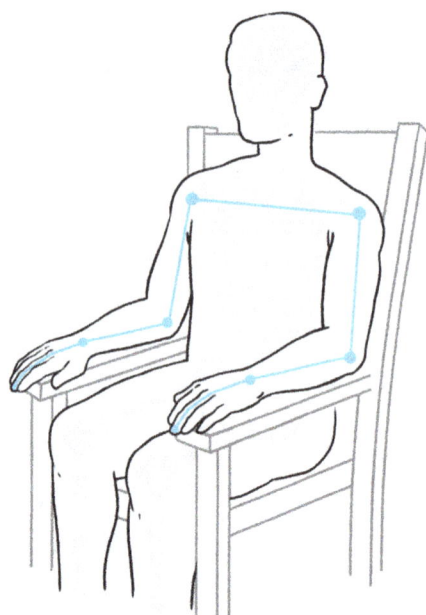

Fig. 2. Directing the arms while sitting in an armchair.

LENGTHENING THE FINGERS WHILE SITTING IN AN ARMCHAIR

In Chapter 7, we directed the arms and shoulders while sitting in a supportive armchair. This is a good way to explore the hand and forearm. We'll begin by reviewing the procedures for directing the arms and shoulders with forearms supported on the arms of the chair. As before, if you do not have an armchair, sit in a straight-back chair with your hands resting on your lap, close to your trunk so that your arms are not dragging your shoulders forward.

Exercise 1, Part 1

Directing the arms in sitting position (Fig. 2)

As in the earlier exercise, we will identify the segments of the upper limb while sitting in an armchair with the arms supported, becoming aware of each piece and putting them together to form a whole.

1. Sitting comfortably in the armchair with your feet flat on the floor, your back supported, and your hands resting on the arm of the chair (or on your lap if you do not have an armchair), allow your trunk to come to its full length, your head to balance forward and up, and your knees to go away from your hips.

2. Be aware of the length of your forearm from your fingertips to your elbows. Take time until you can feel the length of your forearm with your fingers lengthening our of your forearm.

3. Be aware of the length of your upper arms from your elbows to your shoulders.

4. Be aware of the breadth of your shoulders in front and in back.

5. Link up the parts so that you feel the length of your arms from fingertips to elbows, elbows to shoulders, and across your shoulders as a continuous whole. Take your time with this, repeating parts of this exercise as needed, until all the parts come into your awareness and you can clearly feel the segments in part and as a whole.

Exercise 1, Part 2

Lengthening your fingers

Let's now focus on directing the fingers out of the forearm in order to open the hand while supporting your elbows on the arm of the chair. If you do not have an armchair, sit at a desk, turn your chair to face to the left so that you can comfortably place your right elbow on the desk with your fingers pointing upward, and focus on just your right arm alone before facing the other way and focusing on your left arm.

1. Sitting in the armchair, raise your hands so that, with your elbows remaining in contact with the chair, your fingers are pointing to the ceiling (*Fig. 3a*).

2. Turn your attention to your thumbs and each of your fingers, which will begin to come into your awareness. Allow your thumbs and fingers to relax.

3. If your fingers are slightly curled, don't force them to straighten but simply take time to become aware of them and allow them to soften and relax.

4. Begin very gently to straighten your fingers. Do not force them to straighten but simply allow them to uncurl bit by bit.

5. When the fingers are more or less straight, think of them "pointing" upward, as if you are directing energy out of your fingertips toward the ceiling.

6. Continuing to think of your fingers pointing upward, turn your awareness to your forearms from elbows to fingertips so that you are now thinking of your fingers lengthening right out of your forearms. You may notice, as you do this, that your forearm muscles come into your awareness and that your fingers and palms are opening up slightly.

7. Spend a minute or so letting your fingers lengthen and straighten in this way, seeing if you can do so without stiffening or overextending them.

8. Now deviate your hands at the wrist so that your thumbs are in line with your forearms and pointing up to the ceiling (*Fig. 3b*).

9. Take a minute to be aware of your thumbs, and then be aware of the length of your forearms from elbows to thumbs.

10. Think of your thumbs pointing to the ceiling, coming out of the entire length of your forearms as you do so.

11. If you are sitting at a table, face in the other direction and do the same with your left arm.

After doing this exercise over several days, you will find that you will become more aware of your fingers and hands and that, as you get better at "directing" your fingers and thumbs, they will lengthen out of your palms and forearms to allow your hands to open up.

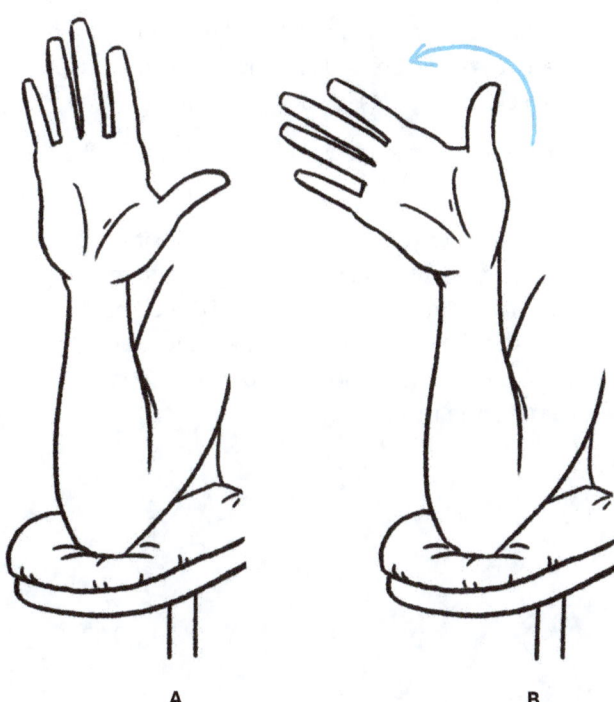

Fig. 3. *Position of hand with (**a**) fingers in line with the forearm, and (**b**) thumb in line with forearm.*

A   B

Exercise 2

Lengthening the fingers by being aware of the joints

In this exercise, we continue to give attention to the fingers as an extension of the forearm, this time focusing on the joints. If the muscles of the forearm act on the fingers at the joints, then it follows that paying attention to the joints will have the reverse effect of stopping the muscles from tightening and aiding in opening the hand.

1. With hands raised and fingers pointing to the ceiling, turn your attention to your right index finger and notice that it has three joints—the knuckle joint at the base of the finger, the middle joint and the distal joint for the last digit (*Fig. 4, blue areas*). Take a moment to be aware of each joint, seeing if you can feel them kinesthetically. As very sensitive instruments, we have a great deal of kinesthetic or proprioceptive feedback from the hands. You will find that, as you pay attention to these joints, each joint will come into your awareness.

2. Now turn your attention to the three joints of each finger in turn, not forgetting your thumb, which has only two joints. Don't worry if you can't feel every joint; just taking time to be aware will bring about improvements, allowing your fingers to soften and unfurl and your palms to open up.

3. After a minute or so, you will find that your awareness has increased and that you can more or less feel all the joints in your right hand.

4. Turn your attention to your left hand and do the same.

5. Notice that, as you become aware of the joints, your fingers will seem to soften and begin to straighten. This makes it easier to "direct" the fingers to the ceiling, as if they have more energy to point even though you are not actively trying to straighten them.

As a manipulative instrument, we have a great deal of control over our hand and fingers. Do you notice that, by focusing on your fingers, you become increasingly aware of each one, and that you can actively extend each finger until, with time, they seem to lengthen and soften? If your fingers are still somewhat curled up, do not force them to straighten but let them remain the way they are and simply pay attention to the joints. Even if you can't feel it happening, being aware of the joints will help the flexor muscles of your forearm to release, which in turn will allow your fingers to lengthen and your hand to open up.

You may also notice that, when you pay attention to your fingers and hands, your kinesthetic awareness of the hands is heightened. As a very sensitive motor and tactile instrument, the hand gives us a great deal of information about the world; it is easier to forget that we are also highly aware of the hand itself. This applies to other parts of the body as well but, because the hand is under direct conscious control and is so highly endowed with sensory and motor nerves, it is one of the easiest parts of the body to work with and to become more aware of.

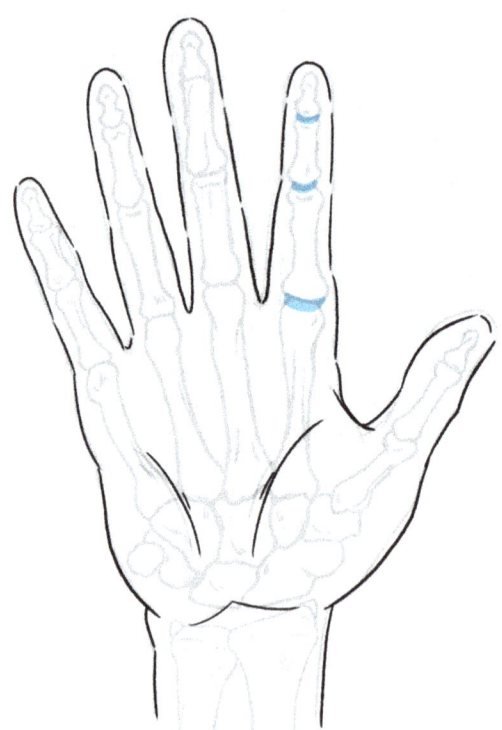

Fig. 4. The bones and joints of the hand: the three joints of the index finger are shown in blue. Each finger has three joints and the thumb has two.

USING THE HANDS LIKE FEET

Let's turn now to the hand itself. We've seen that, although the hands are designed for grasping and manipulating objects, they can also be used for bearing weight, as when we go down on all fours or push a large object with open palms. Many infants go through a phase of crawling on all fours, reenacting that phase of our evolutionary heritage in which all four limbs were used for walking on the ground. As we've seen, using the hands in this way is connected with the coordinated and expansive use of the shoulder in which the extensors are providing active support and the flexors, which tend to contract and interfere with the shoulder and arm, become less active. Although we are all familiar with the hand's fine motor capabilities, we are much less familiar with this more primitive, yet crucial, use of the hand.

When we are on all fours, we support weight generally on the palms, but it is the heel of the hand that bears most of the weight. But where (and what) exactly is the heel of the hand? The heel of the hand is the area closest to the wrist joint and is made up of eight carpal bones (*Fig. 5*). When we think of the wrist, we are likely to think of the place where the wrist watch goes, just above the bumps on either side of the wrist. This is actually not your wrist but your forearm. More accurately, the wrist joint is where the bones of the wrist articulate with your forearm. The wrist also refers to the wrist bones themselves—the carpal bones that form the base of the hand. Anatomy books refer to these as wrist bones (in contrast to the bones of the hand), but these bones form the heel of the hand, so we could say that the wrist is actually part of the hand itself (*Fig. 6*). In this series of exercises, we'll explore the heel of the hand and its role in opening the hand.

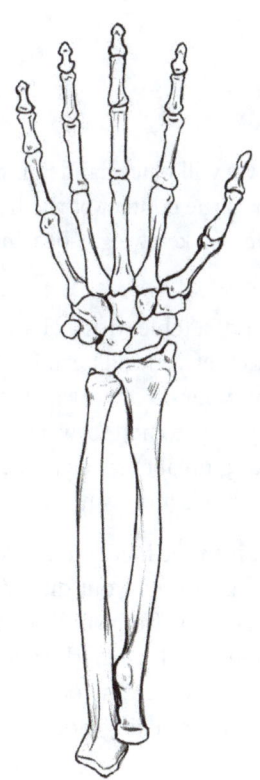

Fig. 5. Bones of the hand and forearm.

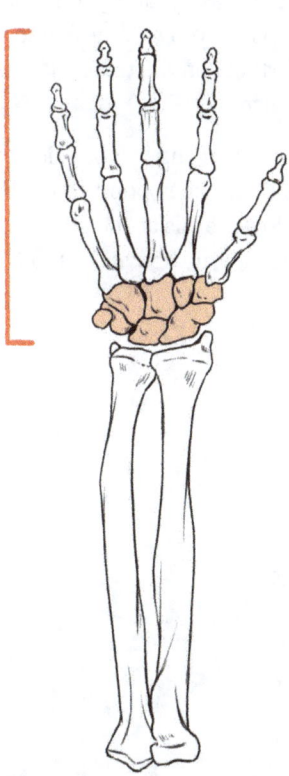

Fig. 6. The eight carpal bones (in pink) that make up the wrist area are actually part of the hand itself.

Exercise 3

Placing the heel of the hand on a table while sitting

In this exercise, we will place hands on the table, paying attention to the contact of the heel of the hand on the table as a key weight-bearing part of the hand.

1. Stand in front of a table with a chair placed behind you so that you will be able to sit at the table. Give your directions so that you are allowing your head to nod forward, your back to lengthen, your gluteal muscles to let go, and your knees to go forward and away.

2. Take yourself into the inclined monkey position and carefully go through your directions, allowing your head to go away from your pelvis and your pelvis from your head to lengthen your back, and your knees to go away from your pelvis and feet so that you are lengthening along the thighs and calves.

3. Let your knees go away and sit in the chair, come back gently from your hips so that you are sitting upright, and carefully go through your directions. If necessary, bring your chair closer to the table so that you will be able to place your hands comfortably on the table without having to extend your arms.

4. With your arms hanging by your sides, straighten your fingers so that they point to the floor and, flexing your lower arms at the elbow, raise your hands so that they are above the table.

5. Keeping your fingers straight, lower your hands so that the heels of your hands contact the table (*Fig. 7a*). Allow your thumbs to relax and contact the table, but see if you can keep your hands and fingers extended and raised slightly above the table.

6. Now lower the rest of your hand onto the table so that your palms and fingers—that is, the whole of the hand—are in contact with the table (*Fig. 7b*).

7. In addition to the heel of your hand, you will now feel your thumb, the pads of your fingers, and the pinky side of your hand, or hypothenar eminence, in contact with the table.

Can you see how the heel of the hand makes contact with the table as a key point of support? If you're clear that the wrist bones hinge in relation to the forearm to contact the table, and that they make contact with the table, this will help your hands to start to open up as you use your hands like feet.

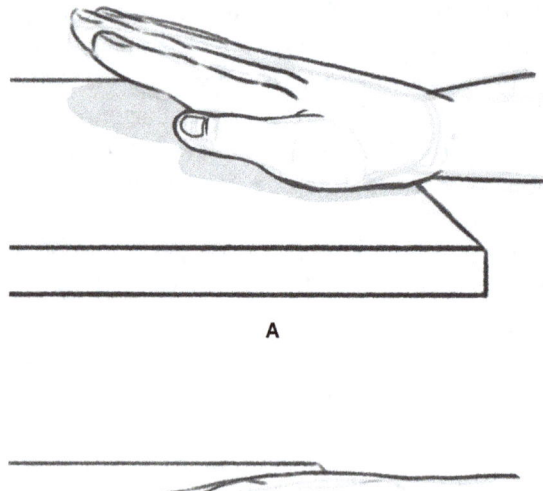

A

B

Fig. 7a. Placing the heel of the hand on table; b. Letting the fingers go on is a more open way of using the hand.

Placing your hand on a wall

In this exercise, we'll again place the palm on a flat surface, observing how the wrist joint lets go to allow the heel of the hand to make contact with the surface.

1. Stand in front of a door jamb so that you have a wall with a surface on which to place your right hand.

2. Straighten the fingers of your right hand so that they are pointing to the ground and, with fingers leading, raise your arm at the elbow and bring your hand very gently to the wall. If only your fingers contact the wall, do not force your palm onto the wall, leaving your hand where it is for the moment (*Fig. 8a*).

3. Now see if you can release your wrist joint to allow the heel of your hand to contact the wall. Do not push the heel of your hand against the wall; simply allow your wrist to let go and see if the heel will naturally go onto the wall (*Fig. 8b*).

4. Notice that, as you allow your wrist to contact the wall, the palm of your hand will now be fully in contact with the wall. Notice also that the wrist bones, functioning as part of the hand, are the key point of contact of the hand with the wall.

Here again we see that, when we use the hand, we tend to be less aware of the heel of the hand than the fingers, which in this case make contact with the wall ahead of the wrist. When we release in the wrist joint and allow the wrist bones, or heel of the hand, to contact the wall—and when we see that the heel of the hand is part of the hand—then we are using the hand as a "foot" and the hand becomes more open.

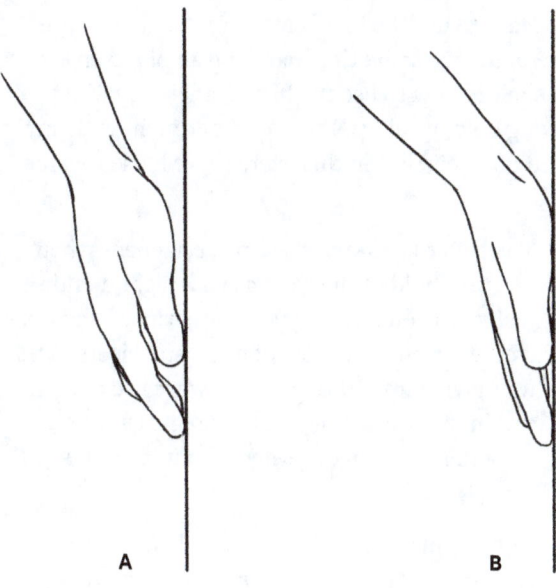

A   **B**

*Fig. 8a. Place hand on wall. **b**. Release at the wrist joint to allow the heel of your hand to contact the wall.*

Exercise 5

Grasping an object using the heel of the hand

To learn to use the hands in a more open way, it is useful to take some time handling an object in order to explore how to use the hands efficiently when taking hold of things. You can experiment with any kind of object, but in this exercise we'll use a water glass.

1. To begin this exercise, see what happens when you take hold of the glass as you might do normally. Do you notice if you have gripped the glass with your fingers? Most of us grasp objects in this way, giving little thought to how we use our hands and in many cases using an extreme amount of tension in the fingers even when it is not necessary (*Fig. 9*).

2. Now try placing the heel of your hand on the glass instead of your fingers. You can do this initially by first raising your right hand. Holding the glass with your left hand, place it against the heel of your right hand (*Fig. 10a*). When you have done this, let your fingers fold onto the object (*Fig. 10b*). (After trying this, you can simply lay the glass on its side on the table and place the heel or palm of your hand on the glass, seeing if you can make full contact with the glass before using your fingers to grasp or hold it.)

3. Do you notice that, when the glass is in contact with the heel and palm of your hand, it takes very little effort to grasp it and feels quite secure in your hand? You may also notice that, with a larger surface area of your hand in contact with the glass, the hand and fingers no longer have to grip the object but can remain quite open.

The universal tendency, when we take hold of objects, is to grip with the fingers. By using the heel of the hand, we regain the ability to contact objects with an open palm, giving us a sense of how open the hand can be and how to use the hand in a more receptive and sensual way.

THE TOPOGRAPHY OF THE HAND

We've seen that the muscles of the forearm, which powerfully flex the fingers and hand at the wrist, are responsible for much of the "grippiness" in the hand and fingers. But the hand itself can become tense and shortened, particularly in the thumb and pinky areas. To fully open the hand, we must pay attention not just to the forearm and the weight-bearing functions of the hand but to the hand itself, and to the parts that become tight and constricted.

We can identify four key areas of the hand: the heel, or region nearest the wrist joint (purple); the thenar eminence, the pad forming the base of the thumb (blue); the hypothenar eminence, the pad forming the base of the pinky (yellow); and the pads at the base of the fingers (pink), which form an arch corresponding to the lateral arch of the foot (*Fig. 11*). The heel of the hand includes the lower part of each pad as well as the gap in between, which is the carpal tunnel.

Fig. 9. When we grasp objects, we usually use our fingers, often using far more tension than is necessary.

A

B

Fig. 10a. Contacting the glass with the heel of the hand; b. Folding the fingers onto the glass.

The Hand   **9**

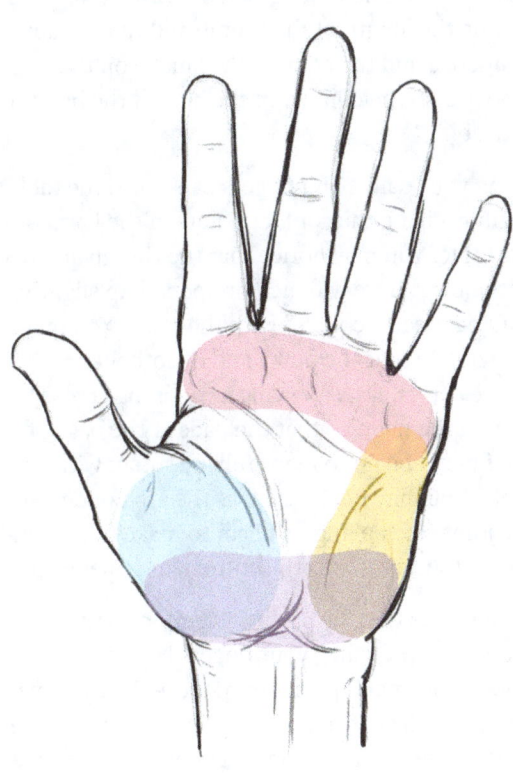

Fig. 11. The topography of the hand.

Exercise 6, Part 1

Opening the hands while placing palms on the table

In this exercise, we will identify the fleshy regions of the hand that make contact when placing the palm on a surface, letting these areas make fuller contact and bringing about more release and openness in the hand.

1. Stand in front of the table with a chair placed behind you so that you will be able to sit at the table, feet slightly apart. Give your directions so that you are allowing your head to nod forward, your back to lengthen, your gluteal muscles to let go, and your knees to go forward and away.

2. Let your knees go away to sit in the chair, come back gently from your hips into fully upright sitting and go carefully through your directions. If necessary, bring your chair closer to the table so that you will be able to place your hands on the table without having to extend your arms.

3. Lengthen your fingers so that they point to the floor, raise your hands at the elbows and place your hands gently on the table, palms facing down and fingers pointing forwards.

4. With your palms placed face-down on the table, notice what parts of your hand are in contact with the table: the heel of your hand, the pinky, the thumb, and the pads of the fingers. You may also feel the contact of the meaty section on the pinky side of the palm (the hypothenar eminence) and the meaty pad at the base of the thumb (the thenar eminence) on the table. Do not try to flatten your palm onto the table; it is normal for the pads at the base of your fingers, which form the arch of the hand, to remain off the table.

5. Again notice the contact of the pads and the meaty parts of the palm on the surface and, without stiffening the joints of the fingers or thumb, direct each finger in turn to lengthen. Also take a moment to be aware of the joints of the fingers and thumbs, as in Exercise 2.

Exercise 6, Part 2

Exploring the contact of thumbs and pinky on the table

The thenar and hypothenar eminence are the muscular pads on either side of the hand that move the thumb and small finger (*Fig. 12*). In this exercise we focus on lengthening and releasing these regions in order to fully open up the hand.

1. With your palms on the table (*Fig. 13a*), rotate your hands slightly at the forearm so that your thumbs and the heels of your hands come up off the table an inch or two and the pinky side of your hand is more fully in contact with the table (*Fig. 13b*).

2. Feel the length of your pinky and the fleshy part of the hypothenar eminence and the contact they make with the table. You may notice how this area of the hand will begin to release and open up, giving you greater contact on that side of the hand.

3. Allow your palm to come back into contact with the table and then raise or extend your fingers off the table so that your thumbs and the heel of your hand remain in contact with the table, with your fingers angling upwards off the table (*Fig. 13c*). In this position, the thumb and the heel of the hand will be fully in contact with the table.

4. Allow the thumb to lengthen out of your forearm, feeling the length of the thumb and the thenar eminence and the contact they make on the table. Notice also the contact of the heel of the hand on the table.

5. Bring your palms and fingers back onto the table, again noticing the contact points of the hand on the table. You may notice that the thumb and heel of the hand have widened or opened up slightly, making greater contact with the table. You may also notice that the pinky and hypothenar eminence can release, allowing a widening across the arch of the hand so that the pads at the base of the fingers begin to make fuller contact with the table. You may notice that, as the arch opens up, the joints of the fingers begin to make fuller contact with the table as the entire hand opens up.

Can you notice that, by paying attention to these contact points on the table, your fingers begin to soften and the palms open up? In our modern lifestyle, we spend a great deal of time flexing the fingers in order to use the hands as motor instruments. In these exercises we have focused on the receptive and sensory aspects of the hand, which tend to become more activated when we use the hands like feet.

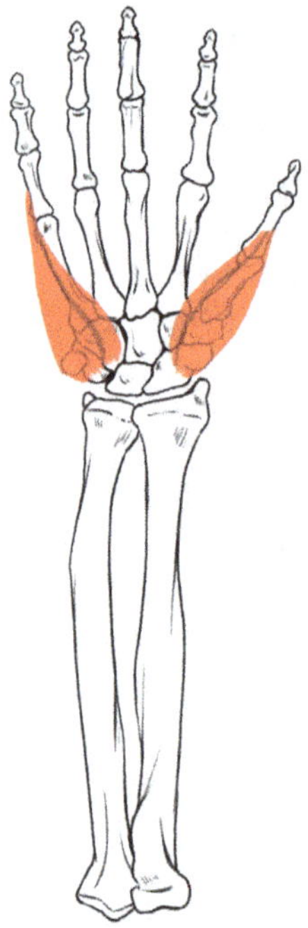

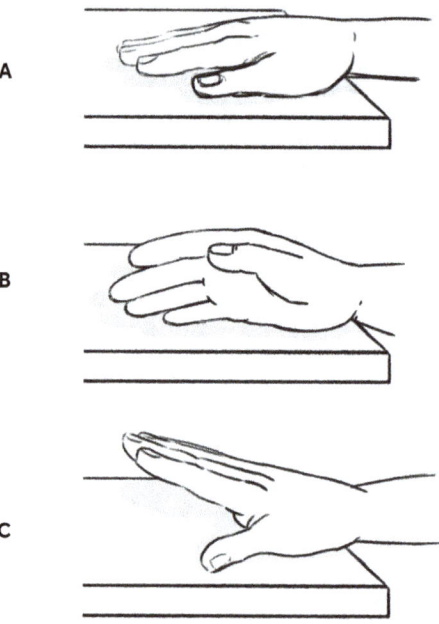

*Fig. 13a. Palm on table; **b.** Forearm rotated with pinky side in contact with the table; **c.** Fingers raised with thumb and heel of hand in contact with the table.*

Fig. 12. The thenar and hypothenar eminences.

Exercise 6, Part 3

Directing the arms and shoulders with palms on the table surface while sitting

Now that we've spent time opening the hands, let's return to the use of the hands and shoulder girdle, connecting the opening of the palms on the table with the widening of the shoulders.

1. With your palms on the table, take a moment to notice the position of your fingers, wrists, and arms on the table. Your fingers are pointing directly forwards, your forearms angle outwards from your hands, and your elbows are going "away" from your wrists (see lines in *Fig. 14*).

2. Be aware of the length of your fingers from your wrists to your fingertips (see lines on hands).

3. Be aware of the length of your forearms from your wrists to your elbows (blue lines on forearms with arrows).

4. Finally, allow your upper arms to go away from each other so that your right upper arm is going away from your left upper arm, and your left upper arm from your right, to allow your shoulders to widen or spread apart (horizontal blue line on shoulder).

Do you notice that, with your fingers lengthening and your palms opening onto the table surface, you can let go in your arms and that the shoulders can widen? This is a key reason why it is important to work on the hands. Allowing your hand to open onto the surface encourages more active engagement of the extensors of the shoulders and arms. Using the hands in this open way has little connection with grasping and therefore enables the hand, arm, and shoulder to work in a completely new and coordinated way.

Further reading:

The Body in Motion, Chapter 6. The Upper Limb

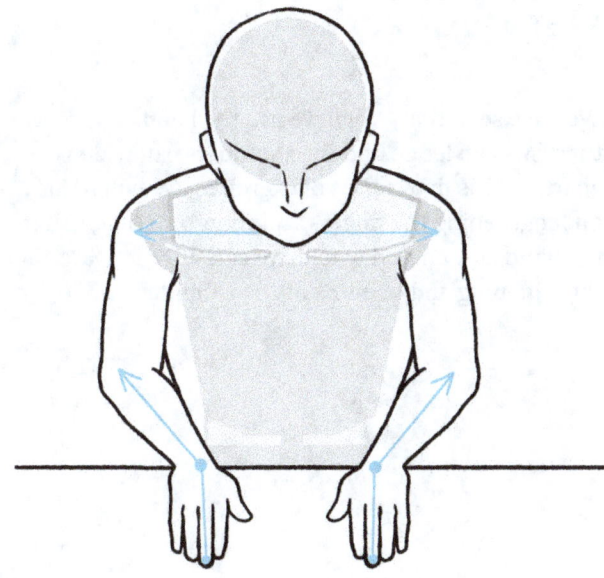

Fig. 14. Directing the arms and shoulders with palms on the table surface while sitting.

USING THE HANDS LIKE FEET REVISITED

We have seen that, when we use the hands like feet, the arms can let go and the shoulders can widen apart. In this final series of exercises, we will focus on lengthening the fingers and thumb so that, using the hand as a unified whole, we can fully activate the widening and opening of the shoulders.

Exercise 7, Part 1

Raising your arms at the elbows and extending your fingers

Let's begin by focusing on extending the fingers and thumb of the hands so that each hand can begin to work as a unit.

1. Standing with feet apart, go through your basic directions.

2. Raise your arms at the elbows and notice that your fingers will naturally tend to curl up (*Figs. 15 and 16a*).

3. Spend a minute or so gently extending your fingers, seeing if you can do so without stiffening or overextending them.

4. If you find it difficult to keep all your fingers straight, spend time straightening each finger individually.

5. As your fingers straighten, try bringing them together.

6. Thinking of your thumbs lengthening, see if you can tuck each thumb alongside your fingers so that the fingers and thumb of each hand are more or less flat and form a single unit (*Fig. 16b*).

7. When you have spent some time doing this, lower your arms, seeing if you can keep your fingers straight.

8. Try this exercise once again, this time seeing if, from the outset of the exercise, you can extend all your fingers with thumb alongside, so that your hand is now functioning as a unit with palms open and fingers fully extended.

When trying out this exercise, it may feel at first that your fingers do not want to fully extend and that it requires effort to keep them extended (*Fig. 16a*). Do not worry about this; as you gain more openness in the hand, your fingers will begin to respond better, the hand will open up and the sense of effort will disappear (*Fig. 16b*).

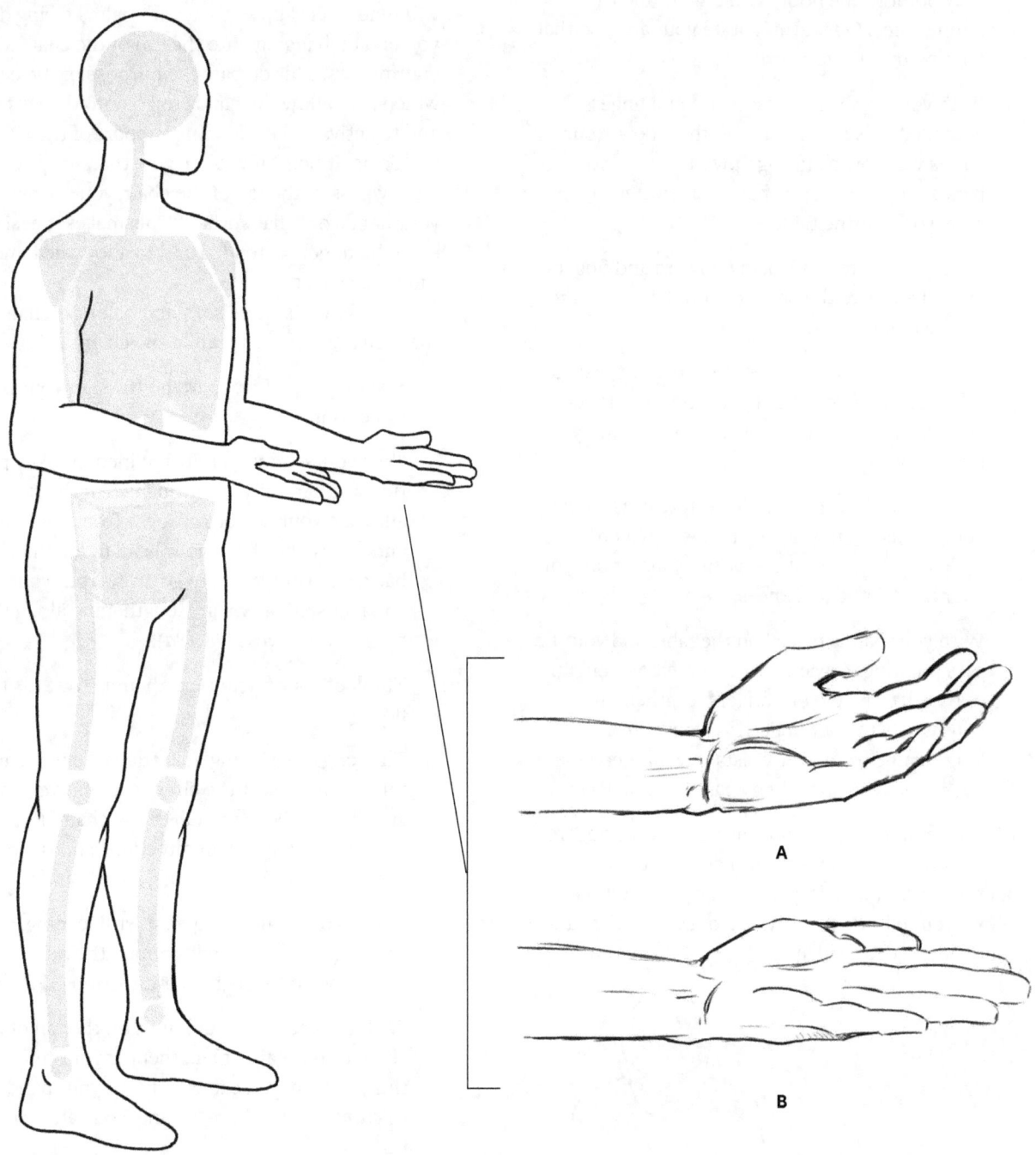

Fig. 15. *Raising hands at elbows.*

Fig. 16. *Using the hand as a foot:*
a. *Fingers curled; b. Fingers extended.*

Exercise 7, Part 2

Placing hands on the table with fingers extended

With your fingers and thumbs functioning as a unit, let's focus now on placing the hands on the table.

1. Sitting at the table, lengthen your fingers so that they point to the floor, with fingers and thumbs in one piece. Outwardly rotate your arms so that your palms face forward.

2. With your palms facing forward and fingers extended, raise your hands at the elbow. Your palms will now be facing upward so that your hands are at or slightly below elbow height, just above or near the table.

3. With your palms still facing upward and fingers extended, place the backs of your hands gently on the table.

4. Repeat your primary directions for your neck to release so that your head goes forward and up, your back lengthens, and your knees go away from your hips.

5. Gently rotate, or pronate, your forearms so that your hands are now facing palms down on the table (*Fig. 17*). Repeat the primary directions for your head, back, and knees.

6. With your palms placed on the table and your fingers pointing forwards with your elbows angling outward, think of your fingers lengthening from your wrists to your fingertips, your forearms lengthening from your wrists to your elbows, and your shoulders spreading apart (*arrows, Fig. 17*).

With your hands functioning as a unit, your fingers lengthening nicely out of your hands, and your hands opening onto the table, you may notice that this allows your elbows to go away from your wrists and your shoulders to widen.

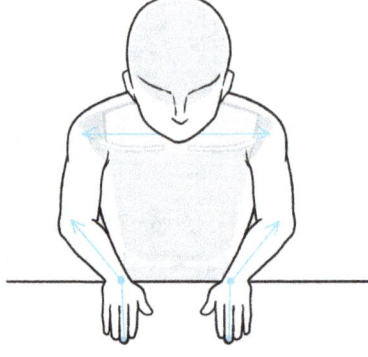

Fig. 17. Directing the arms and shoulders with palms on the table surface while sitting.

Exercise 7, Part 3

Placing hands on the rail of the chair with fingers extended

In this exercise, we will place hands on the rail of a chair while in the inclined monkey position—that is, while standing on two feet. You may find that, without a flat surface for your hands, your fingers will tend to curl up so that, with palms facing down, you end up hanging onto the rail of the chair with your fingers. This defeats the purpose of the exercise, which is to allow the hands to go onto the surface and to activate the widening support of the shoulders and arms. It helps if you imagine that, in spite of the narrowness of the rail of the chair, you are placing your hands on a flat surface. This makes it easier to keep the fingers extended and to allow the hands to function as feet.

To begin this exercise, stand behind a chair so that you are facing the rail of the chair.

1. Standing with feet apart, go through your basic directions.

2. Take yourself into a fully inclined monkey position and carefully go through your directions, allowing your head to go away from your pelvis and your pelvis from your head to lengthen your back, and your knees to go away from your pelvis and feet so that you are lengthening along the thighs and calves (*Fig. 18a*).

3. Think of your fingers lengthening towards the floor.

4. Thinking of your fingers leading the movement, raise your arms at the elbows so that your hands are slightly above the rail of the chair (*Fig. 18b*). Go through your main directions and the directions for your fingers, arms, and shoulders.

5. Lower your hands, fingertips still leading, so that the backs of your hands contact the rail of the chair, and go through your directions (*Fig. 18c*).

6. With the backs of your hands on the rail of the chair, think again of lengthening your fingers. In this position, you can clearly see your hands so that, if the fingers are curling, you can correct this.

7. Take your hands off the rail of the chair and come out of your monkey position.

8. When you have become familiar with this pro-
    cedure, go through steps 1-7 and then try the
    following:

9. Keeping your fingers and thumb in one piece,
    rotate your hands at the forearms so that your
    palms are now facing downwards on the chair
    rail. In this position, your fingers will be fully
    extended so that, even though you do not have
    a flat surface on which to place your hands, each
    hand is resting as a whole on the rail of the chair
    as if on a flat surface.

10. Think of your fingers lengthening from your
    wrists, and then ask for length along your fore-
    arms from your wrists to your elbows so that your
    elbows go away from your wrists.

11. Allow your upper arms to go away from each
    other to widen your shoulders.

12. Take your hands off the rail of the chair and come
    up to standing.

Can you notice that, with your hands placed on the
rail of the chair and fingers extended, your hands are
opening up and that you are now using your hands
like feet?

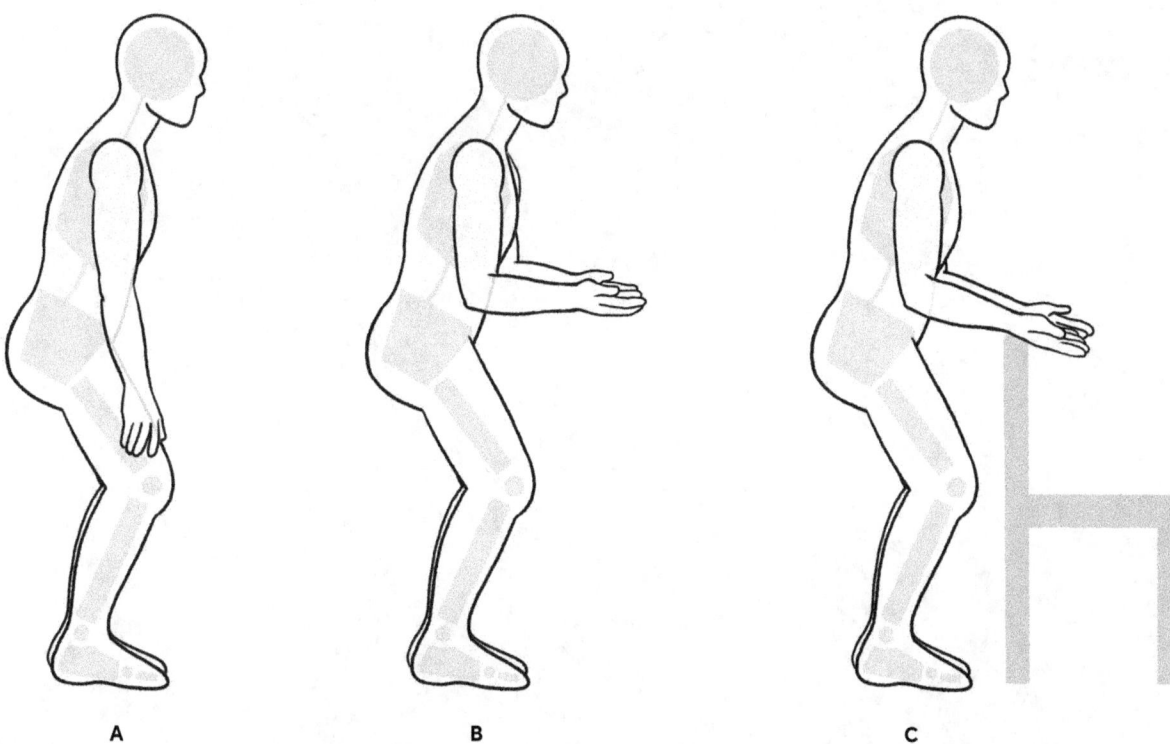

A   B   C

Fig. 18a. Monkey position; *b.* Raising hands at elbows;
c. Placing the backs of the hands on the rail of the chair with fingers extended.

The Hand (Cont.)

Now that we have looked at opening the hand, let's look at the fine motor use of the hand. We've seen that, as an extension of the shoulder and arm, the hand is served by a number of forearm muscles that move the hand and fingers. These extrinsic muscles of the hand, so called because they are not part of the hand itself, act powerfully on the hand and fingers when we forcibly grasp something or hang by our arms. In contrast, the intrinsic muscles of the hand—that is, muscles that are part of the hand itself—are involved in the fine motor movements of the thumb and fingers, such as delicately using a scalpel or threading a needle. These muscles make it possible, when using the hand in fine motor tasks, to flex the fingers and thumb without involving the larger muscles of the forearm and with a minimal amount of tension and interference.

Two key groups of intrinsic muscles are involved in opposing thumb and fingers. The first group are the flexors of the thumb, which form the thenar eminence, or pad of the thumb. These muscles move the thumb in several ways but, most importantly, oppose the thumb to the fingers (*Fig. 1*).

The second group are the lumbrical muscles of the fingers, which are located on the palm and act on the phalanges of the fingers. These muscles flex the first digits of the fingers while simultaneously

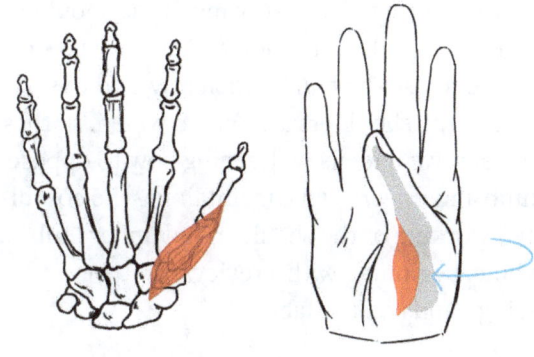

Fig. 1. The muscles of the thenar eminence allow the thumb to move at the wrist to oppose the fingers.

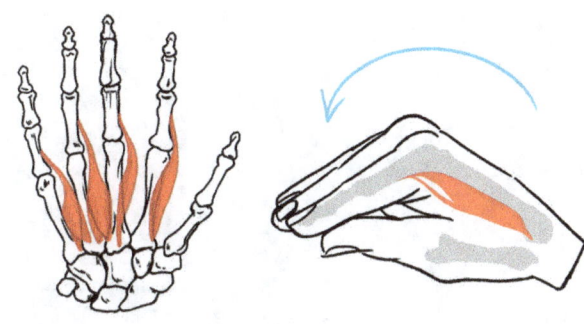

Fig. 2. The lumbrical muscles keep the fingers straight while flexing them at the knuckles.

extending the second and third digits (*Fig. 2*). Just as the thenar muscles make it possible to oppose the thumb to the fingers without involving the forearm muscles, the lumbrical muscles make it possible to oppose the fingers to the thumb while maintaining extension of the fingers and with minimum involvement of the flexors of the forearm.

Opposition of Thumb and Fingers

We've seen that the use of the arm and hand is directly related to the shoulder girdle and that, to use the arms efficiently, we must maintain the widened support of the back and shoulders. This same principle applies to the fine motor use of the hand and fingers, which are designed to flex but must do so with a minimum of tension in the forearm and hand. When we oppose the thumb to the fingers, we want to do so in a way that does not involve narrowing of the shoulders and tension in the arm and hand. This makes it possible to use the hands efficiently, and in such a way that the shoulders are able to widen. In these exercises, we'll focus on learning how to oppose thumb and fingers while maintaining the coordinated working of the shoulder and upper limb as a whole, beginning with a review of sitting and placing hands on the table.

Exercise 1, Part 1

Placing hands on the table

1. Stand in front of a table with a chair behind you so that you will be able to sit down.

2. Coming to your full height, take yourself into the inclined monkey position and carefully go through your directions, allowing your head to go away from your pelvis and your pelvis from your head to lengthen your back, and your knees to go away from your pelvis and feet so that you are lengthening along the thighs and calves.

3. Allow your knees to go away to sit in the chair, and then repeat your primary directions.

4. Lengthening your fingers to point to the ground, raise your arms at the elbow, place your hands palms down on the table and give your primary directions (*Fig. 3*).

5. Think of your fingers lengthening from your wrists, and then ask for length along your forearms from your wrists to your elbows and your elbows to your shoulders (*blue lines*).

6. With your hands remaining fully in contact with the table, allow your upper arms to go away from each other to widen your shoulders (*blue line*).

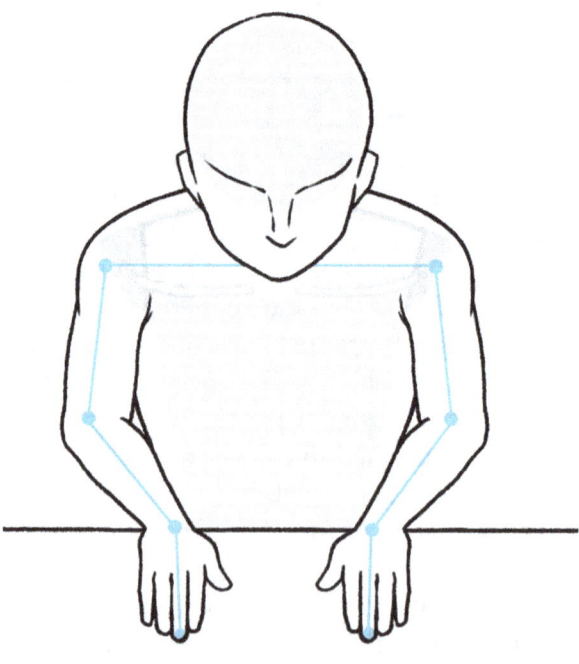

Fig. 3. Placing hands on table.

Exercise 1, Part 2
Raising hands from the table

Let's now look at how to oppose the thumbs to the fingers while maintaining length in the fingers and forearm and widening in the shoulders. The illustration shows only the right hand, but the exercise can be done with both hands.

1. With your hands palms down on the table, think of allowing the fingers of both hands to lengthen from your wrist, not forgetting to include your thumbs (*Figs. 3 and 4a*).

2. Be aware of the length of your forearms from wrists to elbows, your upper arms from elbows to shoulders, and across the width of your shoulders (*Fig. 3*).

3. Extend your hands at the wrist so that your fingers are angled upward at about 45 degrees. When you do this, leave your thumb in contact with the table and keep your fingers more or less together. The heel of your hand will now be in contact with the table and your thumbs will be in line with your forearms (*Fig. 4b*).

4. Think of the length of your fingers from your wrists and the length of your forearms from wrists to elbows.

5. Allow your thumbs to lengthen in line with your elbows.

6. Allow your upper arms to widen apart so that, with the heel of your hand on the table, you are now allowing your fingers and thumbs to lengthen from your forearms, your elbows to lengthen away from your wrists, and your shoulders to widen apart (*Fig. 3*).

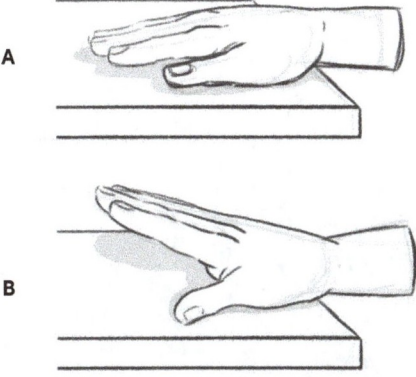

Fig. 4a. Palm on table; b. Raising hand while leaving the thumb on table.

Exercise 1, Part 3
Opposing thumbs and fingers

7. When you have become comfortable with the previous exercises, the next step is to oppose fingers to thumbs, again with both hands.

8. With your palms on the table, go through the directions for your hands and arms (*Figs. 3 and 5a*).

9. Extend your hands at the wrist so that your fingers are angled upward at about 45 degrees, with the heels of your hands on the table and your thumbs remaining in contact with the table (*Fig. 5b*).

10. Give your primary directions, ask for length along the forearm to the elbows from your wrists, and ask for widening of the upper arms.

11. Allow your fingers to lengthen and your thumbs to lengthen out from your wrists and forearms.

12. Flex your fingers at the knuckles so that they point down to the table but remain extended from the knuckles. As you do so, slide the thumb of each hand towards the fingers so that the thumbs will now oppose the index finger (*Fig. 5c*).

13. Give your directions and think of your forearms pulling to the sides.

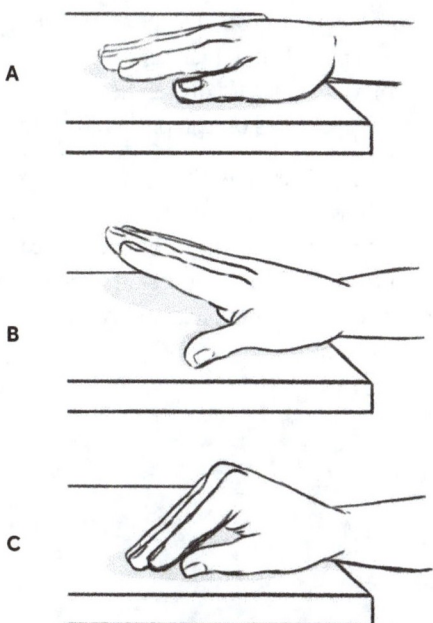

Fig. 5a-c. Opposing thumb to fingers with wrist contacting the table.

Opposition of thumbs and fingers while taking a pen in your hand

The final step is to oppose fingers to thumbs while grasping an object, which of course will involve only one hand.

1. Repeat the steps for going into monkey, sitting, placing your hands on the table, and giving your directions (*Fig. 6a*).

2. Leave your left hand on the table palm down. Extend your right hand at the wrist so that your fingers are angled upward at about 45 degrees, leaving your thumb in contact with the table (*Fig. 6b*).

3. Allow the fingers of your right hand to lengthen and your thumb to lengthen out from your wrist and forearm. Give your directions.

4. Flex the fingers of your right hand at the knuckles so that they point down to the table but remain extended from the knuckles, and slide your thumbs toward the fingers to oppose the index finger (*Fig. 6c*).

5. Go through your primary directions, and add the widening of the upper arms and the pull to the elbows.

6. With your right hand flexed in this way, place a pen between your fingers and thumb (*Fig. 6d*). Experiment with moving the pen by flexing your fingers and thumb and, placing a piece of paper under your hand, see if you can now begin to make lines or shapes on the piece of paper.

Can you notice that, even with a pen held in your hand, your elbows can go outward and your shoulders can widen? This kinesthetic awareness can be applied to all kinds of fine motor skills, including handling tools, playing a musical instrument, and typing on a keyboard.

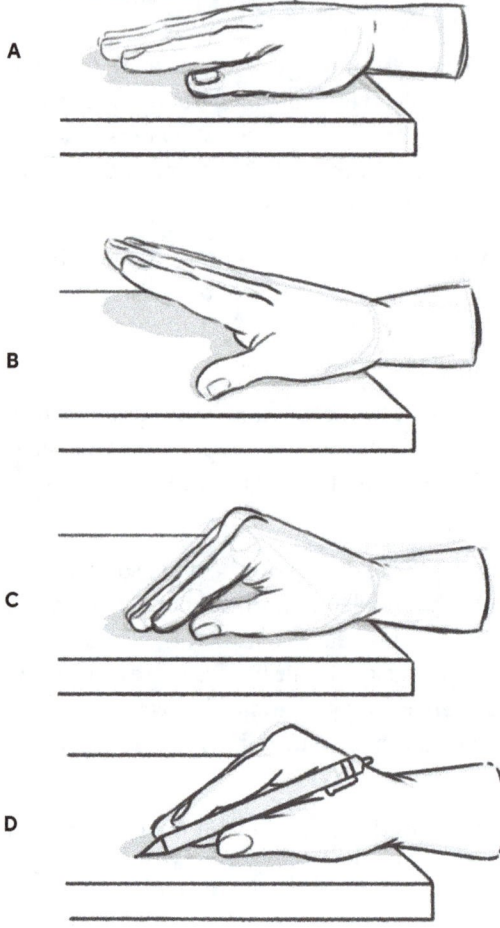

A

B

C

D

Fig. 6a-d. Grasping pen with fingers extended.

Exercise 2

Opposing thumbs and fingers in semi-supine position

Let's now look at how to oppose the thumbs to the fingers while in semi-supine position, which is an ideal position for exploring how to use your hands in a coordinated way while monitoring the body as a whole.

1. Lying in semi-supine, take a moment to be aware of the parts of your body that are supported on the ground.

2. Be aware of your neck, back, and legs.

3. Allow your knees to go up from pelvis and feet.

4. Raise your hands from your elbows so that, with your elbows still on the ground, your fingers are pointing upward (*Fig. 7*).

5. Take a moment to think of your fingers and thumbs lengthening from your wrists and out of your forearms so that your fingers are pointing to the ceiling.

6. Face your palms toward your feet and lower your arms onto your midriff so that your thumbs are in contact your body and your fingers are pointing upward (*Figs. 8 and 9a*).

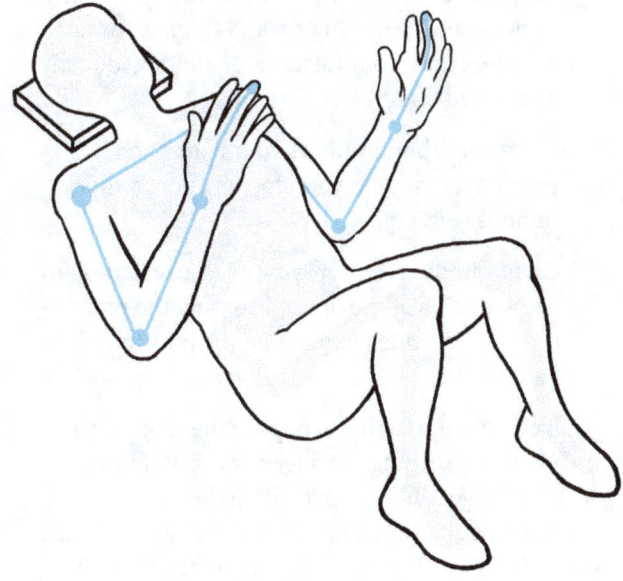

Fig. 7. In semi-supine position with hands raised and fingers pointing upwards.

(continued)

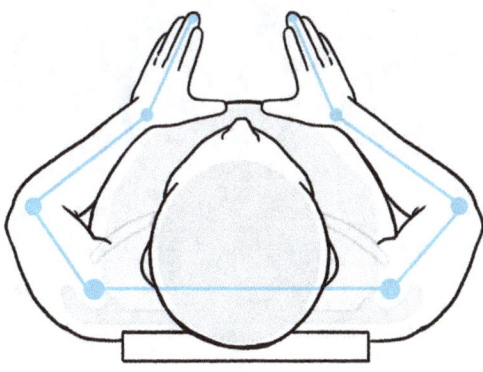

Fig. 8. Hands on midriff with thumbs on body.

7. Direct your thumbs toward each other.

8. Keeping your thumbs in contact with your body, begin to angle your fingers and thumbs toward your feet until your fingers are pointing directly downwards (*Fig. 9b*).

9. Bring your thumbs under your palms and flex your fingers so that your fingers oppose your thumbs (*Fig. 9c*).

10. Give your directions, paying special attention to the widening of the upper arms and the pull to the elbows while maintaining the position of the hands.

It takes a bit of practice to oppose the thumbs to fingers while keeping the fingers straight, but the real challenge is not in controlling the fingers but in maintaining the widening of the shoulders and back while doing so. Practicing this procedure while lying in semi-supine position is an ideal way to explore opposition of thumb and fingers while being able, at the same time, to monitor the head, trunk and legs, and to maintain the directions for the widening support of the entire shoulder girdle.

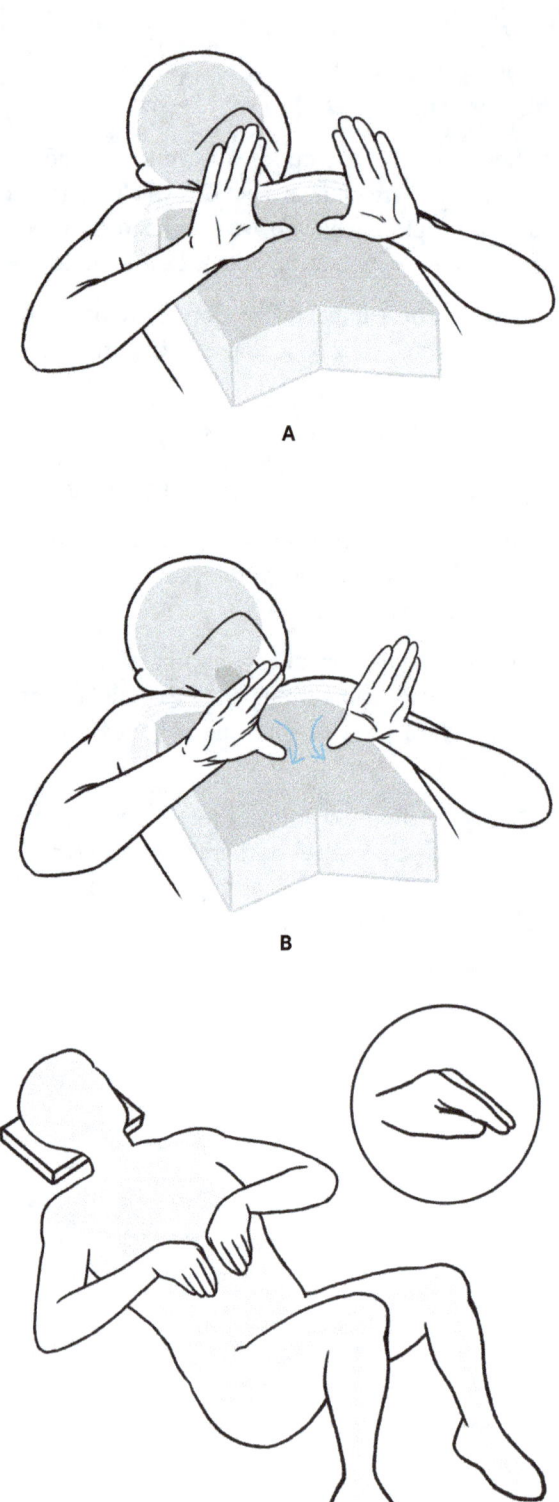

Fig. 9a. Fingers extended with thumbs on body; b. Angling fingers and thumbs downwards to point toward the hips; c. Fingers and thumbs pointing downwards and opposing each other.

The Pelvis, Trunk, and Hip Joints

When we bend at the hips, we tend to sink into the legs, shortening the back and spine. To address this, it is important to be clear, not simply where the hip joints are, but on how the pelvis functions as part of the back and spine as a whole. In this chapter we're going to look in detail at the pelvis and its connection with the back, and explore different ways of inclining at the hips in order to understand how to bend and sit in a way that maintains the length and integrity of the back and trunk.

The pelvis is a bony structure attached to the bottom end of the spine that provides deep and stable sockets for the hip joints so that we can stand on our two legs. This ring-like structure also provides a sturdy framework for muscular attachments to the trunk and legs. Because we are upright, the pelvis also forms a container at the bottom end of the trunk for our innards ("pelvis" is a Latin word meaning "basin") (*Fig. 1*).

In the same way that the scapulae of the shoulder provide sockets for the upper limbs, the pelvic bones on either side of the sacrum provide bony sockets for the lower limbs (*Fig. 2*). But there is a big difference between the scapulae of the upper limb and that of the lower limb. The forelimbs, even in a cat or a dog, need to remain highly mobile in order to absorb shock, which is why they are not directly linked to the spine. Not so with the rear

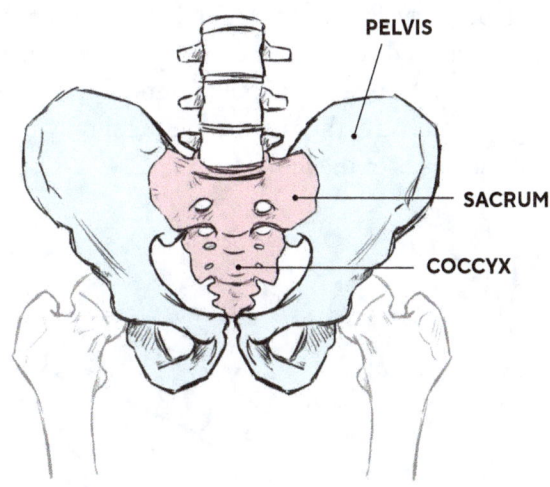

Fig. 1. The pelvis includes the pelvic bones, sacrum, and coccyx.

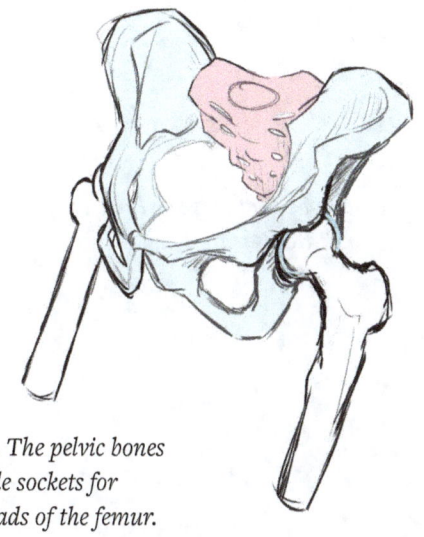

Fig. 2. The pelvic bones provide sockets for the heads of the femur.

123

limbs, which need to convey thrust directly to the trunk. For this reason, the "scapulae" of the pelvis, the two pelvic bones on either side of the sacrum, are directly connected to the spine to form the sacroiliac joint (*Fig. 3*).

This connection of the sacrum with the spine explains why movement of the pelvis, in contrast to the independent action of the scapulae of the shoulder, directly involves movement of the spine. Any alteration of the position of the pelvis has to involve the spine because the two are firmly attached. And you can't really speak of the pelvis without also speaking about the back, since the pelvis functions, for all intents and purposes, as an extension of the back.

If the link between the pelvic bones and the sacrum is critical in four-footed animals, it becomes even more so in humans. When we stand, the weight of the trunk is transferred from the sacrum directly to the pelvic bones, which in turn sit on the heads of the femurs so that, in our upright posture, the trunk is quite literally poised on the heads of the femurs.

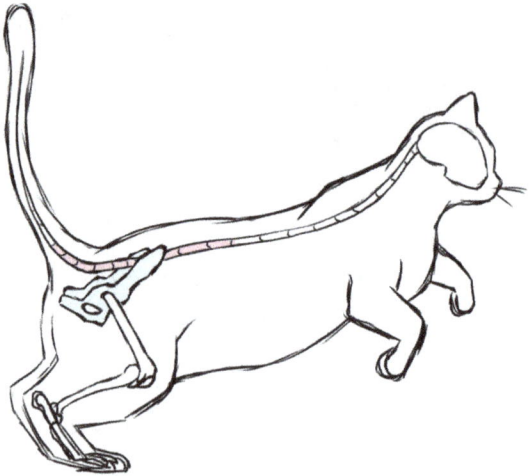

Fig. 3. In animals that move on land, the pelvic bones are attached to the spine.

The Hip Joints

A key function of the pelvis is to provide deep, stable sockets for the heads of the femurs, as shown in *Fig. 2*. But it is one thing to know where the hip joints are and how they work, and another thing entirely to be able to use the legs without compromising the integrity of the trunk. When asked where the hip joints are located, many people point to the pelvic bones—the big, bony rim along the top of your pelvis that forms your waist (*Fig. 4a and b*). Technically speaking, these are not your hips but the crest of the pelvic or iliac bones; the word "hip," as any doctor will tell you, refers not to the iliac crest but to the hip joint, which is much lower than the upper rim of the pelvic bone. The confusion between the two is echoed in the linguistic similarity between the names we use for two very different parts of the pelvis ("hips" versus "hip joints"). In practical terms, this misconception translates into the tendency, when bending or sitting, to create a joint at the waist, which causes the trunk to shorten and collapse. To maintain the proper length of the trunk when bending, we must appreciate that, for all intents and purposes, the pelvis functions as part of the back, and that bending or flexing the trunk at the hips should take place not at the waist but at the hip joints. This why it is so important to know where the hip joints are located and how to use them properly.

There is a corollary to this principle of understanding where the hip joints are located. If the pelvis is connected to the spine, and if bending takes place at the hip joints, then the back of the pelvis, or sacral region of the spine, functions not as part of the legs but as part of the length of the back (*Fig. 5*). Again we see that the pelvis functions as part of the back and must be thought of this way if we are to maintain a fully lengthened trunk.

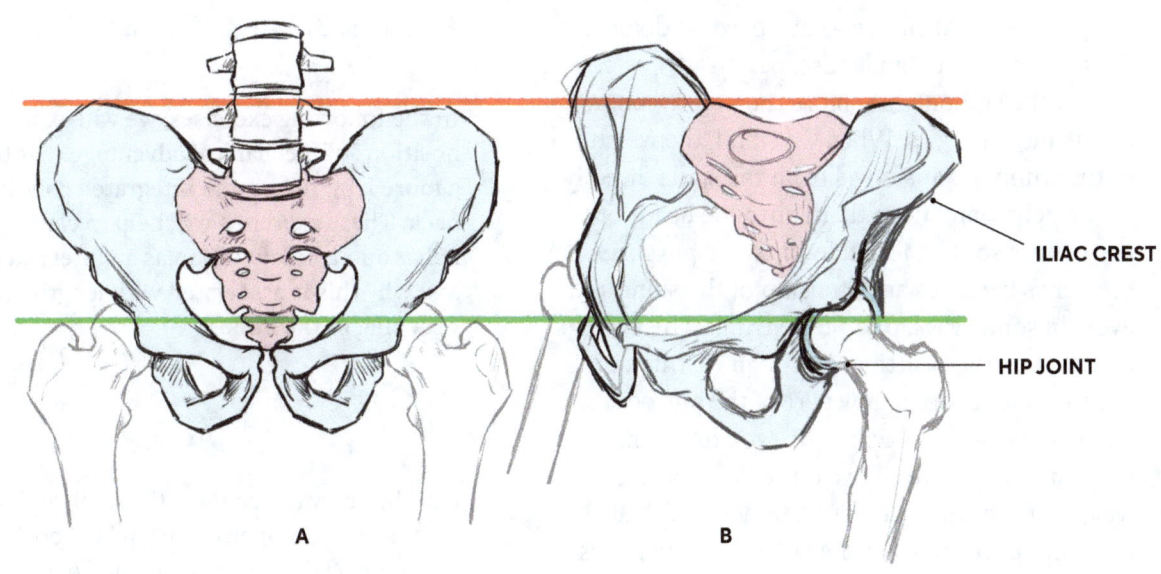

Fig. 4a. We often mistake the crest of the pelvis (the "hip bone") for the hip joints; b. The hip joint is located well below the crest of the pelvis.

The Rockers at the Bottom of the Pelvis Are Our "Feet" When Sitting

The connection of the pelvis with the spine is also directly related to our ability to sit fully upright. When the first primates began to walk fully upright, the spine began to function as a vertical, weight-bearing column that transferred the weight of the trunk onto the legs and feet. This made possible an entirely new form of locomotion that was not only efficient in itself but also freed the arms to function in a new way.

But standing and walking are not the only form of upright posture. We are also fully upright—provided we are not slumping—when we sit in a chair, with our weight supported not on our feet but on the ischial tuberosities of the pelvis, or sit bones (*Fig. 6*). As a form of upright posture, sitting has, in many ways, replaced standing. It is in the sitting position that we perform many of our most complex activities, including using our arms in fine motor tasks such as playing a musical instrument, typing, or using tools. Because sitting in the modern human has become such a universal activity, the chair and table—not to mention couches and other kinds

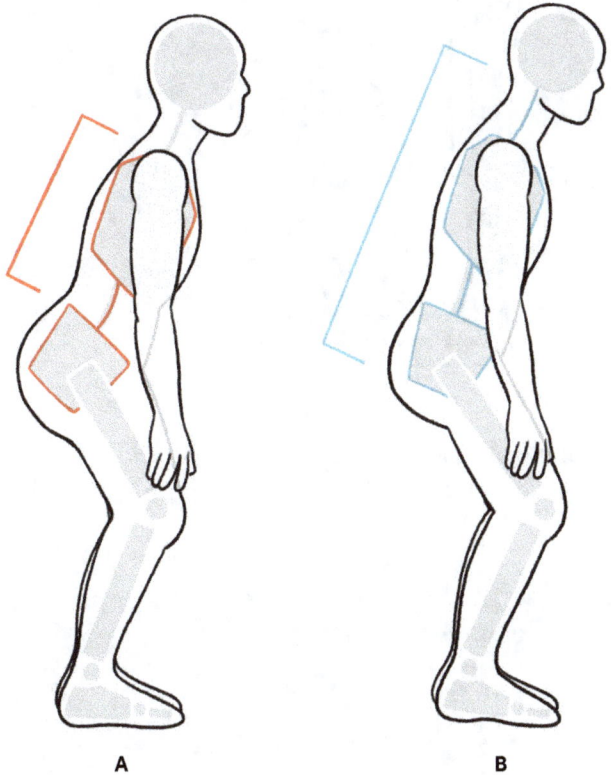

Fig. 5. Identifying the full length of the back: (a) Making a joint at the waist (red bracket) compared to (b) Making a joint at the hips (blue bracket).

of upholstered furniture—have become dominant features of the human landscape.

But the sit bones are more than mere contacts for sitting on chairs. When we stand, the weight of the trunk is transferred from the spine directly to the pelvis, and from there onto the heads of the femurs so that, for all intents and purposes, the pelvis becomes an extension of the spine and even, in some ways, part of the trunk. This linkage relates directly to sitting. Although we think of the sit bones as somehow part of the buttocks and pelvis, they function as direct extensions of the spine. When we sit, we quite literally rest the weight of the trunk on our sit bones, which are not mere projections at the bottom of the pelvis but the bottom end of the spine/pelvis unit. When we sit, we support weight not on our feet but on the rockers of the pelvis, which are our "feet" when we are sitting (*Fig. 6*).

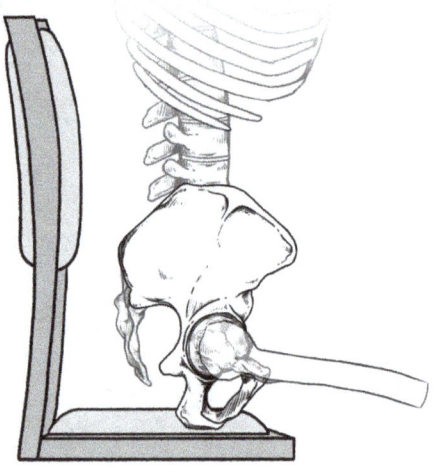

Fig. 6. The sit bones are our "feet" when sitting.

THE PELVIS AND THE BACK

In the following exercises, we will explore various positions of mechanical advantage that bring about a more lengthened and integrated condition of the back. These exercises will help to clarify how the pelvis and trunk function as an integrated whole and why this is associated with lengthening and widening of the back.

Exercise 1

Semi-supine position and the pelvis

Let's begin by returning to the semi-supine position, with the head supported on a pile of books, the upper back and pelvis supported on the floor, and the knees pointing to the ceiling.

1. Lying in semi-supine, take a moment to be quiet.

2. Allow your neck to be free to let your head come out of your back.

3. Let go in your thighs to allow your knees to go up.

4. Let your shoulders widen apart.

5. In this position, two key areas of your back make contact with the floor: your upper back in the region of the shoulder blades, and the back of your pelvis and sacrum. Take a moment to be aware of the contact of your pelvis on the floor, and how it contributes to the lengthening and widening of the back as a whole (*Fig. 7*).

In this position, the trunk is supported on the floor and the pelvis, as the lowest part of the trunk, clearly functions as part of the trunk.

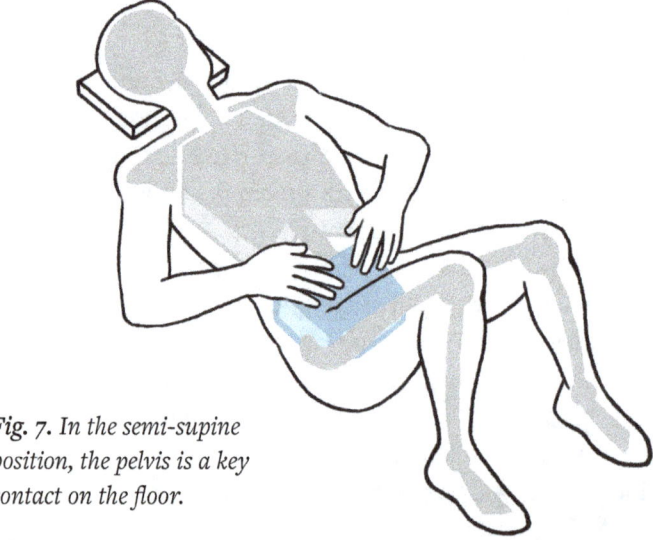

Fig. 7. In the semi-supine position, the pelvis is a key contact on the floor.

Exercise 2

Vertical stance and the erector spinae sheet

We saw in the section on positions of mechanical advantage that, when we assume the vertical stance, the back and spine tend to lengthen. In this exercise, we will perform the vertical stance as a way of becoming aware of the long muscles of the back, the erector spinae group, that runs the length of the back from pelvis and sacrum right up to the skull.

1. Take time to get plenty of length between your hips and head, coming to your full stature without raising your chest.

2. See to it that you are not tightening in the buttocks, thighs, behind your knees, or in your ankles.

3. Allow your knees to release forward so that you go into vertical stance (*Fig. 8*). If needed, come back slightly onto your heels and allow your hips to release while still thinking of allowing your knees to go forward.

4. Once you are in a good, balanced position, think of allowing your head to go forward and up and, without tucking your pelvis, release in your gluteal muscles to allow your pelvis to drop away from your head so that you are allowing your back as a whole to lengthen.

5. Think of releasing in your calves from your heels to behind your knees so that your knees go "away" from your heels. With your knees releasing away from your heels, you may feel some extra release in your back, so that your back as a whole feels more lengthened.

6. You should now feel the length of your back from the base of your head right down to your sacrum and buttocks. What you are now noticing is the erector spinae group of muscles, which run in bundles up the length of the spine from the sacrum right up to the occiput of the skull (*Fig. 9*). Try the exercise a few times and, after a while, you will become more kinesthetically aware of your back as a whole.

After trying this exercise, return to the semi-supine position and spend a few minutes directing your head, back, and knees. Are you now better able to identify the full length of your back? Can you see that your back includes your pelvis, which clearly functions as part of your spine and trunk?

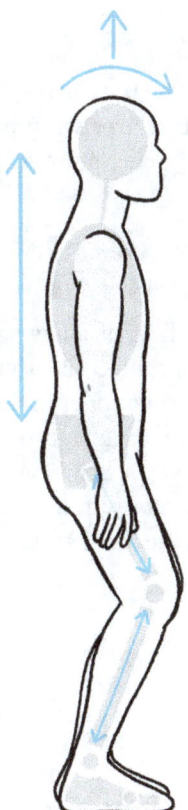

Fig. 8. *Vertical stance.*

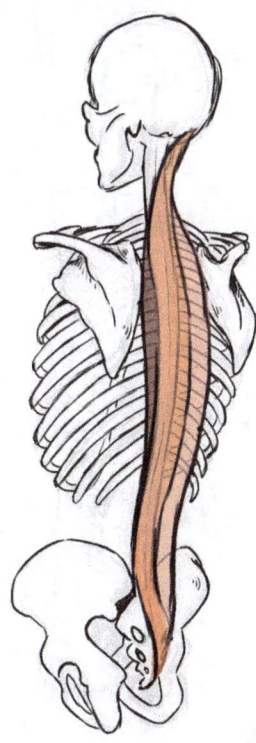

Fig. 9. *The erector spinae muscles connect from the sacrum and pelvis all the way up to the skull.*

Exercise 3

Vertical stance using the wall

In this exercise, the wall is used as a contact point for the upper back and the pelvis, providing support for the back and a reference point for both upper and lower trunk.

1. Stand with your back to a wall, with your heels 3 or 4 inches (8-10 cm) from the wall (*Fig. 10a*).

2. Fall back against the wall, allowing your upper back and pelvis to contact the wall at the same time (*Fig. 10b*). If your upper back contacts the wall first, this means that your pelvis is coming forward and that you are sinking into your legs. Try once or twice more, until your upper back and pelvis contact the wall at the same time.

3. Let your knees go so that you are now in the vertical stance with your back against the wall (*Fig. 10c*).

4. Think of letting your knees go away, your head to go forward and up, and your seat to drop away from your head.

Notice that, in this vertical stance, you can clearly feel your upper back as well as your pelvis, which functions as part of your back. You will also have a heightened awareness of how long your back really is.

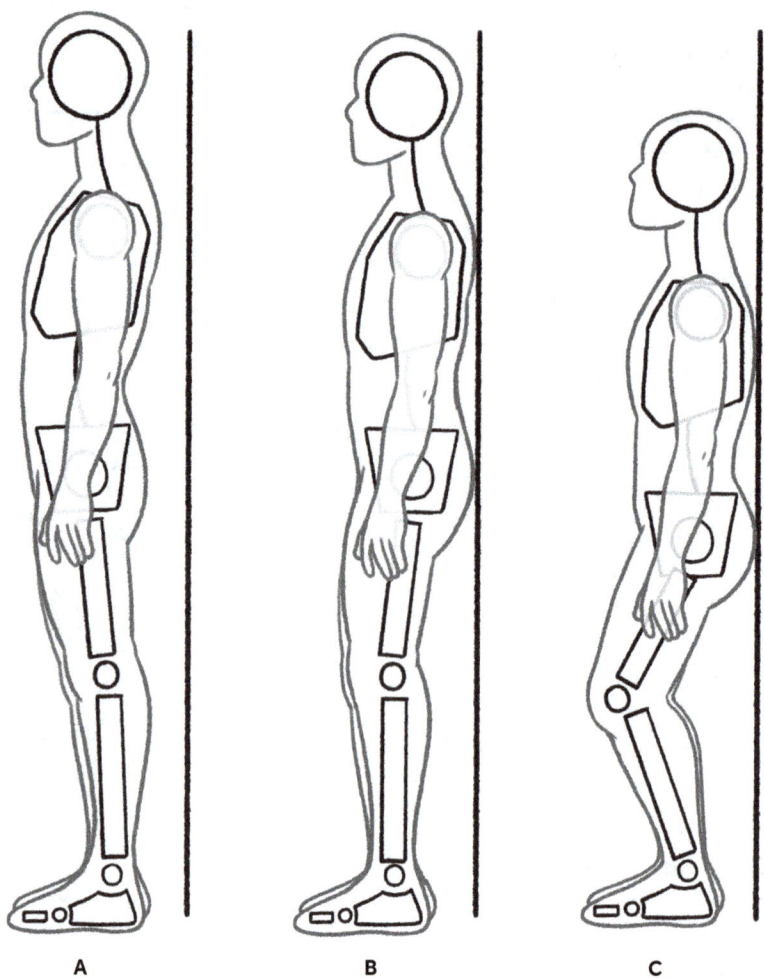

A   B   C

Fig. 10a-c. Vertical stance using the wall.

Sensorimotor Awareness

Exercise 4

Inclined monkey position using the wall

In this exercise, you will go into an inclined monkey position, using the wall as a contact point for the pelvis.

1. Stand with your back to the wall and fall back against the wall (*Fig. 11a*).

2. Let your knees go so that you are in the vertical stance with your back against the wall, and give your directions (*Fig. 11b*).

3. Incline forward at the hips and bend your knees, seeing to it that you do not arch your back or collapse in front—that is, without losing length in your back and trunk (*Fig. 11c*). In this position, your pelvis should still be in contact with the wall.

4. Think of allowing your head to go away from your pelvis and your pelvis from your head so that your back lengthens.

5. Come away from the wall so that you are balanced over your feet and again give your directions (*Fig. 11d*).

Notice that, in this inclined monkey position, your back lengthens between the head at one end of your spine and your pelvis at the other. With your pelvis in contact with the wall and your spine lengthening, you should be able to very clearly feel the entire length of your back, which gives you a much fuller kinesthetic "picture" of your back, which includes your pelvis and extends up to your neck.

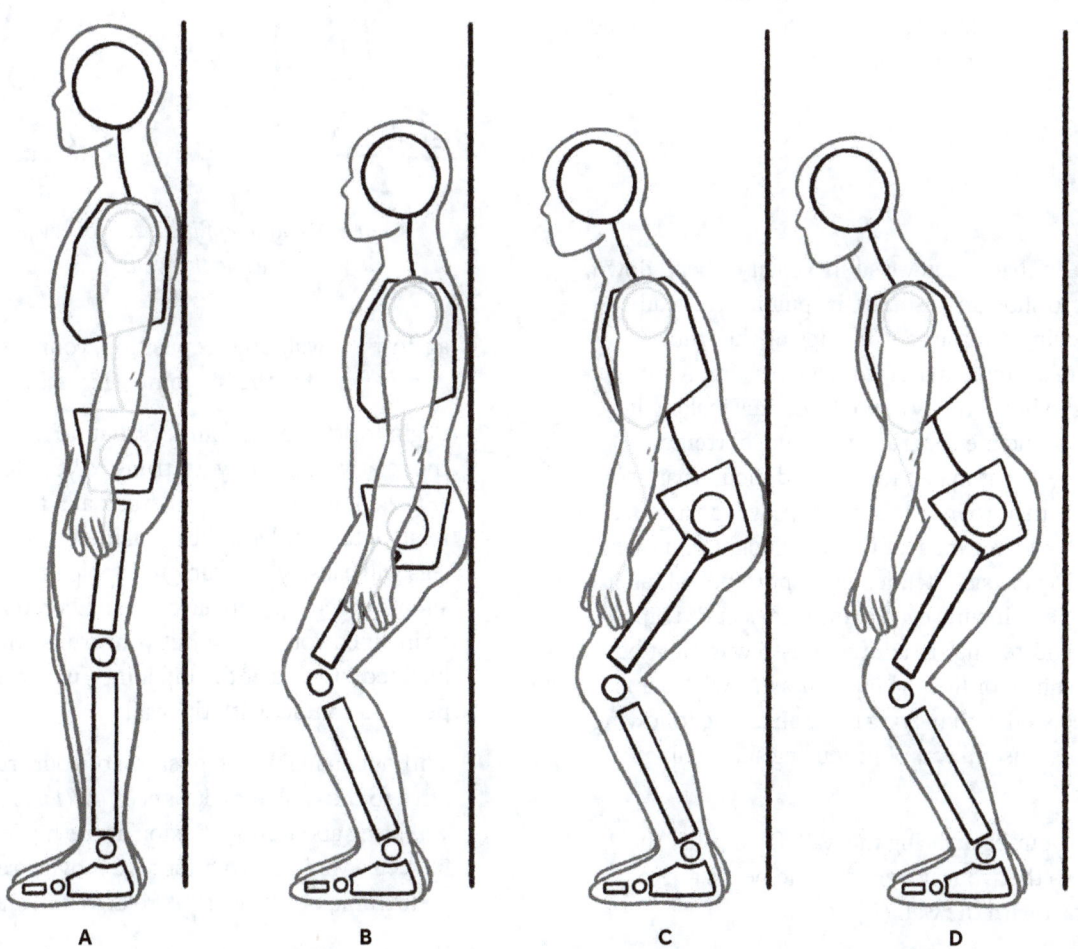

A   B   C   D

Fig. 11a-d. Inclined monkey position using the wall.

Variation 1:
Inclined monkey position against the wall

A simple variation of the previous exercise is to lean against the wall and then to go directly into an inclined monkey position, as follows.

1. With your back facing the wall, fall back against the wall (*Fig. 12a*).

2. Think of allowing your head to go forward and up and your seat to drop away from your head.

3. Allow your knees to bend and, at the same time, incline forward at your hips so that you go into an inclined monkey position, with your pelvis in contact with the wall (*Fig. 12b*).

4. Think of your head going away from your seat and your seat from your head to allow your back, which includes your pelvis, to lengthen.

In this inclined monkey position, it may become clearer that you are hinging not at the waist but at the hip joints. This allows the pelvis to function as part of the trunk, which in turn facilitates the lengthening and widening of the back muscles.

Exercise 5

Going into the inclined monkey position using the wall

We've seen that, when we sit in a chair or bend down, we tend to shorten in stature by pulling the head back, arching the back and collapsing the trunk. It may seem a simple matter to stop this simply by learning to hinge freely at the hips, thus making it possible to incline the trunk without shortening in any way. What makes this more difficult than it appears is that, to incline at the hips we must move the trunk and, for most of us, any thought of moving the trunk evokes the tendency to shorten, making it impossible to incline even a few inches at the hips without shortening. To address this, a way must be found to hinge or flex the hip joints in a way that is not associated with moving the trunk. The following exercise is a useful way of producing such a hinging action.

1. With your back facing the wall, fall against the wall so that your upper back and pelvis are in contact with the wall (*Fig. 13a*).

2. Think of letting your knees go away so that you are in vertical monkey stance with your back

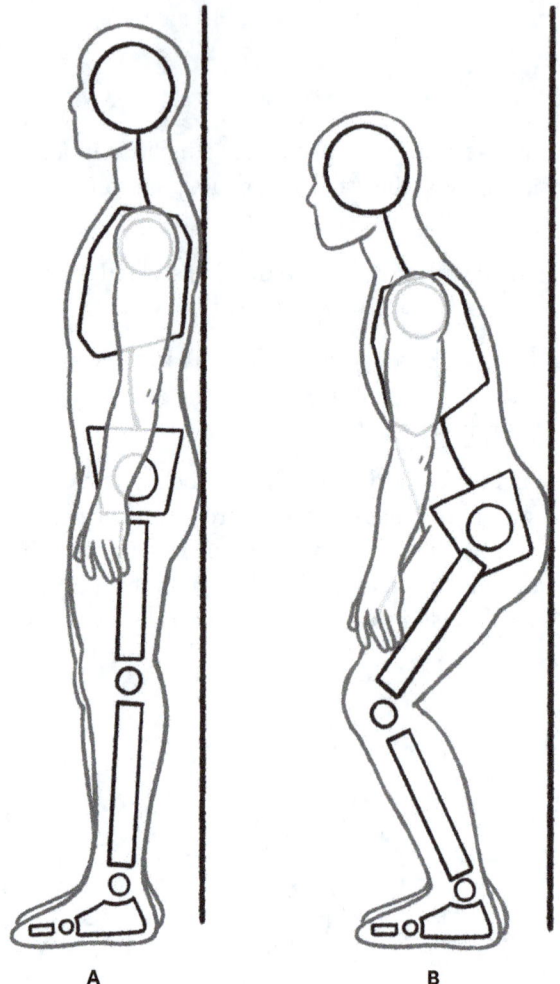

A   **B**

Fig. 12a-b. Variation of inclined monkey position using the wall.

against the wall. In this position, your legs are clearly flexed at the hip joints (*Fig. 13b*).

3. Begin to straighten your legs, but do not change the relative angle of your trunk to your legs (*Fig. 13c*). If you keep your trunk at a fixed angle relative to your legs, the straightening of your legs will cause your trunk to topple forward, as shown in *Fig. 14*. You have not deliberately moved or inclined your trunk, but your trunk will now be inclined forward at the hip joints, with only your pelvis in contact with the wall.

4. Without changing the position of your trunk relative to the wall, let your knees go (*Fig. 13d*). This will bring about more flexion at the hip joints, but in such a way that your legs are moving relative to your trunk, not your trunk relative to your legs.

5. You will now be in an inclined monkey position with your hips flexed.

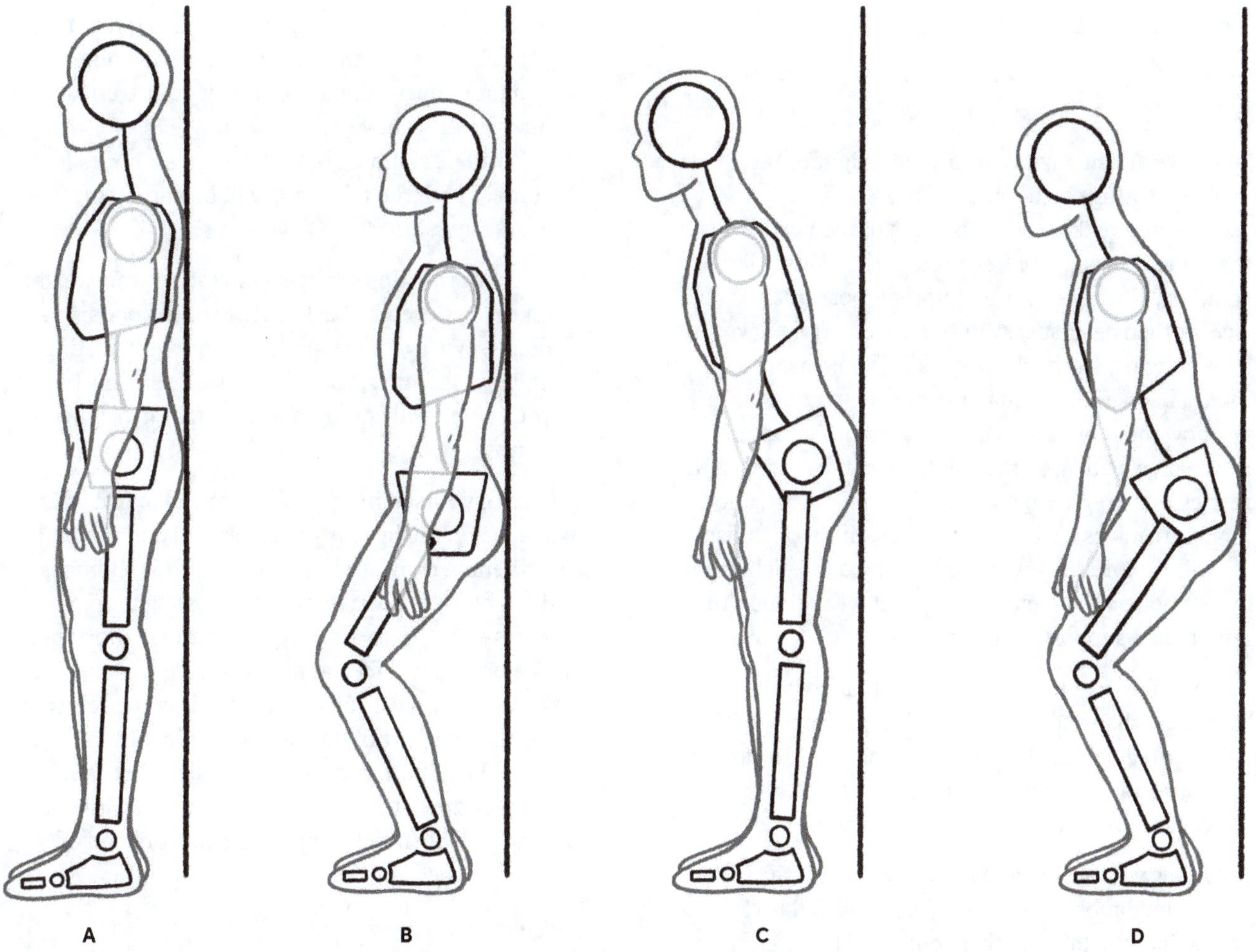

A   B   C   D

Fig. 13a-d. Going into the inclined monkey position using the wall.

6. Think of allowing your head to go away from your pelvis and your pelvis from your head to allow your back to lengthen.

The focus, in this exercise, is on bringing about flexion at the hips by bending the knees rather than moving the trunk. This makes it possible to flex the hip joints in a way that is not associated with moving the trunk. If you are successful in doing this, you will be able to flex freely at the hip joints without disturbing the length of your trunk and without shortening in stature. Your pelvis and trunk will be working in one piece, your knees can go forward from your pelvis and your back can lengthen between your head and pelvis.

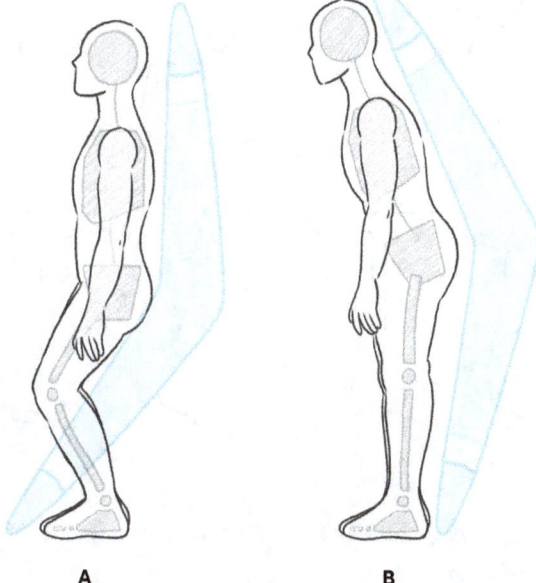

A   B

Fig. 14a-b. Going into the inclined monkey position using the wall.

Exercise 6

Monkey position using a table to support the sit bones

When we are sitting in a chair, the weight of the trunk is resting on the sit bones, which as we've seen are the rockers at the bottom of the pelvis that function as the bottom end of the trunk. Like standing, sitting is a form of upright posture in which we lengthen against gravity so that, even when we are sitting passively, the trunk as a whole maintains internal, lengthened support against gravity. This is not how most of us sit. Once our weight is contacting the chair, we collapse the trunk so that, in addition to resting our weight on the chair, we sink into it, allowing our trunk as a whole to collapse. In this exercise, we will explore the process of resting our weight on our sit bones, but in such a way that we maintain the lengthened support of the trunk.

1. Stand with your back to a table that goes no higher than the tops of your legs (*Fig. 15a*), with your feet about shoulder width apart. Be aware of your feet on the ground and, without lifting your chest up, come up to your full stature.

2. Allow your knees to release and go into the inclined monkey position (*Fig. 15b*). Fall back against the table so that your sit bones are very nearly, if not actually, in contact with the table.

3. Position your pelvis so that you can begin to rest your sit bones on the edge of the table, coming to a more upright posture so that your trunk is now directly above your sit bones (*Fig. 15c*). You will still be standing but, with your sit bones in contact with the table, you will be partly sitting as well (*Fig. 16*).

4. Without thinking of sitting or resting your weight on the table, come back slightly onto your sit bones. With your weight now more fully resting on your sit bones, you will in fact be sitting, but your trunk will continue to maintain its length against gravity.

By placing yourself in a position of mechanical advantage in which the head is going forward and up out of a lengthening trunk and then placing your sit bones on the table, it is possible to support weight on our sit bones—that is, to actually sit—without shortening. Doing this will feel, at first, quite unfamiliar, but it is a very useful way of learning to sit without losing the natural support of the back and spine. In this supported position, you should also be able to very clearly feel the entire length of your trunk, with your sit bones clearly functioning as the bottom end of your entire back and trunk.

Further reading:

Anatomy in Action, Chapter 11. The Hips

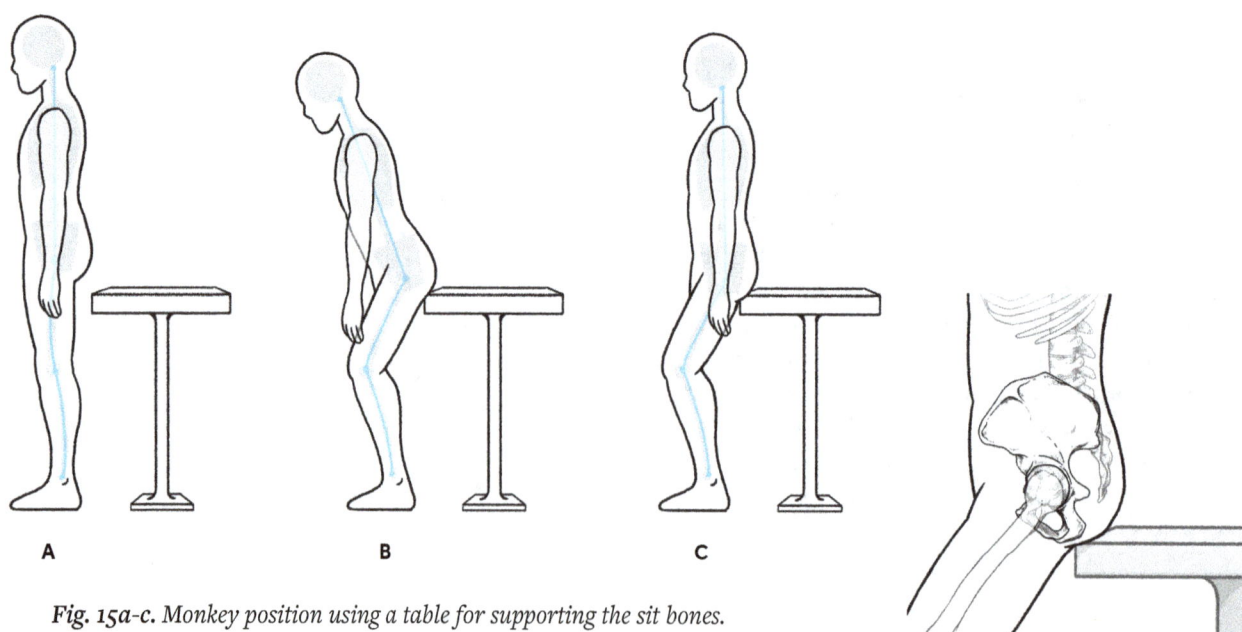

Fig. 15a-c. Monkey position using a table for supporting the sit bones.

Fig. 16. When the sit bones contact the table, we are partly sitting.

KEEPING YOUR BACK IN ONE PIECE IN SITTING

We've seen that the pelvis, which is firmly attached to the spine, functions as part of the back. By exploring the vertical monkey stance, we could see how the two parts work together, allowing the back to function as an integrated whole. The next step in examining this problem is to see what happens when we are sitting and incline forward and backwards in the chair, in which case we tend to shorten the spine, losing the connection of the pelvis and trunk and interfering with the back. By paying close attention to how we perform these actions, we can bring about a much more lengthened and integrated condition of the back.

Exercise 7

Using the monkey position to sit, focusing on the means and not the end

When we sit in our habitual manner, we shorten in stature, pulling the head back, collapsing the trunk and shortening the muscles of the back. By breaking the action down into discrete parts, and by using the position of mechanical advantage as a way of maintaining length at each stage of the action, we can keep the back in one piece as we lower our trunk to the chair and come to upright sitting.

1. Standing in front of a chair with your feet slightly apart, give your directions (*Fig. 17a*).

2. Thinking of releasing the fronts of your ankles, the backs of your knees, and the front of your hip joints, go into an inclined monkey position by falling forward and allowing your knees to bend (*Fig. 17b*).

3. Deepen this position by letting your knees bend until your pelvis is in contact with the chair and, without going any further, go through your directions, allowing your head to go away from your pelvis to lengthen your back, and your knees to go away from your pelvis and ankles so that you are lengthening along the thighs and the calf muscles (*Fig. 17c*).

4. Come back gently from your hips to the upright position by hinging at your hip joints (*Fig. 17d*). Do not perform this movement too quickly, seeing if you can move your trunk in one piece— that is, without throwing your ribs back and shortening your spine or lower back (see next page for more detail).

When you are able to come to the fully upright sitting position without arching or shortening your trunk, you may notice that the muscles of your back have lengthened and spread out and that your back can now function as an integrated whole.

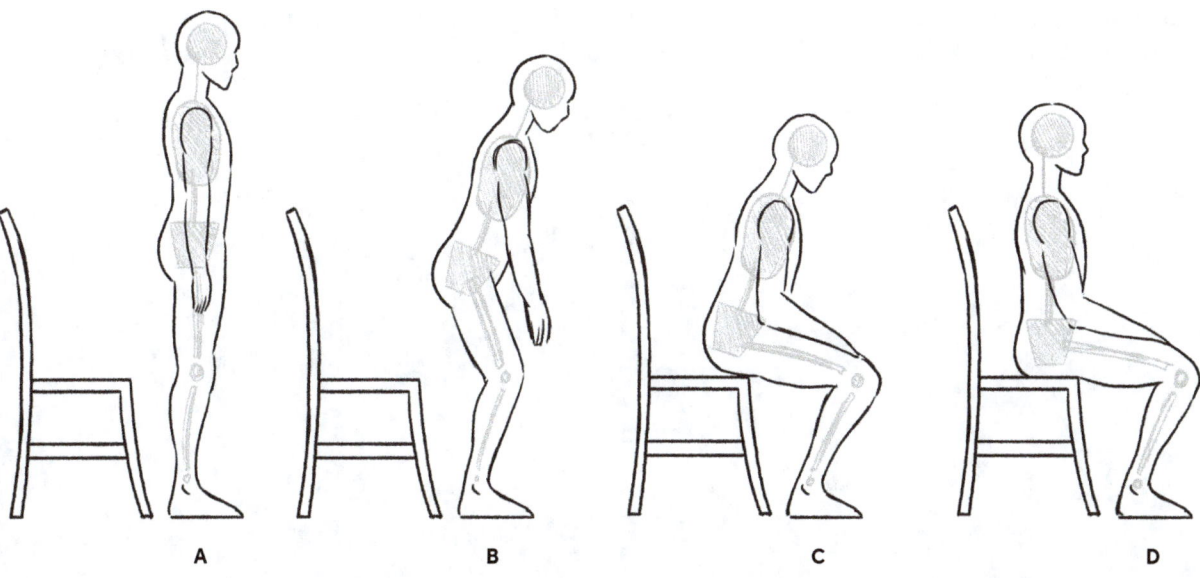

A   B   C   D

Fig. 17a–d. Stand-to-sit, keeping the back in one piece.

Fig. 18. *When we have sat down and are coming back from the hips to the upright position, most of us tend to throw the rib cage backwards, arching the back and shortening in stature. In Figure 18, we can see that, as the trunk comes back as a whole, the rib cage goes back "faster" than the lower back and the lower back shortens. This "breaks" the back into two pieces—the upper back pushing back and the lower back pulling in and arching.*

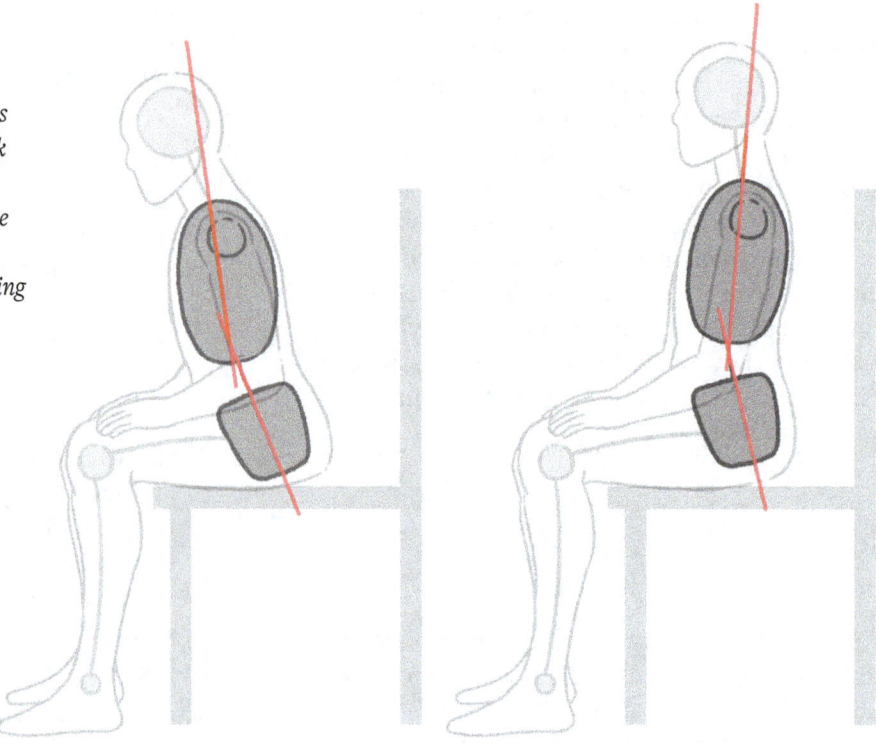

Fig. 19. *When you come back from the hips, take your time, seeing to it that you don't allow the upper back to overrun the lower back. In this way, the back will remain more integrated, the muscles more lengthened, and the back more filled out as a whole.*

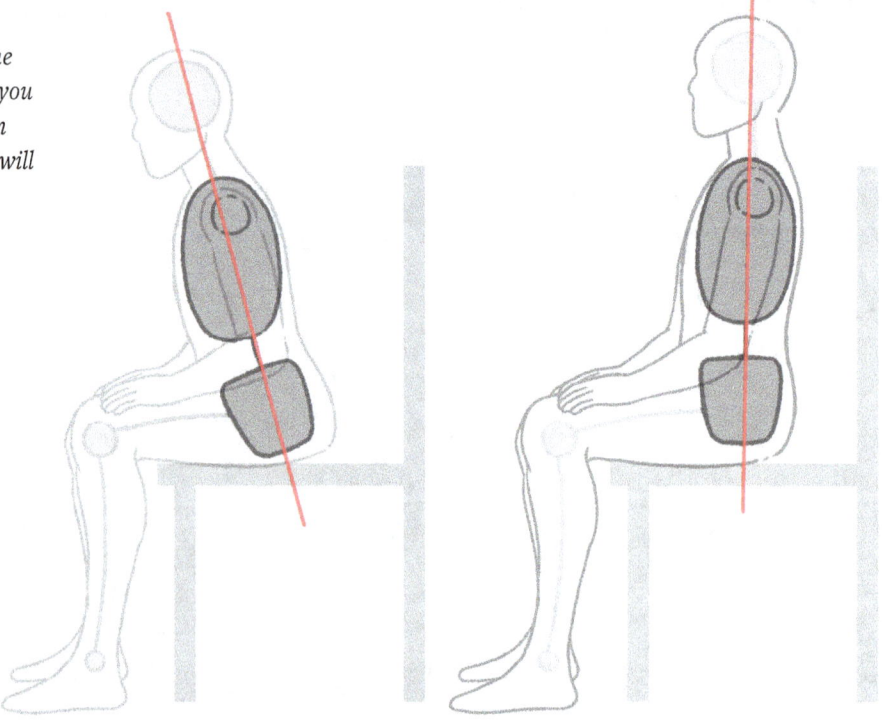

Exercise 8

Going into monkey position using a table for four-footed support

We've now looked at a few ways of bending at the hips while keeping the back in one piece. Another way to approach this is by going into the monkey position and placing your hands on a table so that you are in a four-footed position.

1. Stand in front of a table with your feet shoulder width apart. Give your directions to release your neck muscles so that your head is free to nod forward; see to it that your back is lengthened, that you are not gripping in your gluteal muscles so that your seat can drop away from your head, and that your legs are not braced (*Fig. 20a*).

2. Think of releasing the fronts of your ankles, the backs of your knees, and the front of your hip joints to go into monkey position. Carefully go through your directions (*Fig. 20b*).

3. Place your hands on the table, palms facing down. Again go through your directions, allowing your head to go away from your pelvis and your pelvis from your head to lengthen your back, and your knees to go away from your pelvis and heels so that you are lengthening along the thighs and the calf muscles (*Fig. 20c*).

4. Take your hands off the table and come back to standing.

With your hands on the table so that you are in a four-footed monkey position, you should be able to feel that your back, including the pelvis, can lengthen and widen as an integrated whole.

Further reading:

Anatomy in Action, Chapter 11. The Hips

Anatomy in Action, Chapter 3. Extensors and Head Balance

The Body in Motion, Chapter 7. The Pelvic Girdle

The Body in Motion, Chapter 4. The Spine

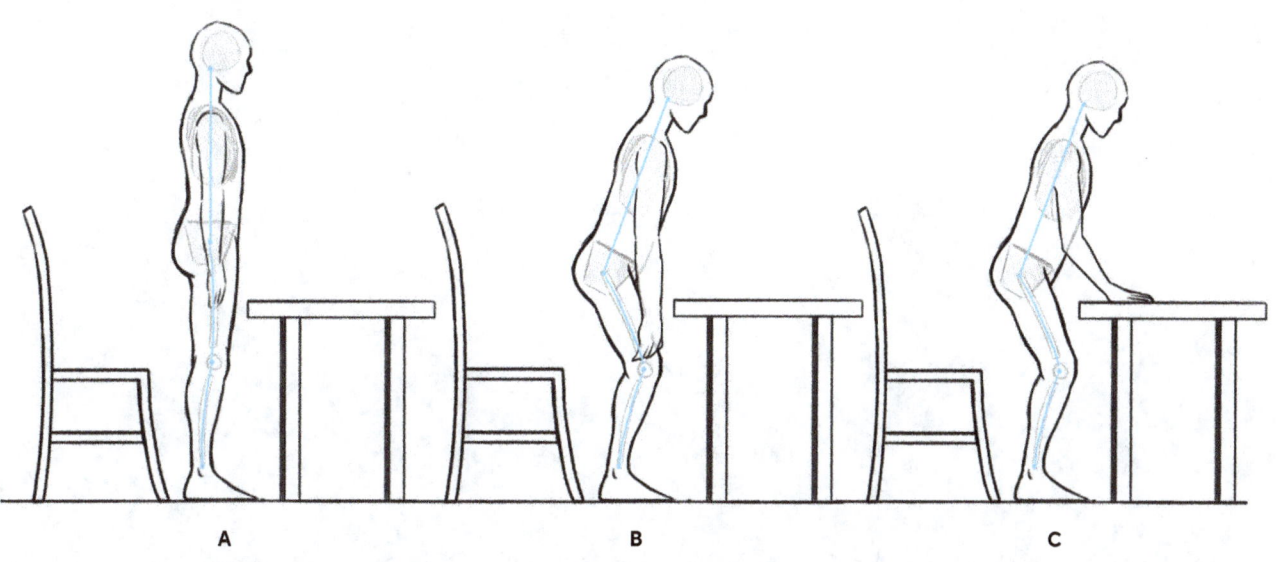

A   B   C

Fig. 20a–c. Going into monkey position using a table for four-footed support.

The Hips, Legs, and Knee Direction

The legs are a particularly important part of the musculoskeletal system. We saw that, when we tighten the shoulders, this interferes at a profound level with the working of the whole system—so much so that, unless we bring about release and widening of the shoulders, we can't expect to restore the working of the musculo-skeletal system as a whole. The same principle applies to the legs. When we shorten in stature, slump, and interfere with the musculoskeletal system in general, the shortening of the legs will be so pronounced that it's really impossible to speak of lengthening in stature, or to experience the coordinated working of the whole, unless we give attention to what is happening in the legs (*Fig. 1a*).

Many of us are familiar with bodywork and relaxation methods that aim to release specific hip or leg muscles, heighten awareness, and bring about greater ease of motion in the hip joint. For anyone seeking to relieve strain and discomfort, such changes seem generally positive and bene-ficial, especially if we feel that we have identified the source of the tension and can do something about it. But it is important to recognize that, in and of itself, removing tension is a somewhat negative approach that accepts tension and dis-comfort as a given, utilizing awareness as a kind of therapeutic process for lessening the tension

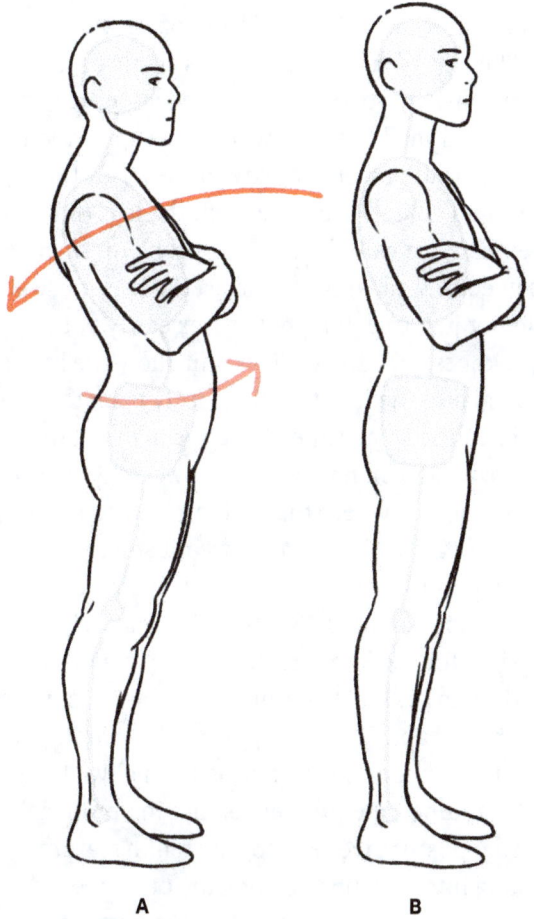

A   B

Fig. 1. In (a) the subject is bracing his legs and sinking into his hips, pushing his hips forward and creating postural lordosis; in (b) the subject is maintaining upright balance with a minimum of strain.

without explaining how the musculoskeletal system is actually meant to work. The truth is that we have a remarkable and natural design and, based on this, our goal should be, not simply to recover from strain but to restore this design and, beyond that, to learn to use the system at a more conscious level so that we can use the legs and other parts of the system easily and efficiently as a matter of course.

To achieve this goal, however, we must have clear and detailed knowledge of how the legs work, what has gone wrong, and how to address the problem. Simply imagining body parts, releasing muscles and fascia, or treating specific tensions will not achieve this goal if, in doing this, we are producing release here or there without fundamentally understanding how we are actually designed to maintain support against gravity and how to restore this function so that we are able to stand and walk with a minimum of effort.

The legs of course support us against gravity. They consist of two segments, the upper leg (or thigh) and the lower leg, which are supported by muscles that powerfully extend the leg at the hip, knee, and ankle. Of course, if all the legs did was to extend, we would have a big problem, since we need to walk and, to do this, the legs must be able not just to extend but to flex easily at the hips, knees, and ankles. This will allow the knees to bend and the legs to swing freely from the hip while, at the same time, the legs can maintain support and, when necessary, powerfully extend.

But here is where the problem comes in. To support the head and trunk, we must extend the legs, but in such a way that they are neither braced nor stiffened (*Fig. 1b*). This makes it possible for the knees to bend easily when we need them to. It also ensures that the leg muscles, which are capable of very powerful movements, aren't working too hard during normal walking and standing. The problem is that in our upright bipedal posture we tend to shorten in stature, sinking into our hips and bracing our knees and ankles in order to maintain upright posture (*Fig. 1a*). At this point, two very harmful things begin to happen in the legs. The first is that, instead of remaining flexible and relaxed, the leg muscles become overworked, and the very thing

we don't want has now happened, which is that the fast-twitch muscle fibers designed to produce powerful movements are now doing the job of maintaining basic postural support. This causes the legs to become habitually braced and over-worked, the joints to become inflexible, and the leg muscles to become habitually shortened and contracted.

The second thing that begins to happen is that the knees, which often become hyperextended, cannot flex and release forward in a way that allows walking to take place easily and effortlessly and instead remain braced to compensate for the lack of flexibility in the muscles and joints. Walking in this way has little to do with a true striding gait and becomes instead a kind of sinking and collapsing into the hips and legs, which can no longer be used in a coordinated way for walking or standing. Walking becomes an exercise in excessive muscle tension that involves pulling ourselves into the ground with each step. In this condition, we no longer know what it means to use our hips, knees, and ankles to walk, bend, and sit but are simply bracing and stiffening our legs in everything we do.

How then do we address these tendencies? We must be clear, to begin with, that reducing this tension through stretching and release will do little to address the problem if, when you return to normal everyday activity, you are continuing to overwork the leg muscles. For such changes to be meaningful, we must bring about release and lengthening in the legs, and we must do this in a way that actually carries over into movement and activity. We do this through the process of "directing" the knees "forward and away." This is more than simply having an image or thought but a form of kinesthetic thinking in which we tell muscles not to shorten so that we stop bracing the legs, which brings about changes that can then be applied in activity. Once you understand how badly you brace and stiffen the hips and legs and are able to stop doing this, you will appreciate that the knee direction is more than an abstract concept but is very definitely meant to address a key part of how we shorten in stature. And because we never tighten the legs in isolation but as part of how we interfere with the body as a whole, the knee direction is critical to the working of the PNR (postural neuromuscular reflex) system as a whole. This is why, if we want to restore the PNR system, it is critical to include the knee direction and to bring about real changes in how the hips and legs are functioning.

Further reading:

Anatomy in Action, Chapter 12. The Leg Spirals

DIRECTING THE KNEES

Because the hips and legs are typically overworked and tense, we need to give special attention to this region of the body. In the following series of exercises, we will identify and bring into our awareness key regions of the hips and legs as a way of releasing tension in these muscles and restoring their proper function.

Exercise 1

Directing the knees and legs in sitting position

In this exercise, we begin with the very simple process of identifying the two main segments of the legs as a way of heightening our kinesthetic awareness (*Fig. 2, blue lines*).

1. Sitting in a comfortable chair with your feet flat on the floor and your back supported, take a moment to be aware of your head, neck, trunk, and shoulders. Allow your trunk to come to its full length, your head to balance forward and up, and your shoulders to widen apart.

2. Turn your attention to your thighs, being aware of the length of your upper leg from your hips to your knees. Notice any tension in your thigh muscles and think of allowing them to let go. Continue to think this until you can feel a change in the muscle tone in your hips and thighs.

3. As you become aware of your thighs, continue to project the thought for your thigh muscles to release by "directing" your knees away from your hips.

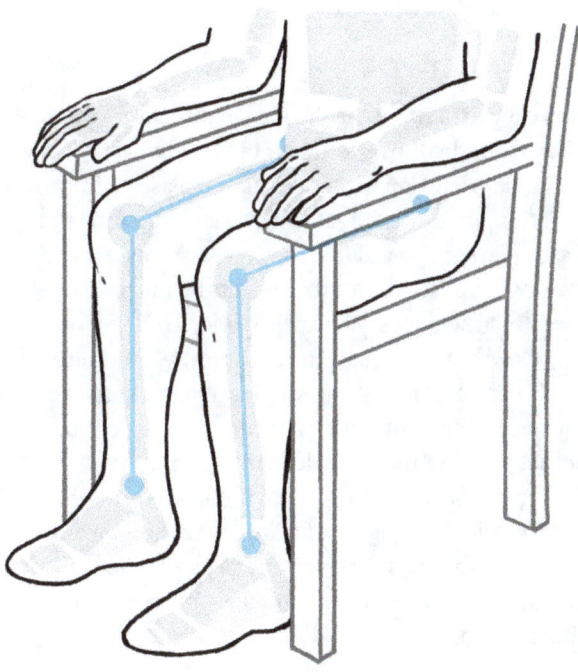

Fig. 2. The leg segments in sitting.

4. Be aware of your feet on the floor. Notice if your feet are tight and let them soften, feeling the contact of your feet on the floor.

5. Notice the length of your lower leg from your heels to the back of your knees along your calf muscles. Continue to be aware of the back of your legs until you feel your ankles and calves letting go or tingling.

6. Continue to direct your knees away from your hips and from your heels, being aware also of the contact of your feet on the floor.

Because the muscles of the hips and legs can become so tight and shortened, it can be difficult to feel or access this part of the body. By taking time to kinesthetically identify each segment of the leg, we can become more aware of our leg muscles and, even more importantly, learn to affect them with our awareness and thinking.

Exercise 2

Directing the knees away in sitting position

It is easy to assume that, when we direct the knees away from the hips, we are employing imagery—in this case of the knee—to facilitate release or improve function, in much the same way that imagining the head floating upward is sometimes used as a way of improving posture. But that is not the purpose of directing the knees. The leg is made up of several muscle groups that become chronically contracted. By directing the knees, we are learning to stop these muscles from contracting in order to bring about actual lengthening and release in the muscles. Directing the knees, in other words, is a form of kinesthetic thinking that facilitates the toning and release of muscles. In this exercise, we explore the key muscle groups that we are learning to affect with this thinking process.

1. Sitting in the chair with your feet flat on the floor and your back supported, turn your attention to your quadriceps muscles, which are the meaty group of muscles on top of the thigh that powerfully extend your leg at the knee (*Fig. 4*). Be aware of the length of your thigh muscles from your hips to your knees, allowing these muscles to release or lengthen. Continue to think this until you can feel a change in tone as the muscles come into your awareness (*Fig. 3*).

2. The second major muscle group on the thighs are the hamstrings, which are on the back of the leg and, when you are sitting, run along the underside of the thigh from your sit bones to the back of your knees (*Fig. 4*). See if you can notice a toning up or tingling as these muscles come into your awareness, and continue to project the thought for the muscles to release by "directing" your knees to go away from your sit bones (*Fig. 3*).

3. The third major muscle group on the thigh are the adductors on the inside of the leg or inner thigh that originate around the pubic bone and run in the direction of your inner knee (*Fig. 4*). As you think of your knees going out and away from each other, these muscles will begin to come into your awareness (*Fig. 3*).

4. As you continue think of your knees going away, be aware of your feet on the floor, noticing the length of your lower leg from your heels to the back of your knees.

5. As you become aware of your thighs, continue to project the thought for your thigh muscles to release by "directing" your knees away from your hips.

After spending some time on this awareness exercise, you may begin to feel a noticeable change in your leg muscles, all of which run in the direction of the knee, attach to the kneecap or, in the case of the hamstrings, cross the back of the knee. With repetition and practice, your thinking will begin to have a distinct and concrete effect on these muscles, and the direction for the knees to go "forward and away" will take on more and more meaning, becoming a kind of shorthand for releasing these muscles of your legs. As the knee direction works, you may also feel your hip and gluteal muscles letting go, your sit bones making a fuller contact with the chair, and your pelvic floor opening up, as if the legs are opening out of your pelvis and trunk.

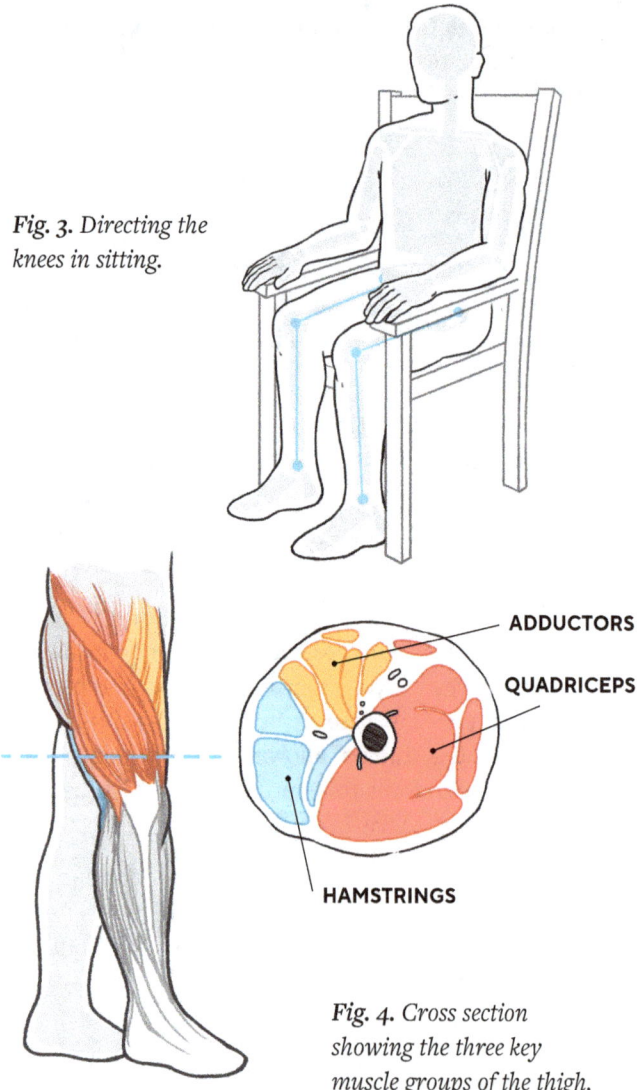

Fig. 3. Directing the knees in sitting.

ADDUCTORS

QUADRICEPS

HAMSTRINGS

Fig. 4. Cross section showing the three key muscle groups of the thigh.

Exercise 3

Directing the knees in semi-supine position

Learning to bring about length in the leg muscles by directing the knees in semi-supine position is one of the most effective ways of restoring length in the legs. As we've seen, however, it is not enough to simply think of the knees going up in space if we have no kinesthetic awareness of the legs to begin with. In this exercise, we will identify, and bring into our awareness, the upper and lower segments of the legs as a way of bringing the legs into our awareness.

1. When you are in the semi-supine position with your knees up, take a moment to identify the two segments of the leg: the upper leg from pelvis to knee and the lower leg from foot to knee (*Fig. 5*).

2. Turn your attention first to your upper leg, which runs from your pelvis in back, which is in contact with the floor, to the back of your knee, and in front from the crook of your hip joint to the top of your knee. See to it that you're not tightening the thigh muscles in back and the muscles on top of your thigh so that you are allowing your knee to go up.

3. Next, notice the lower leg from your feet on the floor to your knee. This segment includes your foot, which contacts the floor, your ankle, the back of your leg to behind your knee, and the front of your leg to the top of your knee. See to it that you're allowing your foot and ankle to let go onto the floor and the muscles of your lower leg to let go so that your knees go up and away from your foot.

4. Take time being aware of each segment of the leg (pelvis to knees and feet to knees), until each segment comes more clearly into your awareness. You may find that you are now becoming more fully aware of your legs including your pelvis, thighs, knees, lower legs, ankles, and feet.

5. With your legs as a whole coming more into your awareness, think of your knees going up from your pelvis and from your feet; the thought for the knees to go up will now include a fairly clear picture of each segment of the leg and its ability to lengthen.

As before, it is useful to give plenty of time to become aware of the leg segments, and to allow each one to lengthen to the knee as the basis for directing the knees upward. The thought for the knees to go up to the ceiling becomes a shorthand that includes the lengthening of both the lower and upper leg.

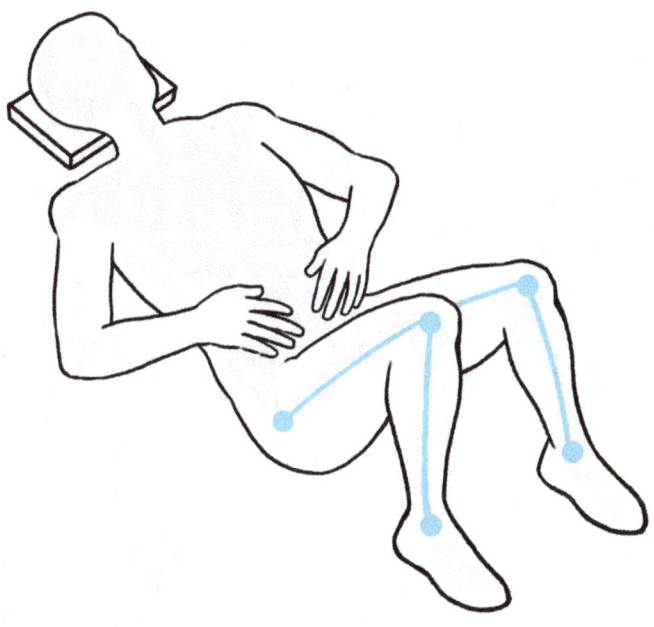

Fig. 5. Directing the legs in semi-supine position.

The Hip Flexors:
The Iliopsoas Complex

The iliacus and psoas muscles, sometimes called the iliopsoas complex, are the primary flexors of the leg at the hip (*Fig. 6*). Iliacus arises from the inner surface of the pelvic rim and, crossing the hip joint, attaches to the lesser trochanter of the femur. The psoas muscle arises from the lumbar spine and, crossing the pelvis, joins up with iliacus to attach to the lesser trochanter. These muscles, acting together, flex the leg at the hip and also assist in flexing the trunk at the hip, as when we perform sit-ups. At a more subtle level, however, the iliopsoas muscles play a crucial role in upright posture. To achieve fully upright posture, the human spine had to develop a lumbar curve, which creates instability in the lower back. If we are shortened and collapsed, the iliopsoas muscle becomes shortened and pulls

on the lower back. In order to restore natural length and support in the trunk, the iliopsoas muscle must release across the front of the pelvis, allowing the lower back to lengthen and in this sense contributing to the lengthened support of the trunk. Roughly corresponding to the freeing of the pectoral region of the chest which allows the shoulder girdle to widen, this release of the iliopsoas muscle across the front of the hip is thus a crucial element in restoring the lengthened support of the trunk.

The iliopsoas complex is also central to the lengthening action of the legs. If this muscle is contracted and shortened, the legs are pulled into the hip and cannot lengthen out of the pelvis. When the knees are "directed" forward, these muscles let go across the front of the hip and pelvis, restoring the natural lengthening of the legs, which can be felt as an increased springiness in the legs.

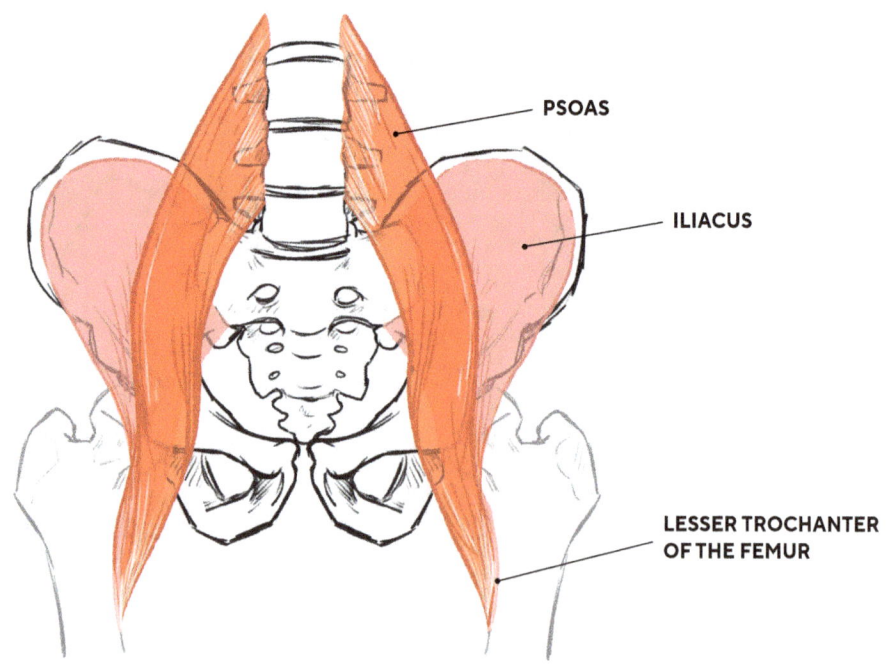

Fig. 6. Hip flexors: The iliopsoas complex.

DIRECTING AND THE HIP FLEXORS

In its habitually shortened state, we normally cannot feel the iliopsoas muscle and its effect on the legs. In these exercises, we support the leg in a way that makes it possible to clearly identify its action and to direct the knee in such a way that this key flexor of the hip can release.

Exercise 1

The action of the iliopsoas muscle

To do this exercise, find a chair that is fairly low so that, while lying on the floor, you can comfortably rest your lower leg on the chair.

1. Lie down in semi supine and place a chair next to your lower left leg.

2. Rest your left leg on the chair seat so that it is fully supported at the calf (*Fig. 7*).

3. Do not hold your leg but let it relax and fall to the side, rotating outwardly. In this position, the flexors of the hip and the adductors of the inner thigh should be completely relaxed.

4. Rotate your leg medially or inwardly so that your knee is more directly over your hip, and you will feel these muscles tighten.

5. Relax the muscles again to let the leg fall outwardly and again rotate your leg inwardly. Can you feel more clearly how the muscles of the hip and inner thigh tighten when the knee is held directly over the hip?

6. Lower your leg onto the ground so that you are in semi-supine position and take a moment to direct your knees.

7. Can you notice that, even in this position, you will tend to hold or tighten the hip flexors and inner thigh and that, by directing your knees, you can begin to access this tension?

8. Repeat the same procedure with your other leg.

After trying this exercise, spend some time in the semi-supine position and direct both of your knees to the ceiling, noticing if you feel any changes in the flexors and adductors of your leg. By thinking of the knees going up but also away from each other, you may feel that these muscles can begin to let go, allowing the knees to come out of the pelvis.

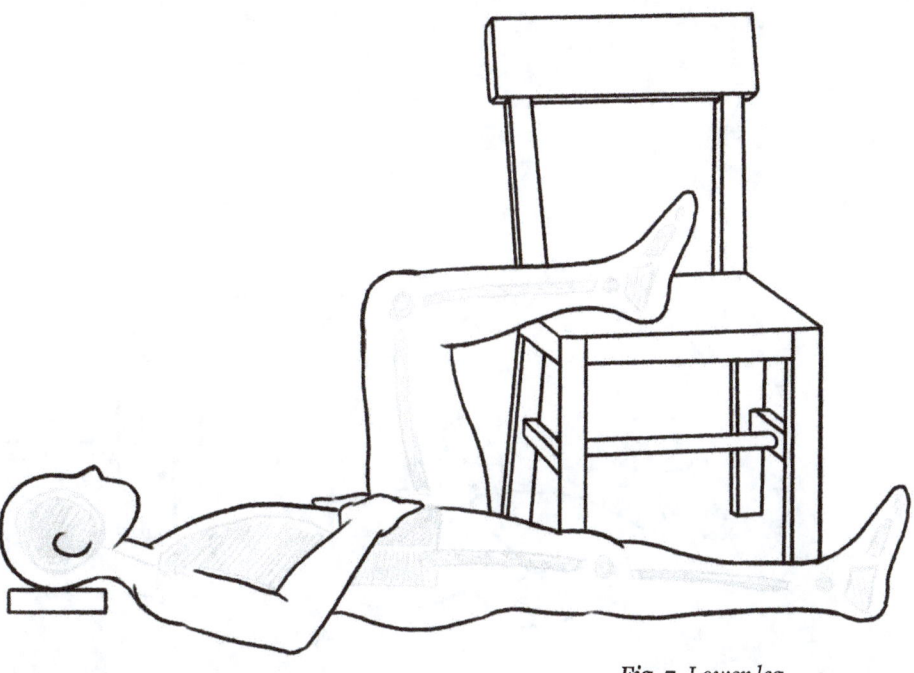

Fig. 7. Lower leg supported on the chair.

Exercise 2

Releasing the hip flexors

When the leg is flexed at the hip and we move the leg, we can identify the tendency to tighten the hip flexors and the corresponding ability to let them go. In this exercise, we explore these movements as the basis for learning how the leg releases out of this crucial region of the hip.

1. Lying in semi supine, place a chair in front of your lower left leg.

2. Place the arch of your left foot on the chair so that your leg is bent at the knee and is aiming toward your chest (*Fig. 8*).

3. Move your knee to the right and left and see if, when you do this, you hold or tighten your hip flexors. Notice also if you tighten the muscles of your pelvic floor, lower back, and inner thigh and allow these muscles to let go.

4. Place your foot on the floor so that you are in the familiar semi-supine position, and direct both of your knees upward. Can you feel a letting go in the hip flexors? In the adductors of the thigh?

5. Place the chair on your other side and repeat the exercise with your right leg.

6. Place both feet on the floor so that you are in the semi-supine position, and direct both of your knees up to the ceiling. You may now be more aware of the tendency to tighten the flexors and adductors of the inner thigh, and their relation to the direction for the knees to go away from the hips.

Directing the knees is not a vague image or concept but is intended to activate the muscle tissues of the hips and legs in such a way that areas that are chronically tight can let go. Shortening in the hip flexors is a key area that must release in order for the legs to lengthen out of the pelvis.

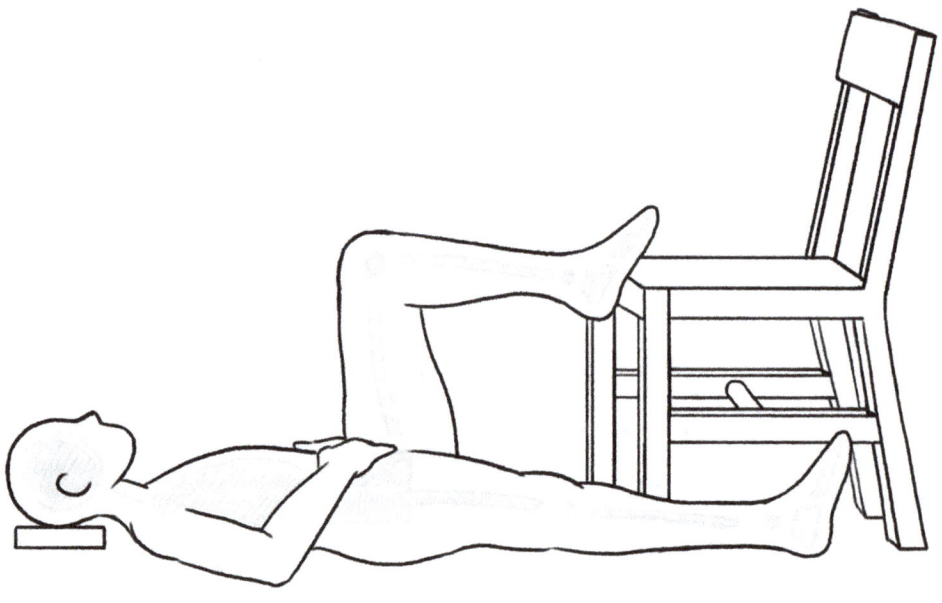

Fig. 8. Variation of lower leg supported on the chair.

LOWERING AND EXTENDING THE LEG

Because the pelvis is attached to the spine, it is not as easy to use leg movements to bring about release in the pelvic region as it is to use arm movements to affect the shoulders, which are far more mobile than the pelvis. In performing the following movements, it helps to remember that these aren't just exercises to be performed in a rote manner but are intended to be part of a process of observing how we tighten in the legs as the basis for bringing about muscular release in the muscles of the hip and thigh. As part of this process, it is important to periodically stop and to "direct" the knees as the basis for recognizing and releasing habitual tensions in the muscles of the inner thigh, the deep muscles of the hip, and the flexors that cross the front of the hip, which correspond to the pectoral region of the shoulders.

Exercise 3

Lowering the leg by leading with the foot (Figs. 9 and 10)

When we straighten or extend our legs, we tend to shorten the hip flexors on the front of the leg and to tighten behind the knees. The following exercise helps to release the hips by maintaining the direction for the knees to go away while lowering the leg into extension. This inhibits or prevents tightening of the hip flexors and the muscles on the back of the leg, ultimately bringing about release in the psoas muscles crossing the front of the hips, the hamstrings behind the knee, and the inner thigh muscles.

1. To begin this exercise, lie in the semi-supine position and direct your your head to go out, your back to lengthen and widen, and your knees to go upward. Give special attention to the knees, thinking of letting go in your hips and thighs to let your knees go upward (*Fig. 9-position 1*).

2. Now begin to lower or extend one leg by creeping the foot forward with your toes. The idea is to move the leg with the foot and to tighten as little as possible in the hips and thighs (*Fig. 9–position 2*).

Fig. 9. *Lowering (extending) the leg.*

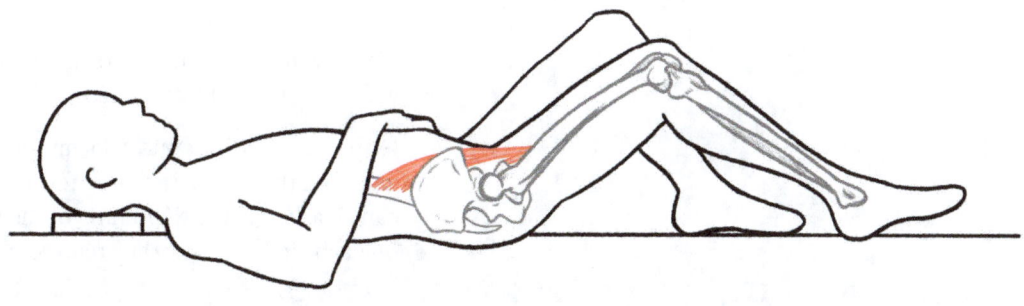

Fig. 10. *The iliopsoas muscle when lowering the leg.*

3.   As the foot advances, continue to direct your knee up and also forward to release across the hip. Be sure not to tighten in the front of the hip and to allow the knee to go away from the hip.

4.   When you cannot advance the foot any further, start to dorsiflex the foot so that you will begin to lead with your heel to lower the leg (*Fig. 9-position 3*). Continue to direct to your knee and to tighten as little as possible in your hip. As the leg extends, the knee will begin to drop because there is nothing supporting it from below. Before advancing the foot any further, give your primary directions, paying particular attention to your knee, which must be directed upwards so that it doesn't drop down toward the floor.

5.   Allowing your heel to slide forward on the floor to extend the leg further, be sure to continue to direct the knee upward and to release across the front of your hip in order to counter the tendency to drop the knee.

6.   Do this exercise in small increments until the leg is fully extended on the floor (*Fig. 9-position 4*), continuing at each point to direct the knee upwards. Allow your leg to lengthen out of your hip and to release in the gluteal muscles.

7.   Continuing to direct the knee, quickly raise your leg at the knee so that the knee is again pointing to the ceiling. Give your directions to your head, back, and knees.

8.   Repeat this process with the other leg and, when you have finished, give your directions to both knees, allowing the thighs and hip flexors to release.

If you have gone through this process slowly and thoughtfully, you should begin to experience release in the hamstrings, the hip flexors, and the gluteal muscles, which allows the knees to go forward and away and the legs to lengthen.

THE HIP EXTENSORS: THE GLUTEAL MUSCLES AND THE "DEEP SIX"

The gluteal muscles are extensors of the hip and stabilizers of the leg at the pelvis. Gluteus maximus is the bulkiest muscle of the buttocks region and powerfully extends the leg. It consists of an upper and lower section, the upper part attaching to the IT (iliotibial) band and the lower part to the shaft of the femur (*Fig. 11b*). Gluteus minimus and medius are abductors of the hip and stabilize the hip when weight is placed on the leg in walking (*Fig. 11a and c*).

There are six deep muscles of the hip: two obturator muscles, two gemelli muscles, quadratus femoris, and piriformis (*Fig. 12*). These muscles spread out from the greater trochanter to form a fan attaching to different points on the pelvis (*Fig. 13*). Acting on the greater trochanter, these muscles are lateral rotators of the hip. When they become contracted, they fix the joint when we are sitting, standing, and walking. When they let go, the hips rotate inwardly as part of the release of the outer or extensor leg spiral.

Exercise 4

Releasing the hip extensors in semi-supine

The gluteal muscles are among the most powerful in the body and, although most of us grip and tighten them unconsciously, we are for the most part quite unconscious of this activity. The following exercise is a simple way of becoming more aware of how we grip in these muscles, which in turn allows the legs to undo out of the pelvis and for the knees to go forward and away. The release of the gluteal muscles also allows the back of the pelvis, where these muscle originate, to open onto the floor, which in turn allows the back, which includes the pelvis, to work more fully.

1.   Lie on your back with books under your head but with both legs fully extended.

2.   Grip or clench your buttocks muscles on one side and then the other. Try this a few times until you can clearly feel the tightening of the hip extensors on each side and how they tend to pull on the leg.

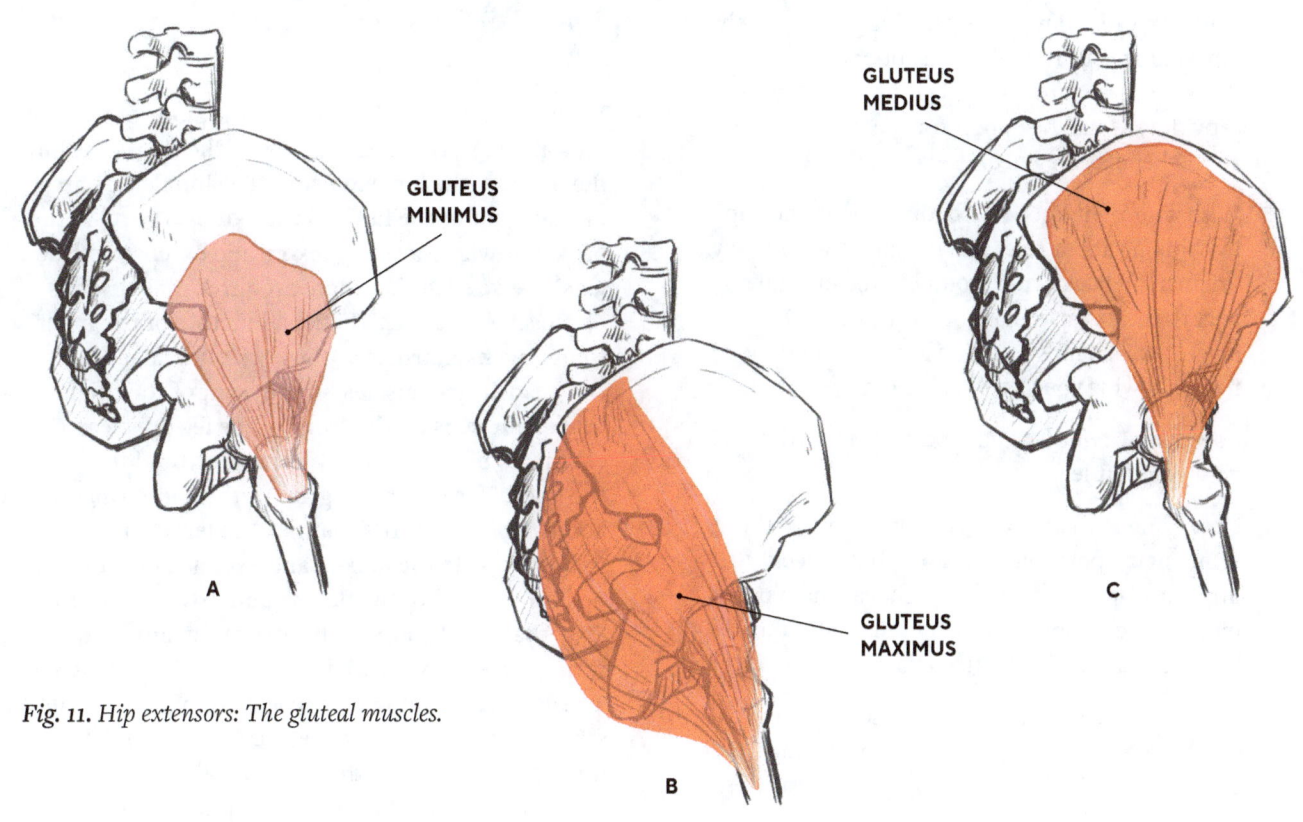

GLUTEUS MINIMUS

GLUTEUS MEDIUS

GLUTEUS MAXIMUS

A

B

C

Fig. 11. *Hip extensors: The gluteal muscles.*

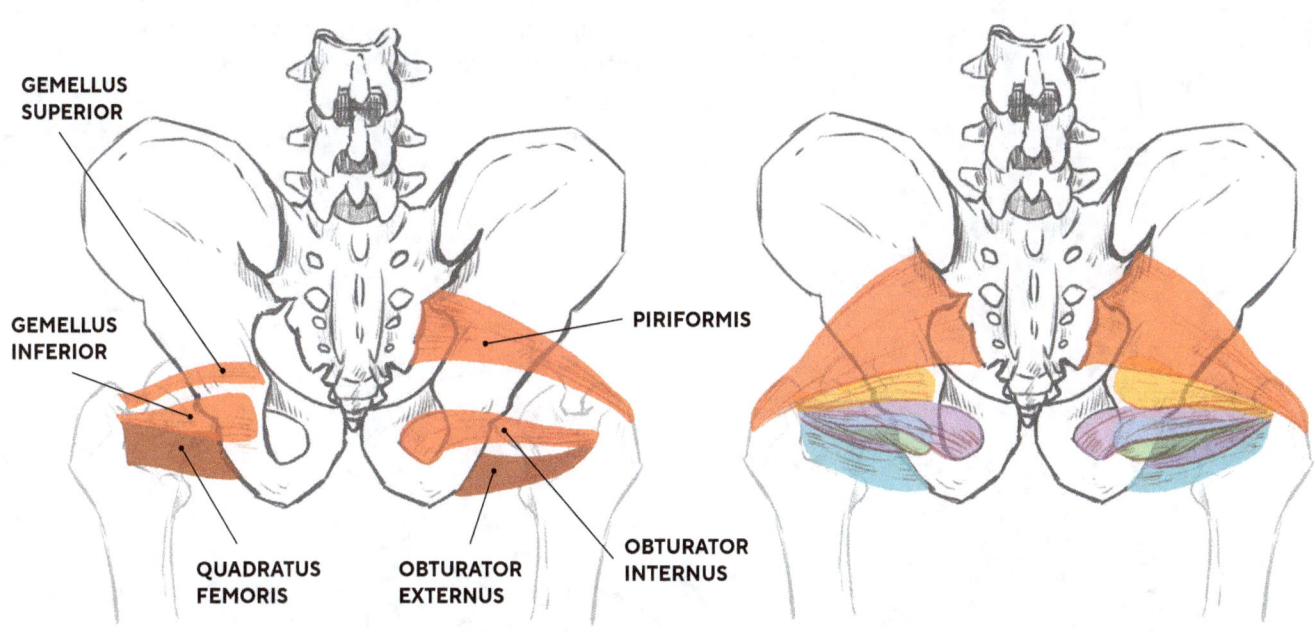

GEMELLUS SUPERIOR

GEMELLUS INFERIOR

PIRIFORMIS

QUADRATUS FEMORIS

OBTURATOR EXTERNUS

OBTURATOR INTERNUS

Fig. 12. *The deep muscles of the hip.*

Fig. 13. *The "deep six" fan out from the greater trochanter.*

3. Bring your right knee up by flexing your leg at the hip, sliding your foot along the floor as you do this so that you aren't simply lifting the leg but providing as much support for the leg as possible as you bend at the knee.

4. With your right knee raised, direct your knee up by thinking about releasing the glutes where they originate in back, wrap around to the hip and connect to the extensors on top of the thigh. Notice if your pelvis tends to widen and fill out on the floor, allowing your leg to come out of the hip.

5. Lower your right leg and repeat the procedure with your left leg.

6. Now bring both knees up so that you are in the semi-supine position, and direct your knees upward. Can you feel that the gluteal and hip muscles are letting go, which in turn lets your knees go "up" and away from your pelvis?

7. Extend your legs one at a time to see if your hip and buttocks muscles are letting go, and raise them once again to direct your knees upward.

By tightening your gluteal muscles and then taking time to let them go, can you notice if you have a tendency to grip them unconsciously and that, as they let go, your knees can come out of your pelvis and your back can work more fully?

THE LEG SPIRALS

We have now looked at three key regions of the hips and legs: the long muscles of the thigh, the hip flexors, and the hip extensors. The hip flexors are on the front of the hip and the extensors are on the back, but where are the flexors and extensor of the legs? We've seen that there are three main groups of muscles on the thigh: the adductors of the inner thigh, the hamstrings at the back of the leg, and the quadriceps muscles on the front of the thigh. The quadriceps on the front of the leg are clearly extensors because they powerfully extend the leg at the knee. The other two groups, the hamstrings and adductors, are flexors that flex the leg at the knee.

But why do the flexors and extensors of the hip not correspond to the flexors and extensors of the leg—that is, why are the flexors of the hip in front while the leg flexors are in back, and vice versa? The answer is that these muscle groups do not run straight up and down the leg but form a kind of double-spiral around the leg (*Fig. 14*). The flexors, which start in front at the hip, spiral inward to the inner and back of the leg (*purple line on rear leg*); the extensors, which start with the gluteal and hip muscles in back, wrap around to the front of the leg (*blue line on advanced leg*). Thus we have two spirals, an inner flexor spiral and an outer extensor spiral, formed by a kind of inward rotation of the leg in relation to the pelvis. We can observe the

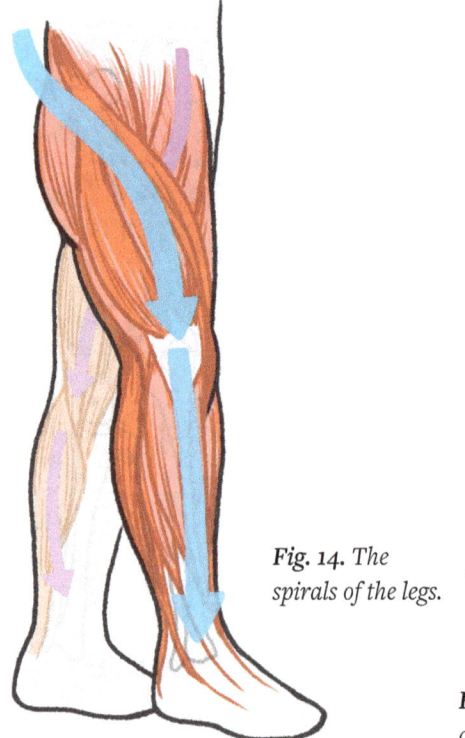

Fig. 14. The spirals of the legs.

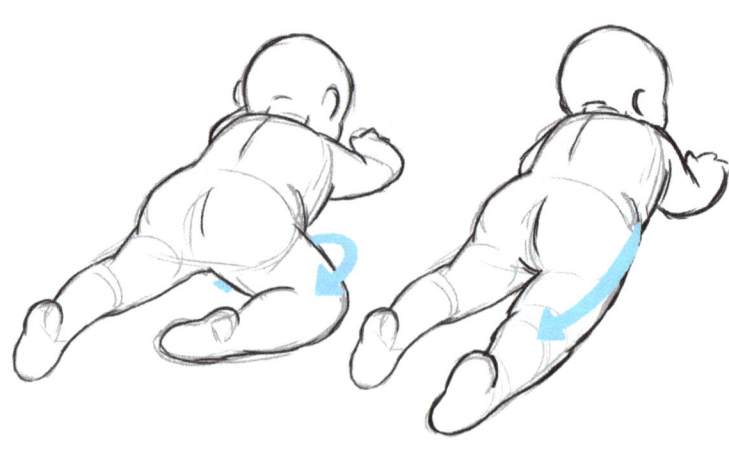

Fig. 15. The spiral action of the legs is clearly visible when an infant crawls.

rotational actions corresponding to these spiral lines when we crawl on our bellies like reptiles: to advance the leg we rotate it outwards; to straighten the leg we rotate it inwards (*Fig. 15*). When we interfere with, or tighten, the outer spiral, we rotate the leg outward; we can see this when we are sitting and the quadriceps muscles pull the knees apart. When we shorten the inner spiral, we pull the knees together, causing a shortening and sinking into the crotch while standing and walking.

The direction for the knees to go away from each other is also directly related to the spiral musculature of the legs. When we bend the knees to walk, this corresponds, in evolutionary terms, to the outward rotation of the legs, which we see most clearly in the reptilian movements of the baby who, when crawling on its belly, rotates the leg outwardly to advance the knee (*Fig. 15*). When we habitually brace our legs, the knee can no longer bend easily, which means that we have not only shortened the leg muscles but also interfered with the ability of the legs to rotate outwardly. The outward rotation that happens when the knee advances requires a release in the inner thigh muscles that corresponds, in upright walking, to the knees going away from each other so that the inner thigh muscles are releasing. This is why, when we think of the knees going forward, we must also allow them to go away from each other, or "forward and away."

Exercise 5

The leg spirals

We saw that, when we pull the knees together and shorten the muscles of the inner thigh, we are tightening the inner spiral. When we pull the legs outwardly, we are tightening the outer spiral. To identify the two spirals, try the following exercise.

1. Sit in a chair with your feet flat on the floor and your back supported. To access the outer spiral, be aware of the buttocks muscles that wrap around from behind to the side of your hip, continuing along the top of your thighs to your knees (*Fig. 16-blue line on right leg*). This will start to undo the outer spiral to allow the knees to go forward from the hips.

2. The inner spiral begins at the front of the pelvis, angling inward to the inner thigh and hamstrings and ending at the inner knee (*Fig. 16—red line on left leg*). To affect the inner spiral, be aware of the length of your inner thigh from your sit bones to your inner knee. This will encourage the adductors and hamstrings to release, undoing the inner spiral and allowing the knees to go forward from the hips and away from each other.

3. Give these directions separately at first, and then put them together to get a clear sense of what it means to direct your knees forward and away.

As you identify and explore the inner and outer spirals, you may become more aware of the tendency to pull the knees both inwardly and outwardly, creating unnecessary tension that interferes with the ability of the legs to lengthen out of the trunk. This gives greater meaning to the knee direction, which is meant to address this shortening as the basis for restoring the lengthening support of the legs.

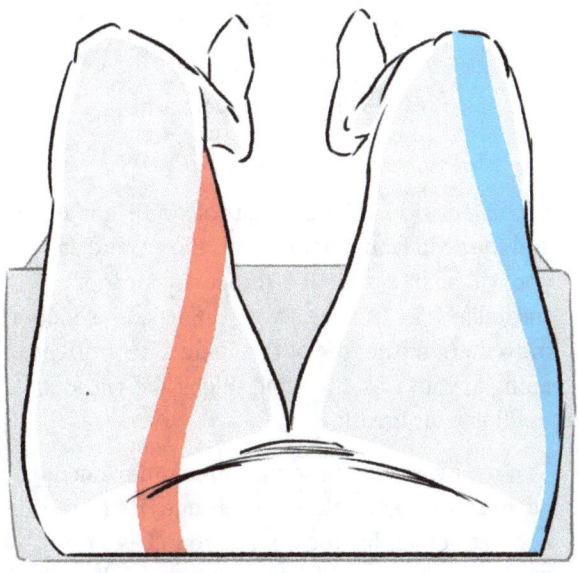

Fig. 16. The leg spirals in sitting.

Exercise 6

Flipper movement of the legs

The flipper procedure with the legs is similar to that of the arms (see Chapter 8) but is more difficult for several reasons. First, most of us have more control over the hand than the foot, making it harder to monitor what we are doing with the foot than the hand. Second, the leg is heavier than the arm. This increases the temptation to use a great deal of effort to move the leg. Finally, the flipper movement of the foot at the ankle requires a more subtle pivoting action than the hand and takes more time to master. The exercise, however, is well worth the effort!

As with the arm, it is useful to consider why we do this movement and exactly what it is meant to accomplish. When we advance the leg, we have to use quite a lot of effort in the muscles of the buttocks, thighs, and back, which generally interferes with the natural lengthening of these muscles. If we can move the leg, not by gripping our muscles but in a more subtle way—that is, by pivoting the foot on the ground and pulling the leg along with it—the leg is passively moved, which makes it possible to prevent the tightening in the hips and thighs and even to bring about release in these muscles.

This movement is directly related to the spiral musculature of the legs. In the prone posture, the only way the leg can advance is to rotate outward. This outward rotation, which corresponds to the splayed position of the legs in reptiles, involves the outer or extensor spiral of the leg. To straighten the leg, or to do the flipper movement in reverse, the leg must rotate inward, which involves the inner spiral. The flipper exercise thus provides a chance to unravel both the inner and outer leg spirals and can be hugely beneficial in restoring a more coordinated condition of the back, hips, and legs.

1. Lie face down on the floor in the reptilian posture—that is, with your head turned to the right side, your right arm advanced with palm facing down, and your right knee advanced (*Fig. 17*). Your left arm will rest alongside your body with the back or dorsal surface of your hand contacting the ground.

2. Take a moment to notice all the parts of your body that are weight-bearing: the left side of your head, your rib cage and pelvis, your left leg, and your right knee and inner leg. Make sure that you're comfortable and able to breathe freely.

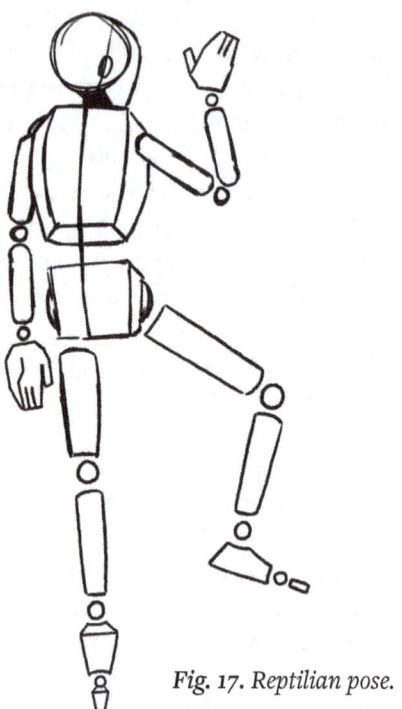

Fig. 17. Reptilian pose.

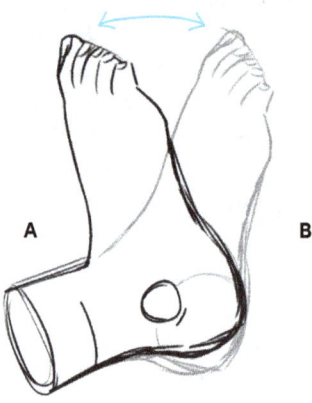

Fig. 18. The flipper movement of the foot at the ankle.

3. In this position, the inner part of your right ankle and foot will be in contact with the ground and you will be free to flex or "flipper" your foot at the ankle (*Fig. 18*). See if you can make this flipper movement of the foot at the ankle without tightening in your ribs, hips, and thighs and without holding your breath.

4. You're now ready to use this flipper movement to advance your knee along the ground. Using the contact of your big toe on the ground as a prop, see if you can now straighten or plantar flex your ankle to advance your knee along the ground

(*Fig. 19*). The idea here is to move the leg, not by tightening your lower back and gluteal muscles but only by using the foot movement. At first, you will want to tighten your buttocks, lower back, and leg muscles to move your leg. When this happens, start over, noticing each time you tighten.

5. One element to pay attention to is the position of the ankle, which must be kept on the ground. As with the flipper movements of the arm, the first movement, dorsiflexion of the foot at the ankle, is preparatory; the second movement, plantar flexion, is active. When dorsiflexing the foot, the leg remains in place on the ground and the foot moves at the ankle, merely sliding on the ground. With the foot dorsiflexed, it is now in position to plantar flex as the basis for moving the leg—that is, to move in the other direction. The inside of the big toe joint (*Fig. 20*) is used as a fulcrum on the ground so that, as the foot is flexed at the ankle, the entire lower leg is advanced on the ground (*Fig. 21*).

6. This sequence is repeated until the knee advances as far as it can go without forcing the hip. You can then reverse the whole procedure (this time using the action of dorsiflexion to pivot the foot and to move and straighten the knee in the other direction) until the leg is fully extended, with the dorsal surface of the foot resting on the ground.

7. When you have finished, compare the freedom of rotation in this leg to the other. Now try the whole sequence turning to the left hand side.

The flipper movement, explored in a thoughtful and patient way, is an invaluable way to undo the spirals of the legs. If you can advance the knee without gripping in the glutes and shortening the flexors, you will bring about beneficial changes in both the flexor and extensor muscles of the legs.

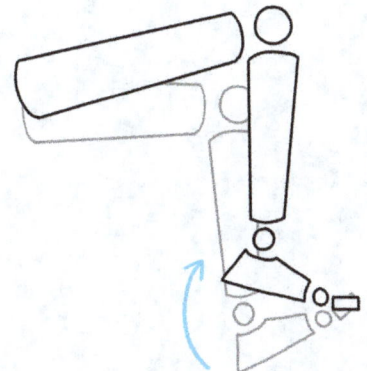

Fig. 19. The flipper movement.

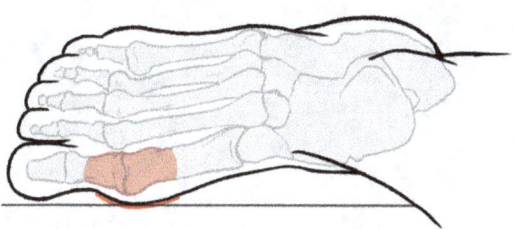

Fig. 20. Contact of the inner big toe on the floor.

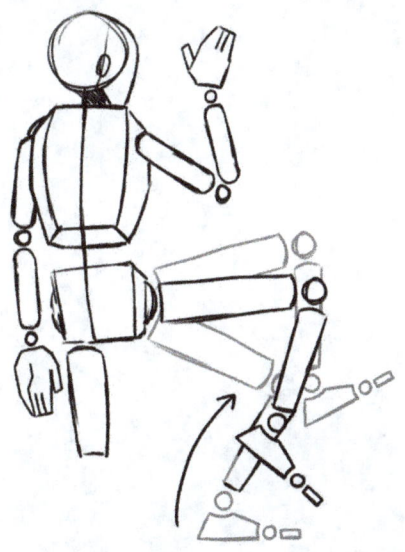

Fig. 21. The movement of the foot at the ankle moves the leg forward.

Activities

13

Sit-Stand and the Means-Whereby Principle

In this series of exercises we will look at the act of getting into and out of a chair, or sitting and standing. Although we take sitting and standing for granted, they are in fact quite complex actions that most of us perform in a very unconscious and harmful way. To sit down in a chair, we must hinge at the hips, knees, and ankles in order to lower ourselves to the chair. Once our sit bones contact the chair, we must then straighten the trunk at the hips so that our weight is shifted over our sit bones and we are sitting upright. These movements are simple enough, but what most of us do instead is to shorten in stature by pulling the head back, arching the back and bracing the legs while aiming our rear ends toward the chair. If you observe these movements closely in someone else, you'll see that these actions amount to a kind of tightening and collapsing of the entire body so that, by the time we are sitting, we have lost the internal, lengthened support of the body. This disengages the muscular system so that, if we then want to sit for any period of time, we are no longer able to do so without slumping on the one hand, or arching our back to hold ourselves up on the other.

As we can see from this simple description, how we sit down in a chair is not just about the act of sitting down but also profoundly affects our sitting balance. Sitting in a chair is one of the most important actions we will ever perform in our lives. We spend hours doing it every day, it's the foundation for many of our most advanced activities, and if we do it badly, this means that we are harming ourselves most of the time. How can we expect to perform this action in a balanced way if, every time we go to sit down in the chair, we shorten and collapse the entire system? By the time we are actually sitting down, we are collapsed and shortened and must either lean heavily against the back of the chair, or else arch our backs and contract further in order to maintain our upright support.

The act of sitting down, then, may seem rather innocuous, but doing it this way is really disastrous when you think about how the musculoskeletal system is designed to work and how badly we interfere with it. No method of relaxation, awareness, or bodywork is going to reverse this state of affairs and get the muscular system working properly unless you stop this habitual action and restore the natural working of the support system, which is why we need to look at this movement in such detail. The good news is that, if you study this action closely, you can turn a very harmful act into the opposite—that is, a means of establishing lengthening muscles and healthy muscle tone; this will take you a long way toward restoring the proper working of the muscular system and healthy muscle function, and enable you to apply this new and healthy way of doing things to a broad range of actions and activities.

There is a final reason why sitting down and rising from a sitting position is crucial to the study of awareness. Many of the actions we have learned so far in this course—going into the vertical stance, directing or sending messages to muscles, and exploring various movements—are rather artificial. This is because, as part of learning to be aware of ourselves, we have to simplify and break down specific actions in order to gain greater control over our actions. Sitting down in a chair is of a different order than these other actions. When we sit in a chair, we are performing a voluntary action—one that is highly ingrained and habitual. These two things—the fact that we perform this action as a voluntary act, and the fact that we perform it in a way that is habitual and stereotyped—make it very difficult to change. You can of course alter how you do it in obvious ways, but if you observe very closely what you're doing, you'll see that in all the fundamental ways it is very difficult to change. Even when you have been equipped with some of the procedures and tools that we have learned here—directing, paying attention, doing monkey position, all of which are part of learning to sit and stand in a more conscious way—it is very hard to put these things into practice because the very thought of sitting down will bring into play our old conception of how to do it, and all the harmful habits that go with this.

It is in relation to this problem that we have to apply a new principle in action, sometimes called the "means-whereby principle," in which we focus not on the end but on the means. That is the real purpose of looking at sit-to-stand: to examine how we perform the action habitually and to learn to perform it more consciously. To succeed in this requires a new attitude about how we do things, as well as the ability to apply the means-whereby principle to real-life actions.

That's why we're going to look at this action in stages, breaking it down into manageable pieces. In Part Five, we'll look at how we can perform the entire action in a more conscious way, as a kind of test case for how we can be more mindful in all our activities.

STAND-TO-SIT, OR SITTING IN A CHAIR

The movement of sitting down in a chair can be broken down into three components:

A. First movement:
Lowering the trunk and inclining forward at the hips (*Fig. 1b*)

To sit down in a chair, we must lower the trunk so that the bottom part of the pelvis, or sitting bones, can rest on the chair. To lower our trunk, we must first hinge at the hips, knees, and ankles so that the trunk is inclined forward, the knees are bent, and the lower leg is inclined at the ankle joint. This is the monkey position and is a key position of mechanical advantage, which we've already examined in some detail.

B. Second movement:
Lowering the trunk to the chair by deepening the monkey (*Fig. 1c*)

To lower the trunk to the chair, the knees, ankles, and hips must flex further; this brings the sit bones into contact with the chair, with the weight of the trunk still mainly over the feet.

C. Third movement:
Coming back from the hips (*Fig. 1d*)

Once the sit bones are on the chair, the final movement is to straighten the trunk at the hips so that the weight of the trunk is brought over the sit bones and you are now sitting fully upright.

Exercise 1

Stand-to-sit using the monkey position

Step 1: First Movement

Let's now take time with each of these movements, building one on top of the other, as the basis for sitting thoughtfully, starting with the first movement.

1. Stand in front of the chair with your feet shoulder width apart (*Fig. 1a*). Give your directions for your neck to be free so that the head is free to nod, the back is lengthened, the gluteal muscles are not gripped so that your seat can drop away from your head, and your legs are not braced.

2. Think of releasing the fronts of your ankles, the backs of your knees, and the front of your hip joints.

3. With your head leading, let your joints release to allow your knees to go out over your ankles and your trunk to incline forward from the hips so that you go into the monkey position (*Fig. 1b*).

4. Go through your directions, allowing your head to go away from your pelvis and your pelvis from your head to lengthen your back, and your knees to go away from your pelvis and feet so that you are lengthening along the thighs and calves (*Fig. 1b*).

5. Come up to the upright position, seeing to it that you do not brace your legs or pull your head back.

Notice that you have performed the first movement of sitting without actually sitting down or even thinking about sitting down. It is important to become fully acquainted with this process, independently of the act of sitting; this first step can then be continued to the second.

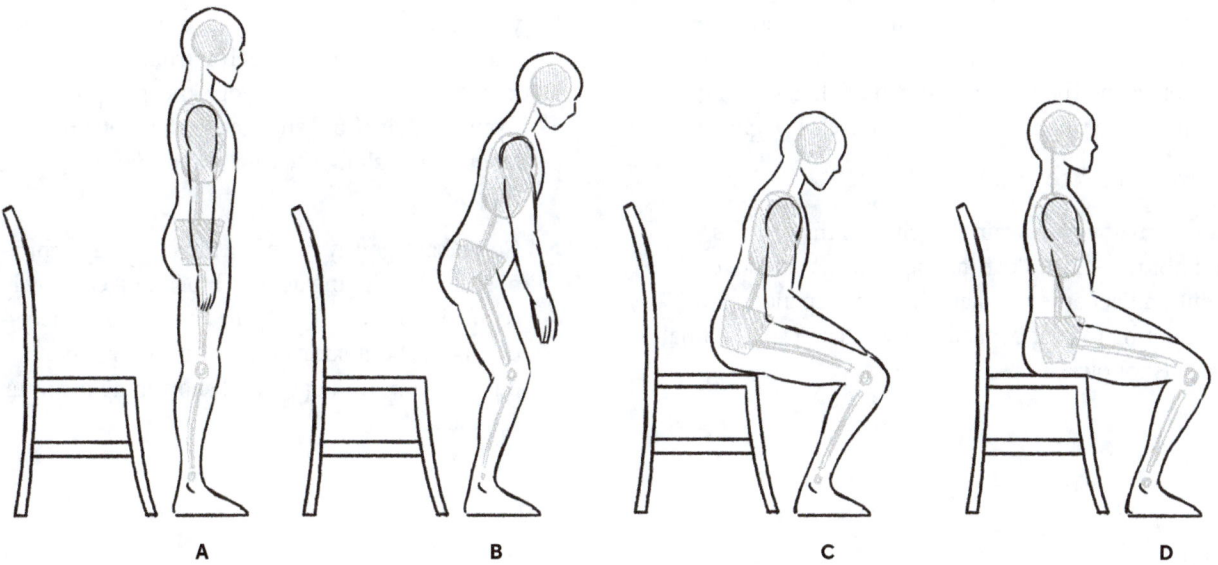

A   B   C   D

Fig. 1a-d. Stand-to-sit.

Step 2: Second Movement

1. Standing in front of the chair, give your directions for your neck to be free so that your head is free to nod, your back is lengthened, the gluteal muscles are not gripped so that your seat can drop away from your head, and the legs are not braced (*Fig. 1a*).

2. Being clear that you do not intend to sit, allow your knees to bend and incline forward from hips so that you are in the monkey position (*Fig. 1b*).

3. Go through your directions again, allowing your head to go away from your pelvis and your pelvis from your head to lengthen your back, and your knees to go away from your pelvis and heels so that you are lengthening along the thighs and the calf muscles (*Fig. 1b*).

4. Deepen the monkey until your seat is in contact with the chair (*Fig. 1c*).

5. Without altering this position, go through your directions, allowing the head to go away from the pelvis and the pelvis from the head to lengthen your back, and your knees to go away from the pelvis and the feet so that you are lengthening along the thighs and the calf muscles (*Fig. 1c*).

6. Come back to standing.

Notice that we are again focusing on the process and not the end. Take time to perform this movement and become familiar with it, independently of completing the act of sitting down. Then try the final step, as follows:

Step 3: Third Movement

1. Stand in front of the chair and give your directions for your neck to be free so that your head is free to nod, your back is lengthened, your gluteal muscles are not gripped so that your seat can drop away from your head, and your legs are not braced (*Fig. 1a*).

2. Being clear that you do not intend to sit, allow your knees to bend and incline forward from the hips so that you are in the monkey position (*Fig. 1b*).

3. Go through your directions again, allowing your head to go away from your pelvis and your pelvis from your head to lengthen your back, and your knees to go away from your pelvis and heels so that you are lengthening along the thighs and the calf muscles (*Fig. 1b*).

4. Deepen the monkey until your seat is in contact with the chair (*Fig. 1c*).

5. Without altering this position, go through your directions, allowing your head to go away from the pelvis and the pelvis from the head to lengthen your back, and your knees to go away from the pelvis and the feet so that you are lengthening along the thighs and the calf muscles (*Fig. 1c*).

6. Come back gently from the hips to an upright position by hinging at your hip joints. Go slowly, seeing if you can move your trunk in one piece—that is, without shortening your lower back, pulling your head back, and shortening in stature (*Fig. 1d*).

When we sit, we shorten in stature both when we lower our weight and when we come back from the hips. The key to the last step in this process is to give time to allow your head to go out of your back, for your back to remain lengthened and widened, and for your knees to go forward and away, before coming back from your hips, which allows your back to continue to lengthen as a whole. If you have performed this action successfully, you will find that there is much less shortening in the back, which will feel more "of a piece." You may also have the sense that, because you have not finished the movement in the usual way, you are sitting in a more active and poised manner—a topic we will look at further in the next chapter.

Exercise 2

Stand-to-sit using a table for four-footed support

Sitting down by using a table for four-footed support is a very useful way of monitoring your back and legs while performing the action of sitting down, as follows.

Step 1: Going into Monkey

1. Stand in front of a table with your feet shoulder width apart (*Fig. 2a*). Give your directions to release the muscles at the back of your neck so that your head is free to nod forward; see to it that your back is lengthened, the gluteal muscles are not gripped so that the seat can drop away from the head, and the legs are not braced.

2. Think of releasing the fronts of the ankles, the backs of the knees, and the front of the hip joints to go into monkey position (*Fig. 2b*). Carefully go through your directions.

3. Place your hands on the table, palms facing down (*Fig. 2c*). Again go through your directions, allowing your head to go away from your pelvis and your pelvis from your head to lengthen your back, and your knees to go away from your pelvis and heels so that you are lengthening along the thighs and the calf muscles.

4. Take your hands off the table and come up to standing.

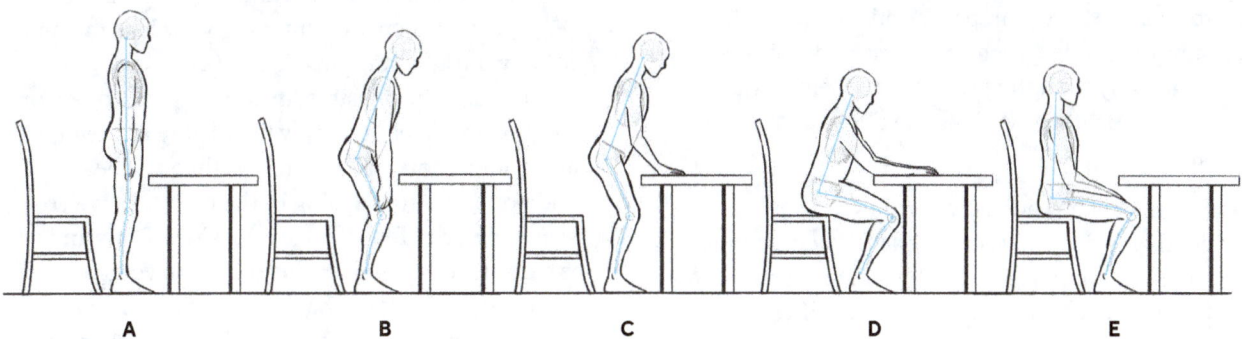

Fig. 2a-e. Stand-to-sit sequence using table.

Step 2: Sitting Down Using a Table for Four-Footed Support

5. Standing in front of the table, give your directions to release the muscles at the back of your neck so that your head is free to nod forward. See to it that your back is lengthened, the gluteal muscles are not gripped so that your seat can drop away from your head, and your legs are not braced (*Fig. 2a*).

6. Think of releasing the fronts of the ankles, the backs of the knees, and the front of the hip joints to go into monkey position. Carefully go through your directions (*Fig. 2b*).

7. Place your hands on the table, palms facing down. Again go through your directions, allowing your head to go away from your pelvis and your pelvis from your head to lengthen your back, and your knees to go away from your pelvis and heels so that you are lengthening along the thighs and the calf muscles (*Fig. 2c*).

8. Deepen your monkey position until (a) your seat is in contact with the chair, and (b) your elbows come onto the table. You will now be sitting, but with the support of your elbows on the table (*Fig. 2d*).

9. Go through your directions, allowing your head to go away from your pelvis and your pelvis from your head to lengthen your back, and your knees to go away from the pelvis and the feet so that you are lengthening along the thighs and the calf muscles.

10. Begin to come back slowly from your hips by gently moving your elbows back, slowly coming to a more upright position by hinging at your hip joints. Do not do this quickly, seeing if you can move your trunk in one piece—that is, without shortening your lower back, pulling your head back, and shortening in stature.

11. You should now have the sense that you have kept more length on your back, that your back is in one piece, and that you are more lengthened in stature.

12. Direct your head up, your back to lengthen and widen, and your knees to go away.

Most of us use a great deal of tension in the legs when we stand, bend, and sit. As a result, we unconsciously brace and grip the legs, which tend to become stiff with age, making it more and more difficult to bend the knees. Learning to "let the knees go away" is a useful way of restoring the flexibility of the legs and also makes it easier to recognize how harmfully we brace and tighten the legs when we perform simple activities like sitting down in a chair or walking.

Although the PNR system is organized primarily around the head and trunk, directing your knees and bringing about release in the legs, which are an extension of the trunk, is a critical part of this system, which can function properly as a coordinated whole only if the legs are lengthening. If you become practiced at this, your legs will become activated and toned, the muscles more elastic and released, and you can begin to use your legs with a minimum of effort.

SIT-TO-STAND, OR RISING FROM A CHAIR

Let's look now at the mechanics of standing up from the sitting position. When sitting, the weight of the trunk is over the sit bones, which are our "feet" when sitting. Standing up from this position involves two basic movements: inclining forward from the hips until your trunk is over your feet (*Fig. 3c*), and then straightening your legs to come to fully upright standing (*Fig. 3d*).

It should be possible, in standing up, to perform the first movement simply by hinging at the hips and coming forward without pulling the head back and arching or collapsing in the trunk. As we've seen, however, few of us are capable of this and will instead forcibly pull the head back to come out of the chair, arching the back, collapsing and shortening in front, and tightening the legs. When we are over our feet and begin to straighten the legs to stand up, we brace and grip in the thighs, further stiffening and shortening in the trunk and pulling the head back rather violently in order to pull ourselves out of the chair. All these movements are not only unnecessary but actually counterproductive, since they prevent the muscles that are needed for standing—namely, the extensors of the back—from working properly.

As a starting point, see if, by giving directions for the neck, head, and back, you can maintain length in the trunk as the basis for inclining forward at the hips, before even attempting to come onto your feet. Breaking the movement down in this way is a crucial part of performing the movement in a coordinated way. Simply hinging at the hips, however, won't solve the problem; the real key to this movement is to spend enough time directing that a new coordination is established based on muscle length, and then stopping the habitual pattern as the basis for performing the action in a new way. As we saw earlier, the goal is not to learn to sit and stand *per se* but to coordinate the system in a new way as the basis for preventing our harmful habits and performing actions more consciously.

Exercise 3

Sit-to-stand using the monkey position

Step 1: First Movement

1. Sitting in the chair, take a moment to give your directions (*Fig. 3a*).

2. Incline forward in the chair a few inches and then go through your directions (*Fig. 3b*). If you feel you have shortened in any way, come back from your hips and start over.

3. When you have taken time to explore this movement, see if you can incline forward so that your trunk is balanced over your feet (*Fig. 3c*). Give your directions in this inclined position, without attempting to stand up.

4. Come gently back to fully upright sitting and give your directions.

Step 2: Second Movement

When you have taken time to explore the first part of the sit-to-stand movement, you will be ready to explore standing from the sitting position.

5. Give your directions in sitting, allowing your head to balance forward, your back to lengthen and widen, and your thigh muscles to let go to allow your knees to go forward and away (*Fig. 3a*).

6. Continuing to direct, incline forward in the chair a few inches and again go through your directions (*Fig. 3b*).

7. Continuing to direct, incline forward in the chair so that your trunk is nearly balanced over your feet, and give your directions (*Fig. 3c*).

8. See if you can now bring your body forward a bit more so that you come over your feet, paying particular attention to the tendency to tighten and shorten in your legs. Stop as often as is necessary to prevent this tightening (*Fig. 3c*).

9. When you have spent time giving directions in this inclined position, go ahead and come over your feet, seeing to it that you are not bracing and tightening in your legs but simply allowing them to straighten as you stand up (*Fig. 3d*).

By taking time to break this movement down, it becomes possible to move in a completely new and effortless way. In this way, you have broken down the act of standing from the sitting position into parts and, by doing so, can prevent much of the shortening and tightening usually associated with this action.

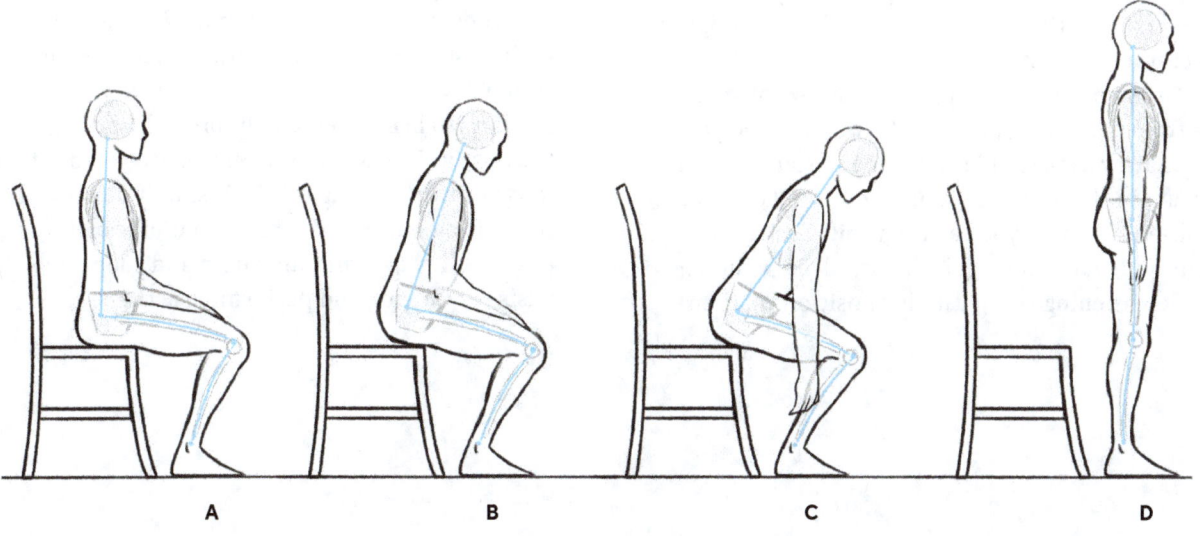

A　　　　　B　　　　　C　　　　　D

Fig. 3a-d. Sit-to-stand.

Directing the Knees Away In Sit-Stand

We have seen that, when we are sitting and stand up, we perform the action in a harmful way, pulling back the head, arching the back, tightening in the legs, and so on. To overcome this, we have broken down the action into discrete steps, taking time to direct the head, trunk, and knees at each stage as the basis for preventing these harmful tendencies. But how exactly do we get out of the chair if we stop tightening muscles? If we come forward in the chair by pulling the head back and arching the back, this is pretty clearly unnecessary, since all we need to do to come forward in the chair is to hinge at the hips. The legs, however, are a different matter. Once we have come forward in the chair and shifted our weight onto our feet, the extensors of the legs must contract, or else we will not be able to support our weight. When we go to raise our trunk in order to stand erect, the leg muscles must contract even more vigorously, or else we will not be able to raise the trunk to the standing position. How else are we going to do all this, if not by actively contracting and shortening our leg muscles?

The answer is that, instead of tightening muscles, we maintain muscle length. To demonstrate this, consider what happens when you assume the monkey position and lower your weight onto your elbows so that you are four-footed. In this position, your legs are doing work, but they are clearly not having to actively shorten because, as part of the overall lengthened support of the body, they lengthen out of the trunk. In this case, the legs support you, but they do it as part of a system of muscle pulls in which muscles lengthen to support you rather than shorten.

The same principle applies to the act of standing from the sitting position. If you can send your knees away as part of lengthening in stature when you are in the four-footed position (we'll call this position A), and if you can then shift back onto the chair with your knees going forward and your legs still lengthening (we'll call this position B), then

why do you need to tighten in your legs when you go the other way—that is, from position B to A? The answer is that there is no need to tighten, because the tension you normally use to support the trunk is being replaced with muscle length, and you now only need to maintain this length as the basis for coming onto your feet. It's as if the body is supported by a series of straps from heel to knee, from knee to hips, and from hips to head. If you don't interfere with the straps by tightening them, the entire strap system assumes the work of supporting the system as a whole, replacing muscular tension with elasticity and effortlessness. This is in fact how the body is designed to work—that is, muscles do not simply contract but lengthen between body parts to maintain body-wide support. And the concept that muscle tension is required to perform this act—or at least the kinds of tension we habitually make when performing basic actions such as sitting down or walking—is simply wrong-headed. To support ourselves against gravity, muscles all over the body lengthen to support us, forming a complex, interrelated system of muscle pulls that rely more on the internal and neural properties of muscles length than they do on active contraction of muscles. As part of this larger system, specific muscles can tighten or contract, but this contraction takes place within a larger whole that distributes muscle support across a wide network, taking the burden off of particular muscles. In this context, the tension we make when we stand up from the sitting position actually interferes with the efficient working of the system, which is why we need to stop this tightening and to direct the parts instead.

When we examine how we perform an action such as standing up from sitting, then, we aren't simply trying to prevent harmful tensions but learning to bring about an improved working of the postural system based on a new concept of how muscles work. Doing this isn't simply a matter of preventing our harmful habits but of learning in a positive way to maintain length and support as the basis for moving and performing actions.

Exercise 4

Sit-to-stand using a table for four-footed support

Using a table as support when rising from the sitting position is an invaluable way of exploring the movement of standing from the sitting position. The support of the arms places us in a four--footed posture, helping to support the back and taking pressure off the legs. This helps the back to lengthen with the knees going away, and is an effective way to reestablish the proper length and support of the back musculature. It is also an invaluable way of exploring, and learning to prevent, the tendency to unnecessarily tighten in the leg muscles when we stand.

1. Sit in front of the table. Give your directions, paying special attention to your knee direction (*Fig. 4a*).

2. Incline forward and place your forearms on the table (*Fig. 4b*).

3. Direct your neck, head, and back; direct to your knees and, without tightening in your legs, come further forward onto your elbows. In this nearly four-footed position, some of your weight is now supported on your arms (*Fig. 4b*).

4. Incline further forward so that you are coming over your feet and can begin to stand. See if you can do this without tightening in your thighs, and while keeping your shoulders and back widening and lengthening (*Fig. 4c*).

5. Now continue to stand up. As you straighten your legs, you will need to come off your elbows and onto your hands, so that you will be in the monkey position with hands on the table (*Fig. 4d*).

6. Come to the fully upright position (*Fig. 4e*).

This exercise is a very good way of establishing length and width in the back muscles as the basis for performing the movement of standing from a sitting position. Because you begin the movement in a kind of four-footed position, it is a good way of exploring how much you tighten in your legs to stand from a sitting position. To overcome the very strong tendency to tighten in the legs, it is crucial to spend time directing the knees away from the hips before attempting to stand up. It takes a considerable amount of time and experimentation to learn not to tighten the legs, but if you spend time on this exercise, you will find that it is well worth the effort.

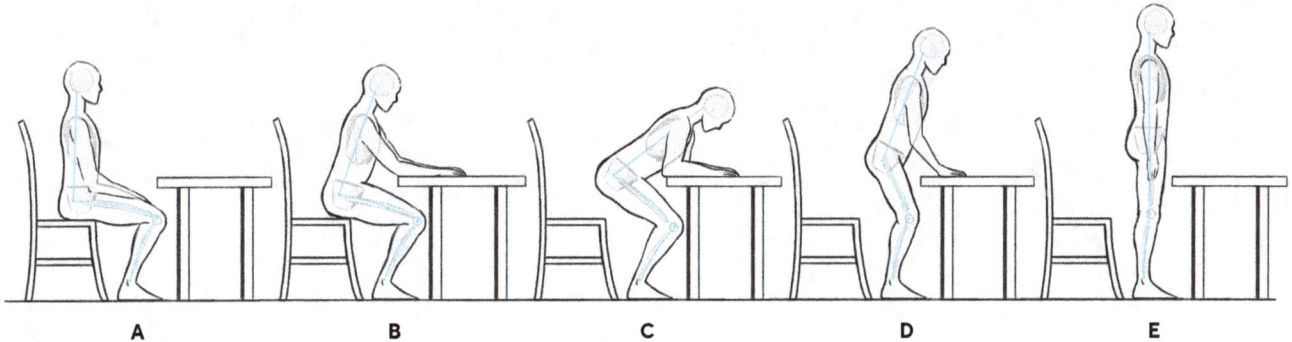

A   **B**   **C**   **D**   **E**

Fig. 4a-e. Sit-to-stand sequence using table.

Sitting Balance

When we think of the musculoskeletal system and how it works, our ability to sit upright in a chair is not the first thing that comes to mind. As the most advanced of the primates, we are capable of an incredible array of skills: the ability to dance, climb, run, fight, make tools, build things, play musical instruments, speak and sing. The ability to sit well, in contrast to these active skills, seems to be little more than maintaining good posture. But just as we are designed to stand and walk fully upright on two feet, we are designed to sit upright on our sit bones. This simple form of upright support is the foundation for many of our most high-level skills, which we perform while balanced on our ischial tuberosities, or sit bones. When we are in good sitting balance, the back and spine are lengthened, the back muscles are nicely toned, and we are capable of sitting, and using our arms in the sitting posture, in a completely effortless way.

Although many animals sit, only humans are capable of sitting in a fully upright or vertical posture. Chimpanzees and other non-human primates are able to sit and even to manipulate tools in a primitive way but, in contrast to humans, they have only a partially-formed lumbar curve that cannot support fully-erect or vertical posture, which requires a fully-developed lumbar curve to counterbalance the thoracic curve. Human infants

begin to develop the lumbar curve at birth, are able to sit at about 6 months of age and to walk at 12 months (*Fig. 1*). By the age of 3 or 4, the child will have a fully-developed lumbar curve and exhibit the ability to perform a complex array of actions in the fully-erect sitting and standing posture.

But exactly how do we sit in a balanced way? Normally we think of sitting in terms of posture, as when we are told to stop slumping and to sit up. But this hardly does justice to the subtlety of sitting, which is really a thing of great complexity

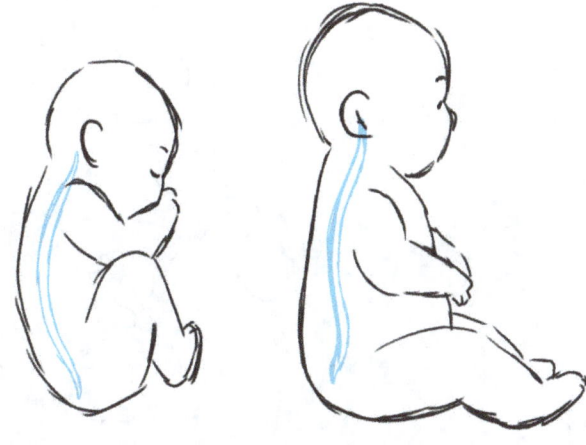

Fig. 1. The spine in a newborn versus a 6-month-old.

and needs to be studied and consciously mastered if we want to maintain our natural poise and coordination throughout life. As children, most of us sit quite beautifully as a matter of instinct; by 5 or 6 years old (and often earlier), children begin to slump harmfully and, to sit upright, must compensate by forcefully arching the back, only to go back into the slump when their back muscles tire. This is more than bad posture; it indicates that the postural system has becoming generally interfered with due to a loss of tone in some muscles and tightness in others. All of this suggests that knowing how to sit well is important not just to our appearance but to our overall health.

When we consider the question of how to sit in a balanced way, it is easy to assume that the lumbar curve is harmful and should be reduced. Is this curve not responsible for why our backs are vulnerable and why, among all the animals, only humans suffer from back trouble? We must remember, however, that the lumbar curve, far from being a liability, is what makes upright posture possible (*Fig. 2*). Try to reduce this curve and

you will immediately see that true upright support becomes impossible: the body will go into a kind of slump, resulting in a definite shortening of stature (*Fig. 3a*). The other extreme is problematic as well: if you deliberately sit up straight by lifting your rib cage, this will cause the back to arch, which also results in a general shortening of stature (*Fig. 3b*). The answer to this conundrum is that the spine must lengthen, but in a way that does not compromise the lumbar curve, which is integral to our ability to lengthen upward against gravity.

One way to think about lengthening the spine is to consider what it means for the entire spine to lengthen from sacrum to occiput. The spine itself is an inert thing and requires the support of muscles, ligaments, and fascia. If we produce this support by lifting the rib cage and arching the lower back, this will not only overwork the muscles of the lower back but will also break the spine at the level of the lumbar vertebrae, preventing the back from lengthening as a whole (see *Fig. 3b*). This isn't sitting fully upright but is a form of shortening the spine. To sit efficiently, we

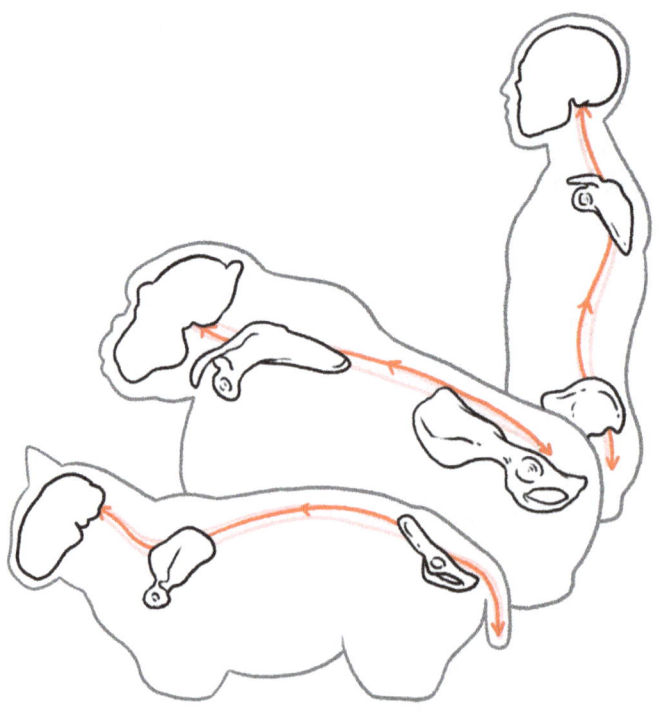

Fig. 2. The lumbar curve makes upright posture possible.

must maintain the integrity of the entire trunk, from the sit bones at the bottom end of the pelvis right up to the skull, thus allowing the spine as a whole to have its full length.

To sit with a lengthened spine also means that the back muscles themselves must lengthen. When you slump, the back muscles stop working and go slack. This may not seem like a bad thing, especially if your goal is to avoid using your muscles entirely. The problem, of course, is that when you sit up, you will have to compensate by arching your back, which means that you will now very definitely overwork your back muscles. You will also shorten the trunk by raising and fixing the chest and rib cage, generally stiffening and shortening in stature. This is why when you habitually slump, your back muscles will be anything but relaxed: to compensate for the lack of natural support, various muscles will be habitually tightened and contracted. To work efficiently, the muscles must maintain the support of the spine, but they must do so by releasing into length so that they can maintain tone with a minimum of effort. For

Fig. 4. Naturally lengthening back muscles in an infant.

this to happen, we must again think about how the musculoskeletal system works as a whole because it is the balance of the head on the spine, and the entire lengthening support of the spine, that allows muscles to let go into length. When these elements are in place, the back can begin to work as a coordinated whole, with the workload distributed throughout the entirety of the back, making it possible to maintain upright support with an absence of effort and strain (*Fig 4*).

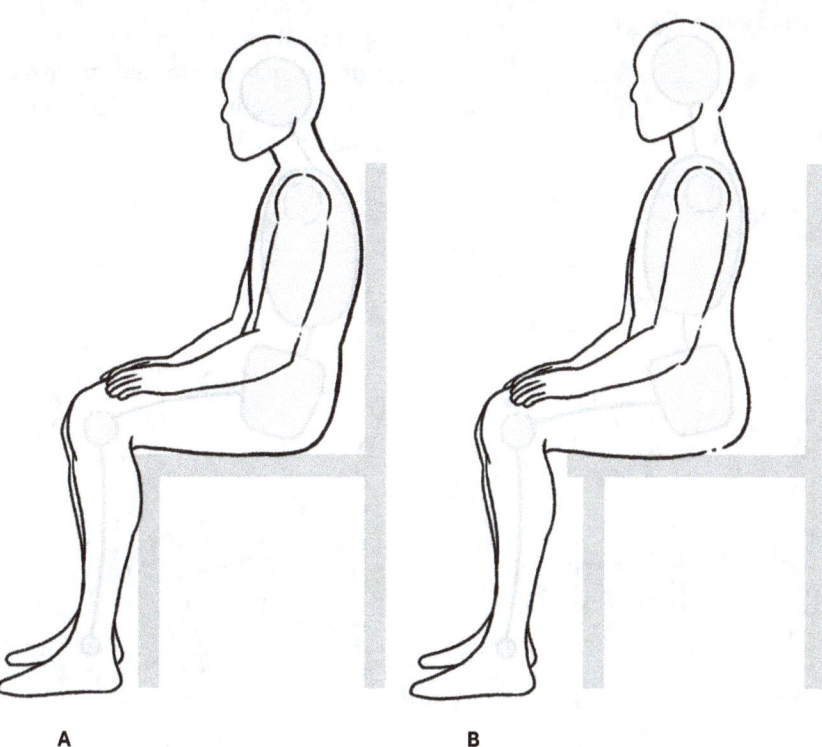

A   B

Fig. 3a. When we slump, we shorten the spine; b. If we sit up straight, we also shorten.

Exercise 1

Using monkey position to sit, focusing on the means and not the end

One of the keys to restoring natural sitting balance is to take time to sit down in the chair from the standing position. We have already seen that, when we sit in our habitual way, we pull the head back, arch the back, and fall backwards onto the chair so that, by the time we hit the chair, we are shortened and collapsed. Given this state of affairs, it is no wonder that, to sit fully upright, we are forced to lift ourselves up, which only increases the cycle of having to sit up, only to collapse back into a slump when we get tired. To counter this, it is very useful to consider how we sit down so that, by the time we touch the chair, we are in balance and can release into length. This gives us a much better chance of getting the whole system to work better, and in fact gives us a very good way of approaching sitting so that, instead of thinking of correcting posture, we can actually think of coordinating ourselves and achieving balanced sitting in this indirect way.

1. Standing in front of a chair with your feet slightly apart, give your directions so that you are allowing your head to nod forward, your back to lengthen, your gluteal muscles to let go, and your knees to go forward and away (*Fig. 5a*).

2. Thinking of releasing the fronts of your ankles, the backs of your knees, and the front of your hip joints, allow your knees to go out over your ankles and your trunk to incline forward from the hips so that you are in the monkey position (*Fig. 5b*). Go through your directions.

3. Deepen your monkey until your seat is in contact with the chair and go through your directions, allowing your head to go away from your pelvis and your pelvis from your head to lengthen your back, and your knees to go away from your pelvis and your feet so that you are lengthening along the thighs and the calf muscles (*Fig. 5c*).

4. Come back gently from your hips to an upright position by hinging at your hip joints. Do not do this quickly, seeing if you can move your trunk in one piece, without shortening your lower back, pulling your head back, and shortening in stature (*Fig. 5d*).

5. Give your directions for your head to go forward and up, your back to lengthen and widen, and your knees to go forward and away.

Notice that, now that you have performed the act of sitting in a thoughtful way, you will tend to be in fairly good sitting balance, neither slumping and heavy nor lifted up and arched in the back. With your spine and back in a more naturally lengthened condition, you will now be able to give your directions and to bring about greater release without collapsing into a slump and losing length.

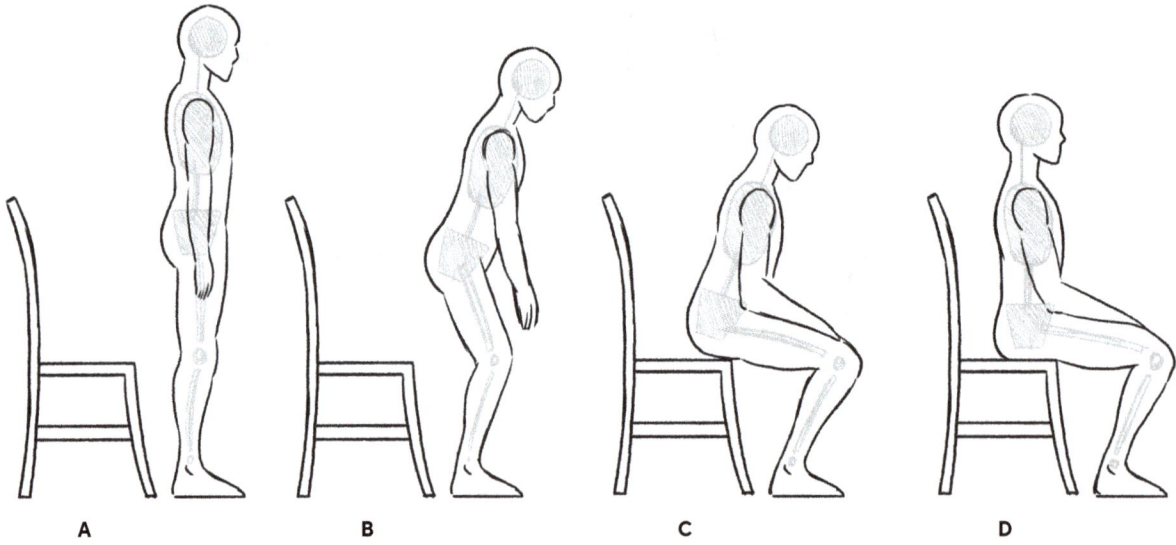

A   B   C   D

Fig. 5. Stand-to-sit: If we are able to maintain length while sitting down in the chair by hinging at the joints, our sitting balance will be improved.

Exercise 2

Balancing over your sit bones and giving directions

Because we tend to become heavy when we sit, it is useful to monitor your sitting balance by gently hinging forward using the hip joints, which makes it possible to keep your trunk poised over your sit bones with your head going forward and up.

1. Sit down in a chair rather quickly and, once you are sitting, observe your sitting balance. Do you notice that, with your weight fully supported on the chair, your hips will tend to roll back so that you are sinking into the chair and getting heavy?

2. Stand up and, this time, carefully go through your directions to sit down, beginning with the monkey position, contacting the chair, and coming back from your hips (*Fig. 6a*).

3. Once you are sitting, give your directions for your head to go forward and up, your back to lengthen, and your knees to go forward and away. If necessary, bring your feet slightly forward; this will make it easier to let go in your ankles and lower leg and to let your knees go away from your hips.

4. Continuing to be aware of both your head and knee directions, hinge at your hips to incline forward in the chair and again go through your directions (*Fig. 6b*).

5. Come back from your hips, continuing to think of your head going forward and up and your knees going away.

6. Do you notice that, when you have come forward in the chair, this helps to keep you poised over your hips, and that it is easier to maintain more active sitting balance?

Although sitting appears to be rather passive, it is in reality an active posture that requires energy to maintain. By directing the head forward and up out of a lengthening trunk and keeping the trunk poised over the sit bones, we can maintain light, effortless sitting balance without shortening, sinking backwards, or having to hold in the hips.

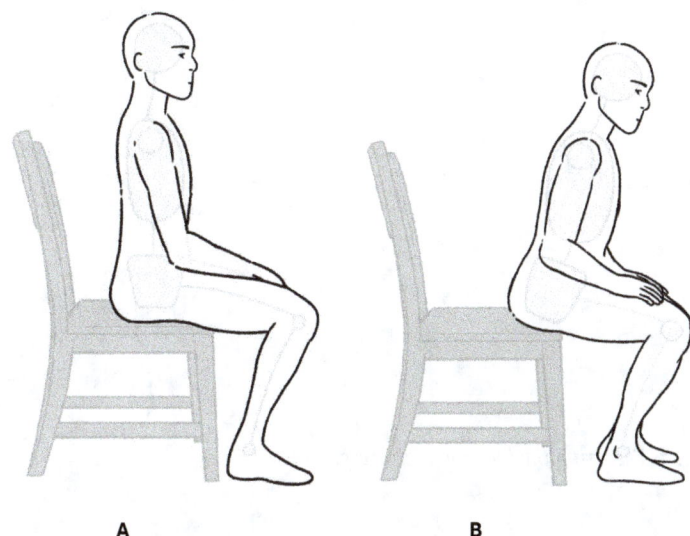

Fig. 6. Inclining forward and maintaining length in the trunk with the head going up and the weight over the sit bones helps to prevent sinking backwards at the hips.

A   B

Exercise 3

Sending your knees away while sitting

One of the most useful things we can do, when sitting in a chair, is to direct the knees away from the hips, which gives the leg muscles a chance to lengthen and helps to activate the PNR system as a whole. When we are sitting, the upper legs are flexed at a right angle to the trunk with the knees pointing directly away from the hips. If we see to it that we are not tightening the thighs and give the knees a chance to go away from the hips—provided we are in good sitting balance and not sinking backwards into a slump—the trunk will lengthen with the head going forward and up, and all the parts will let go into length so that sitting becomes effortless and we are in a state of true poise.

In the following exercise, we explore the process of "sending" the knees away from the hips while sitting. As a purely mental process, the idea of "sending the knees away" may seem vague and intangible, but it is actually a very concrete process and is hugely important in bringing about a condition in which the legs muscles are active, toned, and lengthened.

1. Go into an inclined monkey and give your directions, again not forgetting to think of your knees.

2. Allow your knees to bend so that your seat contacts the chair.

3. Go through your directions and then come back very gently. You should now be in a fairly good sitting balance.

4. Notice that, in this position, your knees are pointing away from your sit bones. If necessary, position your feet so that they are flat on the floor.

5. Give your directions for your head to go forward and up and your back to lengthen. Continue to give your knee directions, allowing your thighs and lower legs to let go, your ankles to release, and your feet to contact the floor (*Fig. 7a*).

6. Continue to think of your knees going forward and away In this balanced sitting position, your legs do not need to tighten in any way and the muscles can lengthen and release in such a way that the knees can go away from the hips (*Fig. 7b*).

7. If you find that you are losing length in your trunk and sinking into your hips, stand up again and start over. This will help to reestablish the upward direction of the head and trunk so that you can return to the process of directing the knees away.

Learning to direct your knees "forward and away" is an invaluable way of restoring the natural working of the legs and of the PNR system as a whole. When you become practiced at this, the PNR system can be activated, and you will be able to stand up onto your feet and walk about, or sit at a desk, without shortening the legs and with the entire system letting go into length.

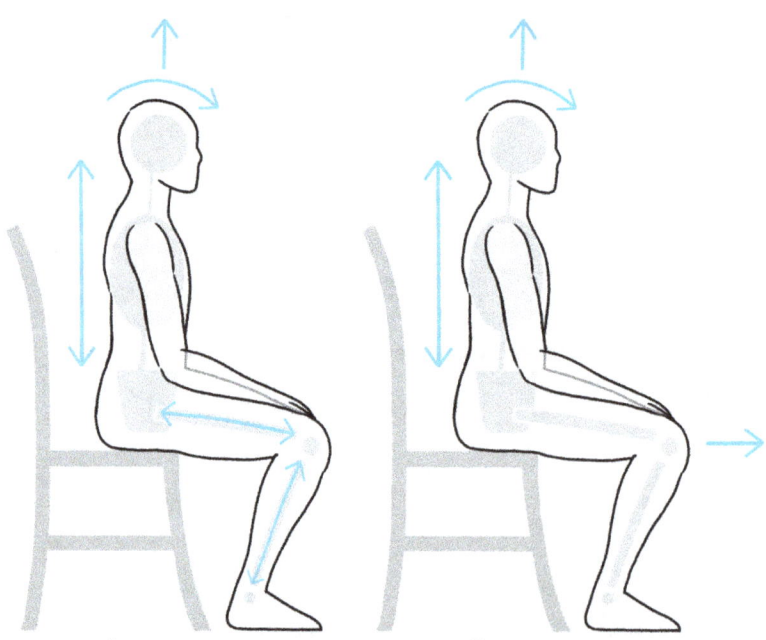

Fig. 7. Directing the knees while sitting.

A B

Breathing and Vocalizing

There are many aspects of the moving body that we have to look at in order to understand how the body works in action. But perhaps no single area is as badly misunderstood, and more neglected, as breathing and vocalization. Innumerable books on bodywork, yoga, and exercise teach bodily awareness and movement and simply leave out breathing and the voice, as if these functions have little to do with the musculoskeletal system. Nothing could be further from the truth. The larynx, throat, jaw, and breathing—and the role these play in vocalization—are completely interdependent with the moving body as a whole. Unless you take these elements into account, you simply cannot expect to gain a full understanding of the moving body. If, for instance, you slump habitually when doing desk work, you will tend to breathe through the mouth and collapse the throat, which will have a profound effect on the musculoskeletal system as a whole. The same applies to vocalization. If you constantly hold your breath when preparing to speak, or constrict your throat while speaking, this will profoundly affect not only your throat but your body as a whole. To restore musculoskeletal health, you must learn to pay attention to how you breathe and how you vocalize.

There are two ways that we interfere with breathing and vocal function. First, if we use the musculoskeletal system inefficiently, this has a generally harmful influence on breathing, which is dependent on the coordinated working of the musculoskeletal system as a whole. We have only to observe someone collapsed in front of a computer to see the harmful effect this has on the throat and respiratory function. Second, when we speak or vocalize, we tend to shorten in stature, using too much tension when we take in air and when we actually produce sound. If we want to use the musculoskeletal system efficiently, it is important to be aware of how we breathe and vocalize, which are as central to the musculo-skeletal system as gross motor movements. We'll begin by looking at how we breathe and at the general tendency to interfere with breathing. Next, we'll look at the nostrils and the critical role they play in breathing and vocalizing. We'll then look at two basic procedures that help to restore natural breathing, and that also serve as a foundation for producing sound effortlessly.

How Do We Breathe?

In order to get air into (and out of) our bodies, we need to make the space inside the thorax get bigger and smaller. Two systems are responsible for these movements. First, the ribs rise like pail handles by moving at the joints where they attach to the spine; this action increases the space within the chest (*Fig. 1*). The uppermost ribs connect in front to the sternum; those below form the costal arch; the last two, the floating ribs, do not attach in front. Because of this, not all the ribs move in the same way, or to the same degree. But most of the ribs rise and widen to some extent, making the space inside the chest get larger; when they return to their lower position, the space gets smaller.

Second, the diaphragm, which forms the boundary between the thorax and abdomen, contracts and flattens out. This increases the size of the lower part of the thoracic cavity (*Figs. 2 and 3*). When the ribs rise and open, the diaphragm contracts and descends; the chest cavity increases in size and air rushes in to fill the lungs. When the ribs return to normal position, the diaphragm relaxes and ascends, air is forced out, and we exhale. We can see, then, that two actions—the movement of the ribs and the diaphragm—are responsible for breathing.

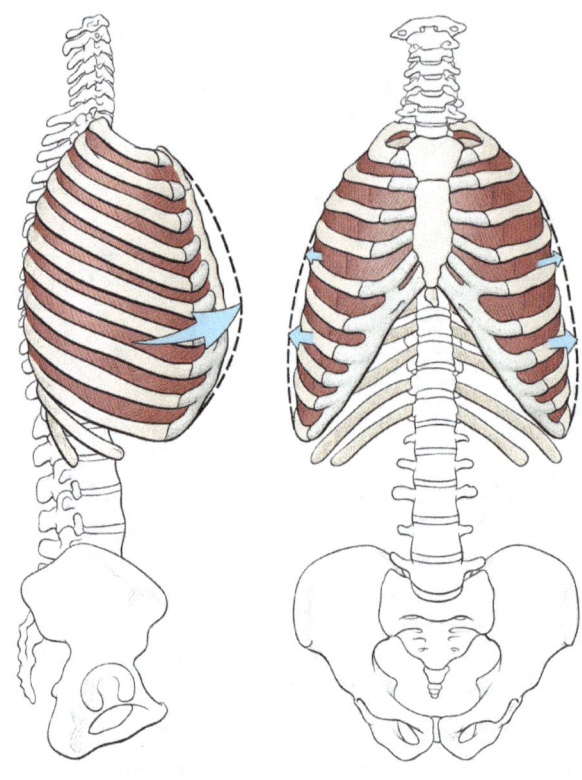

Fig. 1. *Movement of the ribs in breathing.*

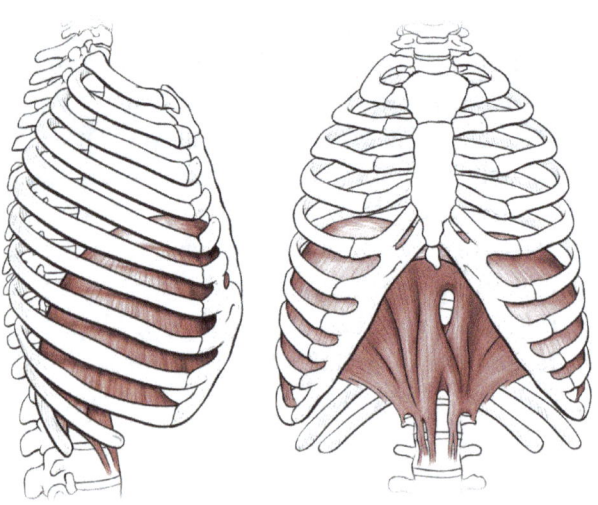

Fig. 2. *The diaphragm.*

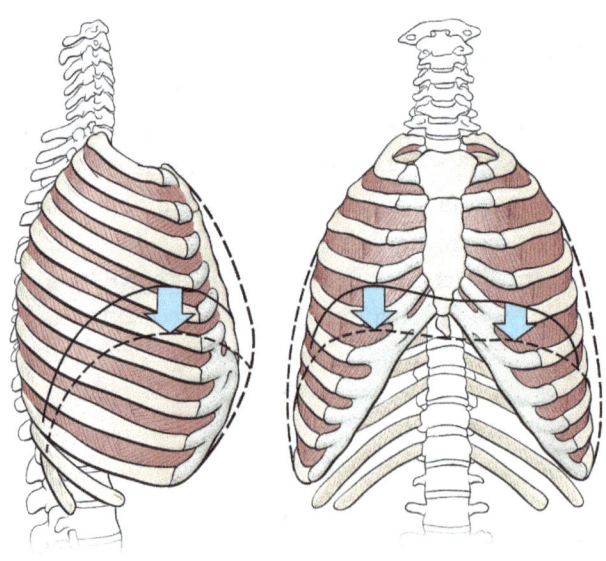

Fig. 3. *Movement of the diaphragm and ribs.*

Although the movements of the ribs and diaphragm take place at a largely automatic level, both are affected by, and dependent upon, the working of the musculoskeletal system as a whole. To understand how, try the following experiment. Hold your pelvic and buttocks muscles and, without letting go, notice how this affects your breathing. Did you hold your breath? Even when you notice this and resume breathing, you may find that you are still unable to breathe fully. Next, try holding or tightening your abdominal, rib, or neck muscles. Again, you will find that this interferes with your ability to breathe fully. In all these cases, it is clear that muscular tension, rigidity or collapse of any kind will profoundly affect your breathing, which is intimately connected with—and dependent on—the efficient working of the musculoskeletal system. To ensure efficient breathing, we have to see to it that we are not interfering with these natural movements by establishing the general conditions upon which breathing depends.

Incredibly, there is almost no discussion of this fact in most books on breathing, which focus almost entirely on the specifics of how to breathe more fully, the action of the diaphragm, or the benefits of a particular type of breathing, but almost entirely omit discussion of the key components upon which all these factors depend—namely, the efficient working of the musculoskeletal system as a whole. To breathe efficiently, we must focus not on breathing itself but on the body as a whole—how it works, how to restore its natural functioning, and how we interfere with it when at rest, in activity and, perhaps most importantly, when vocalizing.

Exercise 1

Observing how we interfere with breathing

Although breathing and vocalizing are intimately connected with musculoskeletal function, our muscular and vocal habits are so ingrained and unconscious that we do not normally notice what we're doing to interfere with our breathing. In the following exercises, we will begin to explore the connection between the musculoskeletal system, breathing, and vocalization.

1. Lying in the semi-supine position, breathe normally, noticing the air flowing in and out through your nostrils.

2. Now stiffen your neck or pull your head back against the books. Did you hold your breath?

3. Go back to normal breathing for a minute and again hold your breath, this time noticing if you have tightened your neck, stiffened your chest, or raised and fixed your ribs so that your back is making less contact with the floor.

The exchange of air into and out of our lungs, or what we call breathing, depends upon the movements of the ribs and diaphragm. If we shorten in stature and create muscular tension, this affects the shape of the thorax and reduces the flexible movements of the ribs and diaphragm, thus interfering with breathing.

Exercise 2

Observing harmful habits that interfere with breathing

1. Sit quietly in a chair, noticing the breath flowing in and out through your nostrils as you breathe normally.

2. Now stand up. Did you do anything to interfere with the natural flow of breath through your nostrils when you got up to move?

3. Walk slowly in a circle and bend as if to pick something up from the floor. Did you stop breathing when you were walking about, or when you bent down?

4. Stop walking and, standing in position, tighten your feet and legs. Now tighten your neck and stand at attention. Did you hold your breath when you did either of these?

5. Sit down in the chair and, while you are sitting quietly, tighten your buttocks and pelvic muscles. Did you hold your breath?

Breathing depends on the movements of the ribs and diaphragm, but these movements, in turn, depend on the coordinated working of the body as a whole. Anything we do to interfere with the musculoskeletal system will interfere with breathing. When we learn to restore the natural working of the muscular system, we restore natural breathing.

Exercise 3

Observing patterns of tension that interfere with breathing

Although we are constantly and habitually interfering with our breathing, it is hard to perceive our own habits clearly, or even to believe that we are doing anything to interfere with breathing during our everyday actions. A useful way to understand these harmful habits is to identify them in someone else; when we see objectively how someone else interferes, we learn by association what we are doing in ourselves. (Note: A classroom is ideal for making such observations; in a live online class, students can observe each other visually in breakout groups.)

1. To begin, partner up with a fellow student or friend who will sit or stand while you, as the observer, will stand next to her with a hand placed on her upper back.

2. Ask your partner to take a deep breath. What did you see and feel? Did she lift her chest, stiffen her neck, or fix her ribs?

3. Ask your partner to sit up straight. Did she stiffen her chest or ribs?

4. Place your left hand on top of your partner's head and your right hand on her back. Ask her to breathe normally and to give her directions. Does this have an effect on her breathing?

Because breathing takes place automatically, we assume that it is somehow unaffected by the harmful way that we perform actions. When we observe someone else's harmful habits, we can begin to see the kinds of things we are doing in ourselves to interfere with our breathing. We can also see that the key to improving our breathing is not to try to breathe more fully (which will generally interfere with breathing) but to bring about the general improvements in coordination upon which breathing depends.

Exercise 4

Lying quietly and giving directions in the semi-supine position

1. Lying in the semi-supine position, take a few moments to notice the air going in and out through your nostrils.

2. See to it that you are not stiffening your neck or pulling back your head; allow your back to lengthen and fill out and send your knees up to the ceiling.

3. Notice if, as your muscles release and your nervous system quiets down, your breathing gets easier, including the movements of your ribs and diaphragm.

Breathing is based upon the free movements of ribs and diaphragm, which is why direct attempts to improve our breathing are not nearly as important—or as effective—as making sure we are giving time to restore the natural conditions upon which breathing depends.

NOSTRIL BREATHING

One of the most useful things we can do to restore normal and healthful breathing—and to learn to stop interfering with our breathing when we are speaking or moving about—is to notice the air going in and out through our nostrils and to see to it that we do not interfere with this automatic flow of air. We have two ways of taking in air—through the mouth and through the nostrils (*Fig. 4*). When we need to get as much air as possible, we can of course open the mouth in order to maximize the intake of oxygen. But as a rule, we should not normally breathe through the mouth, which functions mainly as a way of taking in food and for speaking and vocalizing (*Fig. 5*). For normal breathing, we should primarily use our nostrils, which have evolved specially for the purpose of taking in air (*Fig. 6*).

As a dedicated passageway for taking in air, the nasal passages are specially adapted to filter out foreign particles and to moisten and warm the air. Breathing through the nostrils also slows down the flow of air into the lungs, which enhances oxygenation of the blood. In contrast, mouth breathing tends to be shallow and quick; when we take air through our nostrils, we breathe more fully and engage more of the lungs. Breathing through the nasal passages also releases nitric oxide molecules into the inhaled air, which act as "airborne messengers" in the cardiovascular system that, among other things, regulate blood pressure, increase oxygen uptake in the lungs, and boost immune function. All these benefits are lost when we breathe through our mouths.

Because most of us spend a great deal of time in sedentary occupations, we tend to breathe habitually through the mouth, collapsing the palate and generally interfering with natural breathing. Learning to breathe through your nostrils is a good first step in addressing this tendency. When you breathe through your nostrils, your mouth should be closed with your tongue naturally arching in your mouth and contacting the hard palate (*Fig. 7*). Breathing freely through your nostrils, with your tongue in this "resting position," is a good way to ensure that you are not holding your breath.

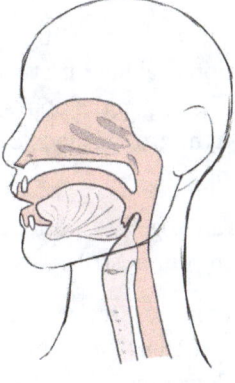

Fig. 4. The mouth and nasal passages.

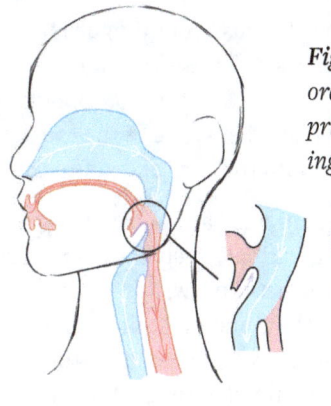

Fig. 5. The mouth and oral passageway are primarily used for ingesting food and water.

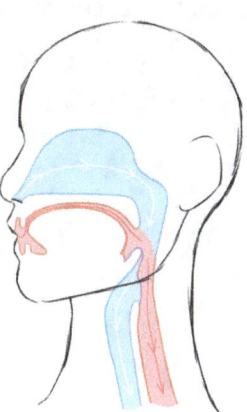

Fig. 6. We are designed to breathe primarily through our nostrils.

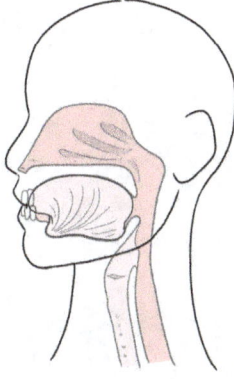

Fig. 7. The resting position of the tongue when breathing through the nostrils.

Exercise 1

Nostrils, tongue position, and breathing

To begin this exercise, spend a few minutes lying down in the semi-supine position, making sure that your neck is free, your head is resting on the books, your back is fully supported on the ground, and your knees are going up to the ceiling.

1. Making sure that your lips are together, notice the air going in and out through your nostrils.

2. Open your jaw and observe the position of your tongue, which will naturally arch in your mouth with the tip touching your lower teeth (*Fig. 8a*).

3. Now close your jaw. Because your tongue is arched, the body of the tongue will now contact your hard palate (*Fig. 8b*). During quiet breathing, this is the natural resting position of the tongue, which forms a seal with the hard and soft palate.

4. When the tongue is in this natural "resting position" and you are breathing freely through your nostrils, this means that the jaw, lips, tongue, and throat are left alone and breathing will be unimpaired. Consciously being aware of the breath going through the nostrils in this way thus provides a good starting point for not interfering with the mechanisms of speech.

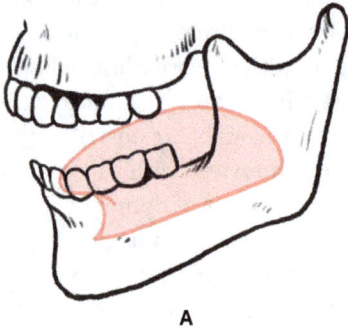

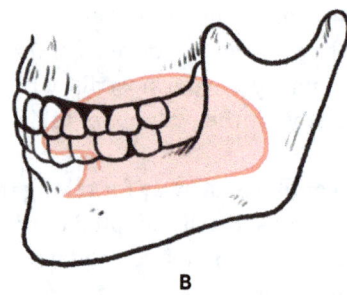

Fig. 8a. The position of the tongue with the jaw open; *b.* Resting position of the tongue with the jaw closed.

Exercise 2

Non-doing and speech movements

In this exercise, we explore the movements involved in speech and learn to use the jaw, lips, and tongue without tightening the neck, pulling back the head, and shortening in stature.

1. Spend a few minutes lying down in the semi-supine position, making sure that your neck is free, your head is resting on the books, and your back is fully supported on the ground.

2. Notice the breath going in and out through your nostrils. With your jaw closed (*Fig. 9a*), make sure your lips are together and your tongue is naturally arching in your mouth.

3. When you're satisfied that you are leaving the system alone nicely, see if you can open your jaw while continuing to breathe through your nostrils (*Fig. 9b*). Notice if you have stiffened your neck muscles, tightened your throat, or held your breath. Opening the jaw is, of course, one of the elements of speech and is therefore closely associated with the basic pattern of misuse. Learning to open the jaw without interfering with your head balance and without disturbing the flow of breath in and out of the nostrils is critical to coordinated speech.

4. When you can move your jaw comfortably without tightening your neck and without interfering with the flow of air through your nostrils, try moving your tongue, lips, and the muscles of your face. If you can do this without interfering with your breathing and with your overall muscular system, you are well on your way to being able to speak in a coordinated fashion and can begin to apply this in everyday speech.

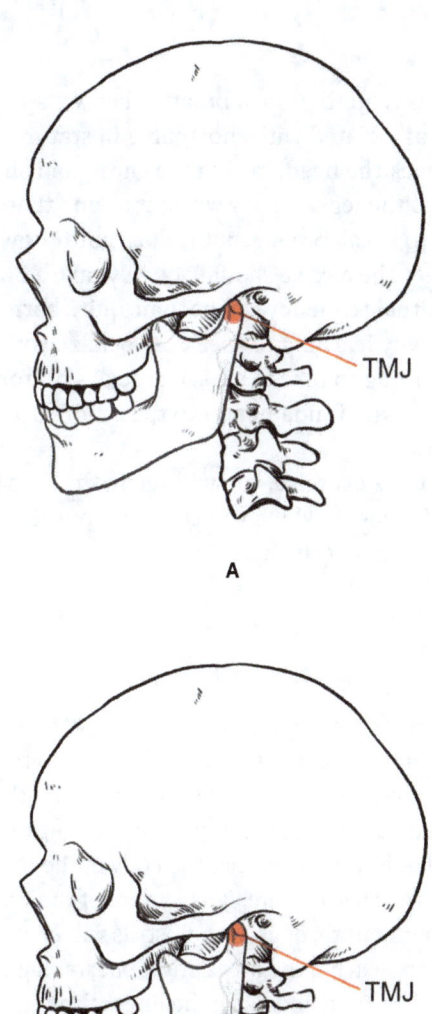

Fig. 9. The jaw hinges at the temporomandibular joint (TMJ): a. Jaw closed; b. Jaw open.

OBSERVING HABITS OF VOCALIZING THAT INTERFERE WITH BREATHING

Most of us tend to gasp in breath when we speak, which is associated with shortening in stature, pulling back the head, raising the chest, and shortening into the legs. It goes without saying that we need air to speak or sing, but it does not follow that, to get the air, we should actively take a breath. This habitual tendency can become quite harmful, which is why learning to speak or vocalize without actively trying to take in air is a crucial skill for voice users and fundamental to the art of effortless vocalization.

To do this exercise, you will recite the first line or two of a poem, which you can write out if you don't know one by heart.

Exercise 1

Identifying the tendency to gasp in air

One way to break the habit of taking breath when preparing to speak is to sit quietly and to breathe normally through your nostrils with your mouth closed and your tongue in its natural "resting position"—that is, arched so that the body of the tongue contacts your hard palate. Being aware of the breath going in and out through your nostrils will ensure that you are leaving the breathing alone; taking this as a starting point, and using the lines of the poem you have memorized, try the following exercise.

1. Sit in a chair and, making sure your lips are together, allow the breath to flow freely through your nostrils.

2. Spend some time being aware of the breath flowing in and out through your nostrils.

3. Now speak the first line of your poem. Did you notice if you prepared to speak by sucking in or gasping in air? Did you stiffen your neck or raise your chest?

4. Stop for a moment and return to quiet nostril breathing. Continuing to be aware of the breath going in and out through your nostrils, now simply *think* of speaking the line. Can you notice more clearly that, in preparation to speak, you tighten your neck or hold your breath?

The first step in learning to prevent the habitual pattern of tension that interferes with vocalization is to identify it. This is not difficult to do if we take the time to stop and to give directions, in which case our harmful habits will stand out more clearly.

Exercise 2

Inhibition and reciting text

It may seem that, to speak or sing, it is necessary to actively take in air. Singers in particular will often find it hard to believe that it is possible to produce sound without taking a breath in preparation in order to have enough air. But drawing in the breath is actually a harmful habit that interferes with the musculoskeletal system as a whole. In this exercise, we explore the process of using nostril breathing as a way of identifying when we interfere, and taking the time to recite a line or two without making any unnecessary preparatory movements.

1. Lying in the semi-supine position, give your directions.

2. Notice the breath going in and out through your nostrils. Make sure your lips are together and your tongue is naturally arching in your mouth.

3. Without interfering with this natural flow of air, speak one line and then close your mouth and let your lips come together so that the breath will again come in and out through your nostrils.

4. Allowing the air to continue to go in and out through your nostrils, speak the second line and let your lips come together. Notice if there is any change in the quality of sound you produce when you do.

5. If you can speak one line of the poem without taking a breath, try reciting several lines of the poem, seeing to it that, when you begin a new line, you close your mouth so that the air enters your nostrils and doesn't come in through your mouth.

6. Again notice the change in the quality of your voice when you do this.

Learning to allow the air to go in and out through your nostrils as the basis for producing sound is an invaluable exercise for preventing unnecessary interference with the breathing system and with the throat while speaking, and provides a crucial foundation and point of reference for becoming aware of unnecessary and harmful habits in normal, everyday speech.

THE CONTROLLED EXHALATION

We've seen that, when we vocalize, we tend to actively take in air, which is part of the general tendency to shorten in stature and to interfere with the musculoskeletal system as a whole when speaking or singing. The first step in addressing this tendency is to restore the general conditions on which breathing depends, which will ensure that the back is full and supported, the thorax is open and flexible, and the ribs and diaphragm can move freely.

But what about vocalizing itself? How do we ensure that breathing can take place in a full and supported way if we interfere with our breathing when we vocalize? The answer is that, instead of focusing on getting air into our lungs, we must focus on letting the breath out. And we must do this in such a way that the exhalation is extended so that, instead of collapsing and pressing air out of the lungs, the air is released slowly or in a controlled manner—otherwise known as a "controlled exhalation." A simple way of understanding the controlled exhalation is to think of it in terms of not holding the breath. If you lift a heavy object or prepare to speak, you'll notice that the initial response is to stiffen and hold the breath. If, at the moment you begin to hold the breath, you instead stop and let the breath out slowly through your lips or teeth, you are performing a controlled exhalation. Controlling the exhalation in this way allows us to shift our attention away from holding or taking breath and to focus instead on letting the breath out—that is, on not stiffening and holding the breath.

Controlling the breath in this way is beneficial for several reasons. First, focusing on letting the air out of your lungs reverses the tendency to fix the ribs and tighten the diaphragm—that is, to stop holding the breath. Second, letting the air out has the general effect of quieting and calming the nervous system. In this context, the controlled exhalation is a re-educational procedure for allowing a free breath flow by letting the breath out instead of holding it, and letting it out slowly instead of collapsing or shortening to exhale. At a more advanced level, the controlled exhalation provides the basis for producing sound in a coordinated way—a topic that we will touch on in a moment, and which is covered in more detail in the resources listed below.

Exercise 1

The controlled exhalation

1. Sit comfortably in a chair, back supported by the back of the chair and feet flat on the floor. Notice the breath going in and out through your nostrils.

2. Without altering your breathing in any way, make a whooshing or "sss" sound for several out-breaths in a row. Don't take in air to do this; simply let the air come in on its own, and make sure you are breathing through your nostrils on the in-breath.

3. Finally, be sure not to turn the controlled exhalation into a sigh by collapsing during exhalation, which may seem relaxed but is in fact collapsing the chest and has little to do with coordinated breathing or vocal production. A true controlled exhalation can be brought about only when one has the clear intention to prolong the out-breath in a steady way and maintains a coordinated, energized state of the muscular system while doing so.

Exercise 2

Controlled exhalation in semi-supine position

1. Lying in the semi-supine position, give your directions for your neck to be free, your head to go forward and up, your back to lengthen and widen, and your knees to go up.

2. Notice the breath going in and out through your nostrils.

3. Without altering your breathing in any way, produce a controlled exhalation by blowing through your lips.

4. After giving your directions for a few more minutes, do a series of controlled exhalations, making sure that you are allowing the air to come in through your nostrils between exhalations.

5. After trying the controlled exhalations in the semi-supine position, try doing a series of controlled exhalations in the inclined monkey position.

Further reading:

Breathing and the Voice

Your Body, Your Voice

Pointers:

You may find, when you try this procedure, that the exhalations last only a second or two, but there is no need to worry about this. If you insist on producing a long and slow exhalation, you may get a longer out-breath but you will only interfere with the entire process by preparing to take breath and then creating tension during the out-breath.

Be sure, when you finish each exhalation, to breathe through the nostrils on the in-breath. During normal breathing and speech we tend to gasp in air through the mouth; allowing air to come in through the nose by consciously preventing the tendency to take the air in through the mouth tends to restore a normal breathing pattern.

It is crucial, when controlling the exhalation, not to manipulate your breathing in any way. Although a controlled exhalation is focused on the out-breath and not the in-breath, just thinking about the procedure will tend to invoke the desire to breathe in and then, during each subsequent inhalation, to take a long slow breath in preparation for the next exhalation. Breathing in slowly in this way is a form of "doing," and it means we have become subconsciously preoccupied with taking breath—precisely the thing we are trying to avoid. A true controlled exhalation can be performed only when we honestly recognize that we are beginning to take in air, resist the tendency to actively breathe in, and focus instead on the exhalation and not on the in-breath. When we do this, the air will come in relatively quickly, not slowly.

Exercise 3

The whispered "ah" while sitting

1. With your feet flat on the floor, and sitting comfortably in the chair, notice the breath going in and out through your nostrils. This is a good way of ensuring that you are not interfering with your breathing.

2. Without altering your breathing in any way, open your mouth and produce an "ah" sound by whispering. Remember that the "ah" vowel should sound open, like when the doctor holds down your tongue and asks you to say "ah." It is also prolonged, so that you are clearly intending to produce the sound.

3. Do several of these in a row, not taking breath between "ah's" and allowing the air to come in by itself.

Exercise 4

Performing a whispered "ah" in monkey position with hands on table

1. Stand in front of a table with your feet comfortably apart and go through your directions (*Fig. 10a*).

2. Take yourself into monkey position and carefully go through your directions (*Fig. 10b*).

3. Place your hands on the table, palms facing down (*Fig. 10c*). Release your neck to let your head go forward and out, and think of your head and pelvis going away from each other to lengthen your back.

4. Produce several whispered "ah's" in a row, being sure not to take in air to prepare. Make sure you have a clear intention to produce the whispered sound, but do not try to prolong the sound or to use effort of any kind.

5. Try another series of whispered "ah's," taking time to brighten your face and to open your throat, improving on the quality of the sound as you proceed.

6. Take your hands off the table and come out of monkey.

Exercise 5

Whispering text

When you have spent time progressing through the previous exercises, you are ready to try reciting some lines while in monkey position. Remember that when we speak, we tend to depress the larynx, to shorten in stature, and to use too much breath pressure. These exercises are designed to make it possible to prevent these harmful tendencies by replacing them with the coordinated elements of the whispered "ah." Using the text of the poem you have memorized, try the following exercise in both semi-supine position and while in monkey position.

1. Standing in front of the table, take yourself into monkey position and carefully go through your directions (*Fig. 10b*).

2. Place your hands on the table and give your directions to release your neck to let your head go forward and out, and think of your head and pelvis going away from each other and knees to go away (*Fig. 10c*).

3. Produce a series of controlled exhalations, making sure that you're not taking breath between exhalations but focusing entirely on the out-breath.

4. Without taking breath, whisper the first line of text.

5. Bring your lips together and let the breath come in through your nostrils.

6. Try whispering the next line, starting over again from step one if necessary.

Notice that, when you whisper the line of text, you are actually performing a whispered "ah," but with the addition of articulated speech. Utilized in this way, the whispered "ah" provides the foundation for speaking or singing based on the coordinated working of the body as a whole.

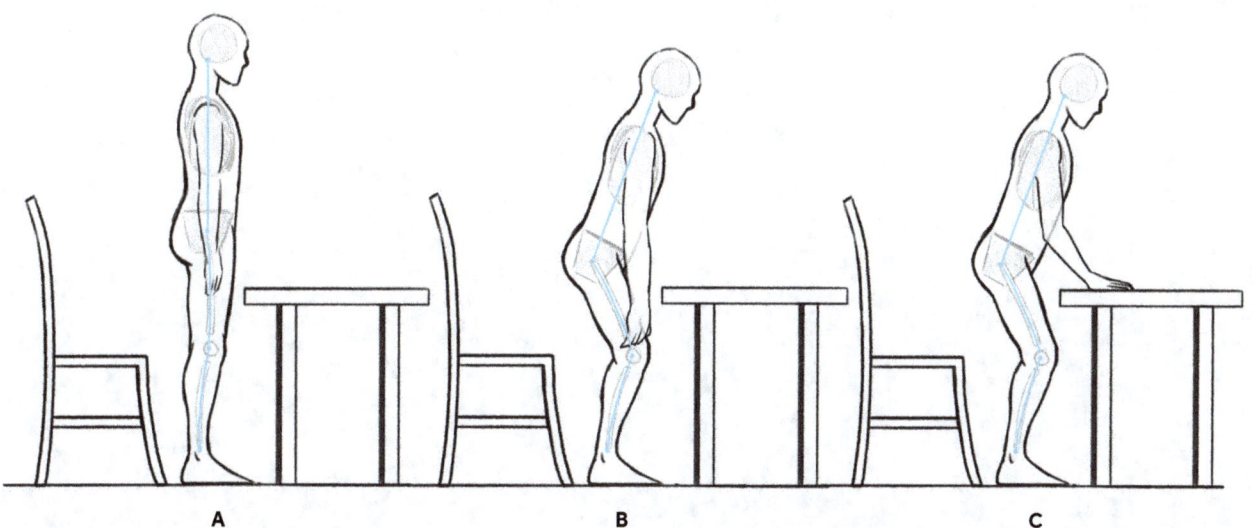

A   B   C

Fig. 10a-c. Performing a whispered "ah" in monkey position with hands on table.

Walking

Let's look now at walking—how it takes place naturally, how we interfere with it, and how to restore our natural poise in walking. In order to perform a movement—any movement—lots of things have to happen, lots of muscles have to do work, controlled at various levels in the nervous system. But the really complicated thing, the thing that is not so easy to understand, is how they all work together. Walking has been studied in great detail because it's so fascinating and complicated—what muscles do what, what actions have to take place, how we walk by falling and catching ourselves. But the most important thing is the hardest to see because it's so basic, so fundamental, that we can analyze the whole thing to pieces and still miss this essential element, the overriding piece that makes the whole thing possible, that makes it possible to stand and to move on two feet in the first place.

So what is this basic element that we must have as a background for walking, this basic system that makes it all possible? It's the overall lengthened support of the body against gravity, which as we've seen is organized around the head and trunk. In order to support ourselves to walk forward in space, the lengthened relationship of head and trunk allows the whole system to maintain upright posture in an effortless, light way, with the head leading a lightly supported trunk, and without any bracing, stiffening, or collapse in the pelvis and legs. What happens, when most of us perform this movement, is that we interfere with our basic upright posture in a really serious way by shortening in stature and using too much tension in our hips and legs. And because this interference is so habitual and ingrained, we don't even realize it's happening. Over time, we collapse and stiffen so badly while walking that, by middle age, many of us can no longer walk properly but have to make a set of very harmful compensatory actions in order to walk forward in space. Given this set of circumstances, the only way to restore natural, efficient walking is to remove this interference, which is why the study of walking must include, not just body mechanics but the study of upright support, which is the real key to understanding how to walk efficiently.

What Is Walking?

Walking—that is, the ability to move forward in space in a vertical posture with the legs swinging underneath the body in a striding gait—is a unique form of locomotion found nowhere else in the animal kingdom. Other animals can walk on two feet but, even among the primates, only humans can walk in a fully upright, vertically-poised posture, with the various body segments stacked one on top of the other, and with the head and trunk rotating around a vertical axis and arms swinging freely at the shoulders (*Fig. 1*).

In order to walk, our legs swing underneath the trunk in a pendulum motion, and the head and trunk come over the advancing leg so that the body as a whole moves forward in space. These two actions are sometimes described as a double pendulum. The first pendulum is the action of the legs, which alternately swing from the hip (*Fig. 2*). The second pendulum involves the entire body and is actually upside down. As the advanced foot is planted on the ground, the body as a whole swings over the foot like a reverse or upside-down pendulum to advance in space (*Fig. 3*).

A less obvious but essential component of walking is the action of the knee, ankle, and foot. In order for the leg to swing from the hip, the leg must bend at the knee, allowing the heel to come off the floor as the ankle bends and the foot flexes at the big toe (*Fig. 4*). When this happens, the foot rolls off the floor, the leg swings forward, and we take a step. In vigorous walking, the legs are more actively extended at the hip, knee, and ankle. We are not normally conscious of this unless we hit a slippery patch while walking and the foot slips, at which point it becomes clear that, in vigorous walking, we are actively pushing off as we extend the supporting leg.

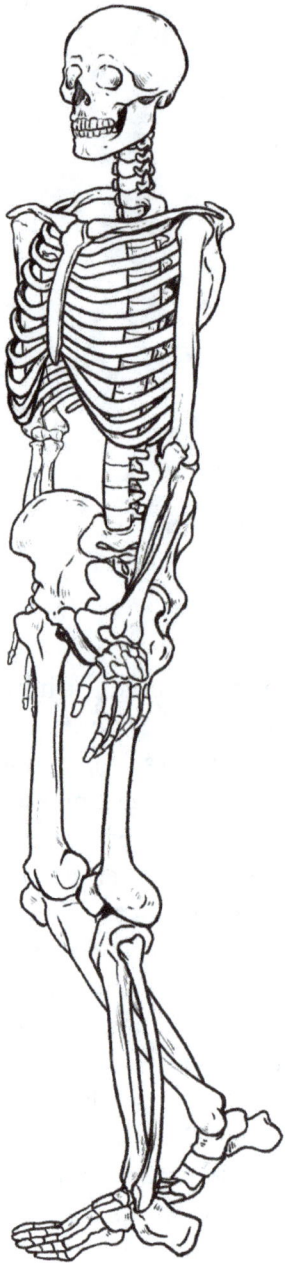

Fig. 1. Walking fully upright with a striding gait.

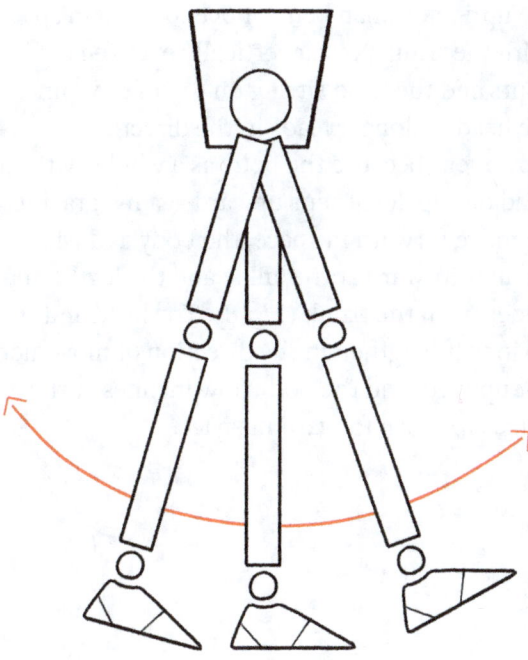

Fig. 2. Pendulum action of the legs swinging at the hip.

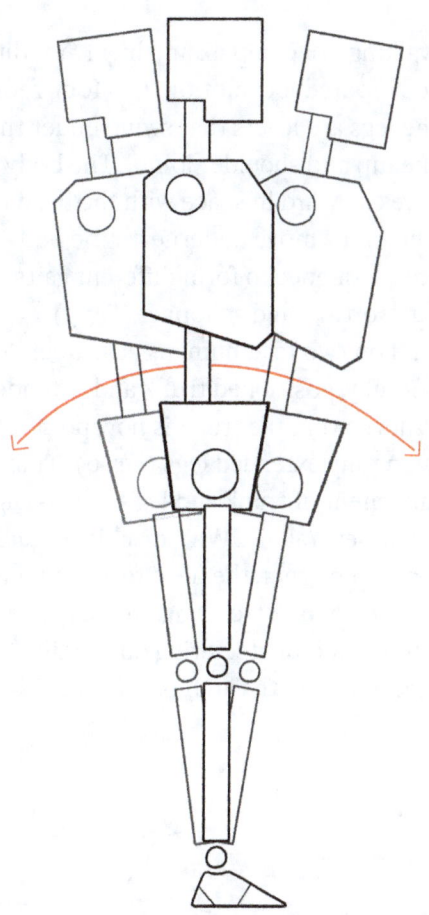

Fig. 3. Reverse pendulum action of the entire body from the ankles.

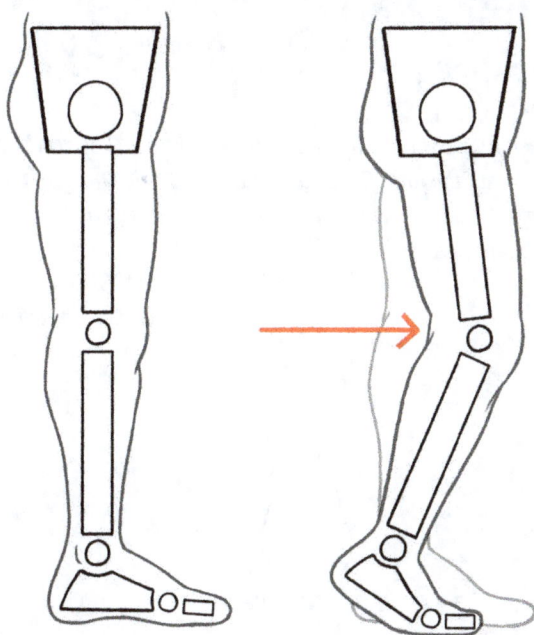

Fig. 4. When we walk, the leg swings from the hip, but the knee going forward is the key to this action. The release of the knee allows the heel to come off the ground, the foot to roll off the floor, and the leg to swing under the trunk.

Upright Posture and the Striding Gait

Human walking is a complex and highly modified form of four-footed locomotion. In a four-footed animal, the legs are levers that swing under the body at the hip and shoulder joints. The body as a whole moves forward in space with the head leading, and the limbs move underneath the body in a coordinated sequence to form different gaits such as walking, trotting, and galloping (*Fig. 5*).

To stand on two feet, humans have upended the horizontally-positioned trunk and extended the leg struts so that the trunk is now poised vertically on fully extended legs (*Fig. 6*). This vertical arrangement of trunk and leg struts is highly unstable, like several SEGWAY machines stacked one on top of the other, the head teetering on top of the spine, the trunk teetering on the heads of the femurs, the femurs teetering on the tibia, and the tibia teetering on the arch of the feet (*Fig. 7*).

Given this vertical arrangement, how does the upright human being move forward in space? With the trunk poised vertically over the hip joints and the head sitting on top of the spine, the head no longer leads in the direction of movement because the body as a whole, with the head on top, lengthens upward against gravity. To move forward in space, the body as a whole inclines forward at the ankle and the legs swing underneath the trunk (*Fig. 8*). The head and trunk no longer lengthen in the direction of movement but upward, and the body now inclines at the ankles to move forward in space.

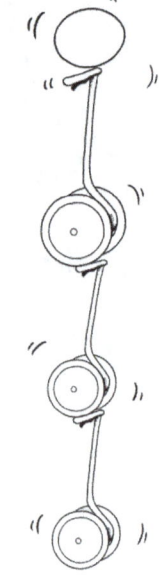

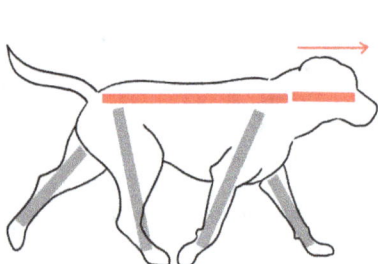

Fig. 5. Action of the limbs in a four-footed animal.

*Fig. 6. To stand on two feet, humans have upended the horizontally-positioned trunk of the four-footed animal (**a**) and extended the leg struts so that the trunk is now poised vertically on fully extended legs (**b**).*

Fig. 7. The vertical arrangement of trunk and leg struts in the human being is like several SEGWAY machines stacked one on top of the other.

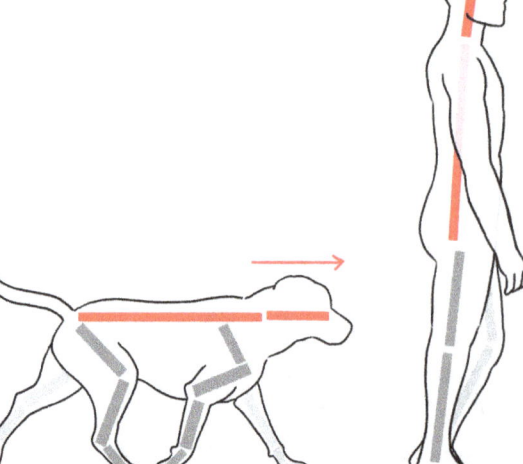

Fig. 8. To move forward in space, the body as a whole inclines at the ankle and the legs swing underneath the advancing trunk.

The Ankle Joint and How We Are Poised On Two Feet

The most obvious function of the ankle is to move and position the foot in relation to the lower leg—that is, to dorsiflex and plantar flex the foot (*Fig. 9*). When we push off the ground when walking, or if we raise our weight on our toes, we are plantar flexing the foot. We also saw that, with the foot fixed on the ground, the muscles on the lower leg that act on the foot now stabilize the lower leg in relation to the foot, which is essential to our postural support and balance on two feet.

But these actions represent only a part of what the ankle is for. In our upright vertical posture, the entire body is poised on two feet as the basis for moving in space. When we take a step, we must bend the knee and flex the ankle in order to advance the leg, but we must first incline at the ankles in order to initiate the forward movement of the body as a whole (*Fig. 10*). For this to happen, the lower leg—and the entire body with it—must be free to incline at the ankle, in which case we are not moving the foot in relation to the lower leg but allowing the lower leg to move in relation to the foot.

This action of the leg at the ankle is central to the act of walking. Although we must stabilize the lower leg in relation to the foot as the basis for maintaining upright posture, we must also be unstable in order for movement to take place, and this instability is actually part of how we are designed to move on two feet. If we shorten in the legs, brace the knees and stiffen our feet, this interferes with our ability to move freely at the ankle and thus compromises our upright poise. Freedom at the ankle joint is thus an essential component of our upright design.

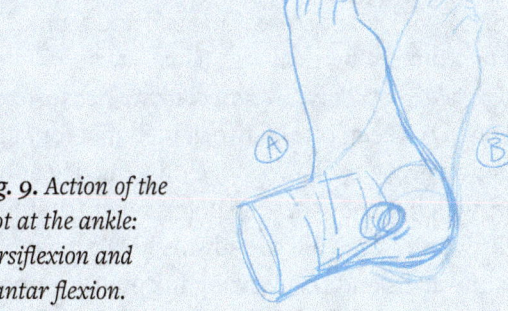

Fig. 9. Action of the foot at the ankle: dorsiflexion and plantar flexion.

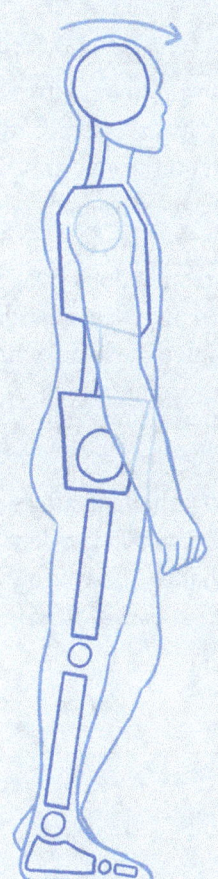

Fig. 10. The body as a whole is poised at the ankle joint and inclines forward at the ankles when we walk.

The Spiral Aspect of Walking

A final aspect of walking that must be mentioned is the spiral aspect of the trunk and the corresponding movement of the limbs. In our vertically-poised posture, the head and trunk rotate around a vertical axis. This rotational design is directly involved in walking because, although we keep our body oriented in a forward direction as we walk, we move only one leg at a time, which means that the pelvis must rotate slightly every time a leg is advanced. To balance this, the arms and trunk swing in counter-opposition to the legs, which helps to maintain stability but also means that the trunk counter-rotates as we walk (*Fig. 11*).

When we change direction or look around, we also engage the spiral musculature and the ability to rotate on a vertical axis, since we turn by rotating the head on the spine and by rotating the body slightly. The act of walking, then, involves subtle spiral movements of the trunk, enabling us to move with tremendous ease, flexibility, and skill. Our poise on a vertical axis also expands our visual field, since the head, which rotates so freely on top of the spine, aided by movements of the eyes themselves, can be easily turned to give us a 360-degree visual field. Our human upright posture is an altogether amazing design, and the spiral musculature, which is oriented around this vertical axis so that the body is always free to rotate, is an integral part of this design.

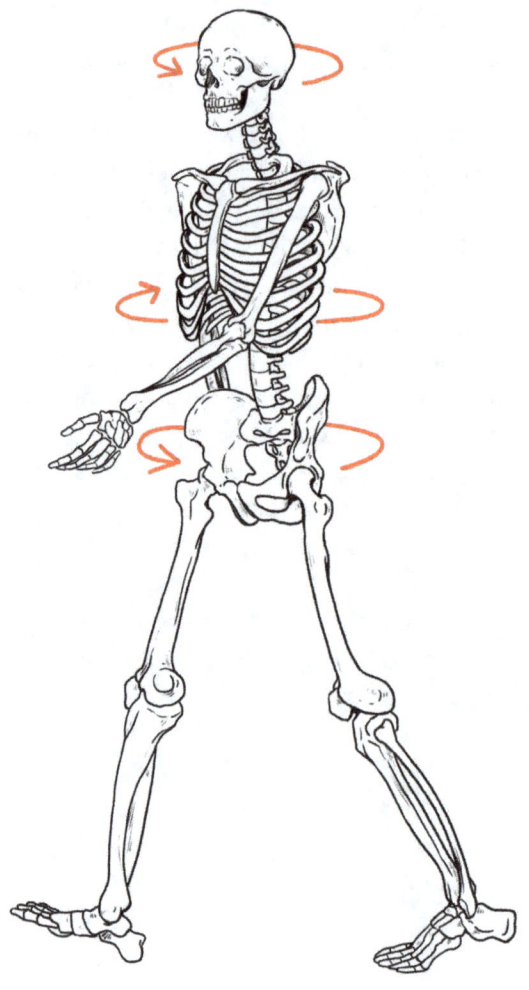

Fig. 11. *The spiral action of the body in walking.*

Walking and Our Tensegrity Design

Let's return now to the question of how to walk without interfering with our natural poise. As we've seen, the body as a whole is designed to lengthen against gravity and is poised at the ankle joints to allow forward movement in space. As the trunk inclines forward, the knee of one leg is bent, the foot rolls off the ground and the leg swings under the advancing trunk. When we take a step in this coordinated manner, the movement of the leg is entirely secondary to the lengthened support of the body as a whole, which functions as a tensegrity system designed to lengthen against gravity as we bend at the joints and the legs swing underneath the body.

In walking, the average adult interferes with these actions by shifting weight onto the supporting leg, sinking into the hip and shortening in stature while advancing a leg. The entire body becomes tensed and shortened, breathing becomes impaired, and the legs and hips are stiffened and braced. Young children walk very lightly on their feet because they support themselves easily against gravity and do not shorten or use unnecessary tension when they walk. Adults, in contrast, use a great deal of unnecessary tension when they walk, often performing the activity in a very labored and harmful way. Yet few of us think about how we walk, or how to walk in a more efficient and mindful way.

To reestablish a natural striding gait the body as a whole must lengthen against gravity—a process that, as we've seen, is based on our larger tensegrity design. A key element in this design is the forward balance of the head, which counterbalances the pull of the extensors muscles at the nape of the neck. The spine and back muscles remain lengthened while the weight comes forward to advance a leg. The body as a whole thus continues to lengthen upward even while advancing forward. In a four-footed animal, the head is cantilevered to maintain length on the neck muscles while the spine lengthens horizontally—that is, in the direction of movement. In humans, the balance of the head counterbalances the extensor muscles of the back so that the head goes up and the spine lengthens along its vertical axis—in other words, we lengthen upward to move forward in space. This upward movement, not the action of the legs, is the key to coordinated walking.

Exercise 1

Observing shortening in stature using vertical monkey with your back against the wall

We saw earlier that, when we stand from the sitting position, we shorten in stature. In this exercise we observe how we shorten in stature when taking a step to walk.

1. Standing with your back to the wall, fall back gently against the wall so that both your upper back and pelvis are in contact with the wall (*Fig. 12a*).

2. Allowing your knees to bend, go into vertical stance (*Fig. 12b*).

3. Now gently push yourself forward from the wall with your arms, not changing the basic orientation of your head, upper back, and pelvis (*Fig. 12c*).

4. Again taking care not to change the orientation of your head, upper back, and pelvis, come very gently to the fully upright posture (*Fig. 12d*).

5. Now take a step with your right leg. Did you shift your weight over your left leg? When you shifted weight, did you bring your pelvis forward and sink into your left leg?

The tendency to shorten in stature is the basic problem in walking, which is not simply about body mechanics but about our natural lengthened support against gravity. When we walk or take a step, we interfere with this natural support by shifting our weight over the supporting leg and shortening in stature.

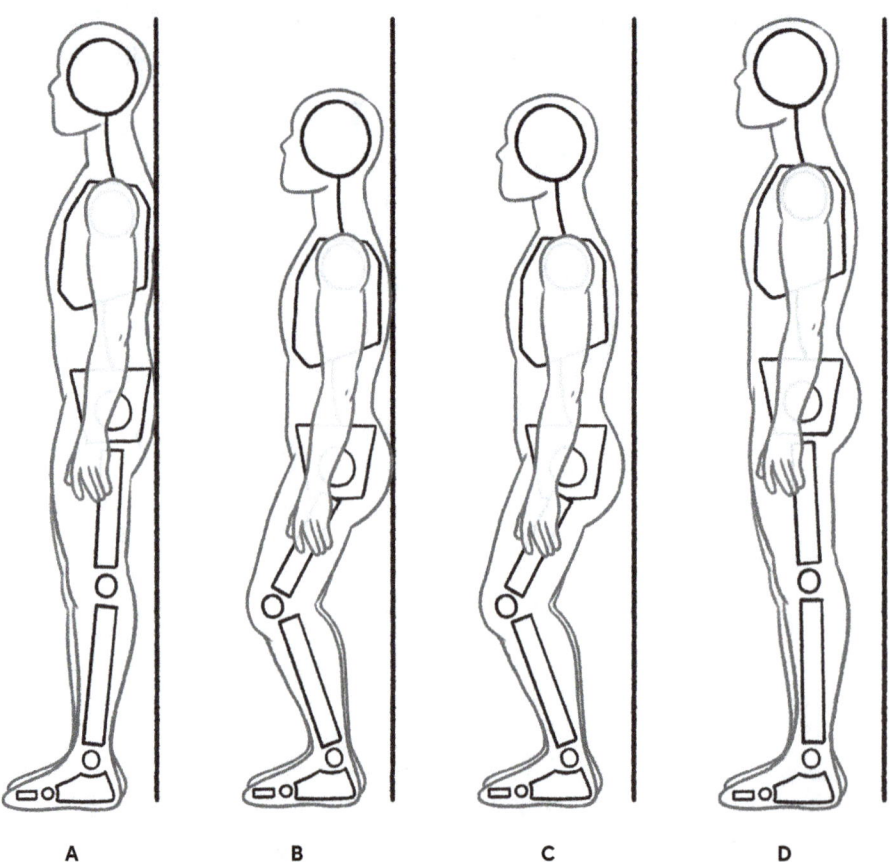

A   B   C   D

Fig. 12a-d. Observing how we shorten in stature when we walk, using vertical stance with your back against the wall.

Exercise 2

Bending the knees in walking

We've seen that, when we take a step to initiate walking, we tend to shorten in stature and brace the legs, which in turn prevents the joints from working. To stop creating this unnecessary tension, we have to regain the ability to allow the knees to bend while maintaining the length of the body as a whole. In the following exercises, we explore the process of bending the knees as the basis for walking in a more coordinated way.

Part One: Letting your knee go and raising your heel to walk

1. Stand with your feet shoulder width apart (*Fig. 13a*). Give your directions for your head to go up, your back to lengthen and widen, and your gluteal muscles to let go.

2. Bend your right knee so that the heel of that foot comes off the ground, allowing the weight to go onto the ball of the foot so that you are not shifting your weight onto your left foot but keeping your weight evenly distributed between both feet (*Fig. 13b*). Being able to do this is not difficult but may take a minute to figure out, so take a moment to explore this action before going on to the next step.

3. When you are able to raise your heel without shifting weight, bring the heel down so that you are again standing normally on both feet as in *Fig. 13a*.

4. Repeat this procedure with your left foot, raising the heel while continuing to support weight on the ball of the foot, and then lowering the heel.

5. See if you can alternate sides, raising one heel and then the other. There should be no shift of weight because, while each heel is off the ground, the ball of the foot still carries weight. Play around with this for a minute or two until you can do it comfortably.

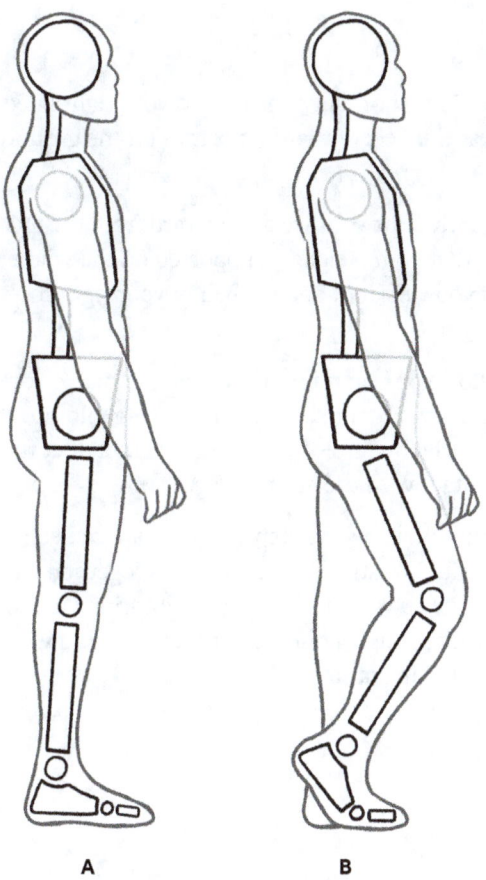

A   B

Fig. 13a-b. Letting a knee go to raise the heel.

Part Two: Shifting your weight forward to take a step

1. Standing normally, again bend your right knee so that the heel of that foot comes off the ground (*Fig. 14a*).

2. Gently shift your weight forward from the ankles so that your weight is supported on the whole of your left foot and the ball of your right foot (*Fig. 14b*).

3. Allow your right foot to advance so that it comes under your trunk. Your right foot should now be slightly forward of your left, with both feet fully in contact with the ground (*Fig. 14c*).

You have now taken a step and, if you have been successful in putting these elements together, will have done so without shifting weight from side to side, without using unnecessary tension, and without shortening in stature.

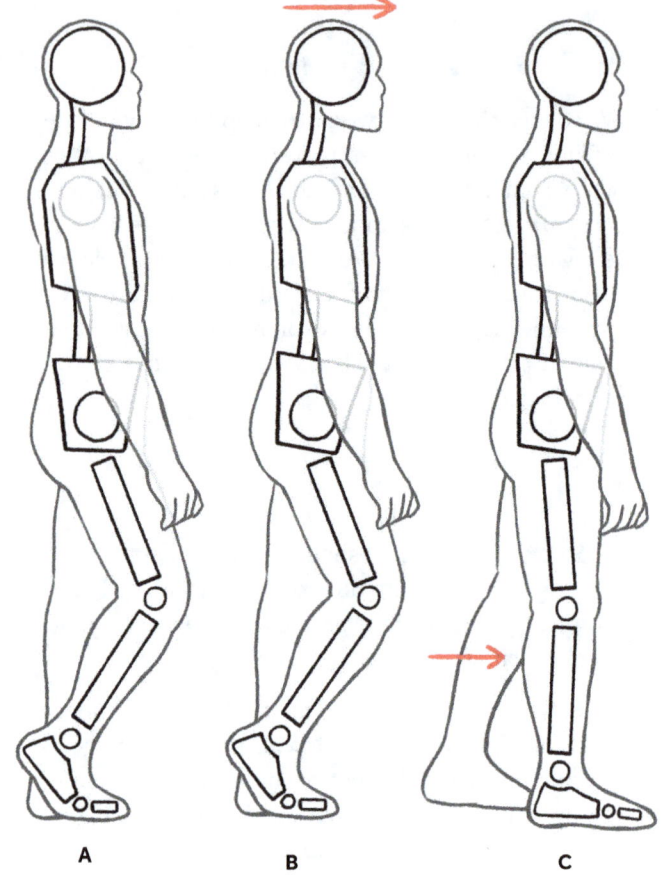

A   B   C

Fig. 14a-c. Letting the knee bend and shifting weight to take a step.

Exercise 3

Exploring walking using chairs for support

In the last exercise, we broke walking down into three component steps: (a) bending the knee as the basis for advancing the leg; (b) inclining the body as a whole at the ankles; (c) advancing a leg to take a step. A very useful way of exploring these movements is to place a chair on either side and to place hands on the chair rails, using the rail of the chair as a point of contact and support while doing these movements, as shown in *Fig. 15*. This exercise is a variation of the previous one, but here we will look at these movements in a different sequence, exploring each one singly before putting them together.

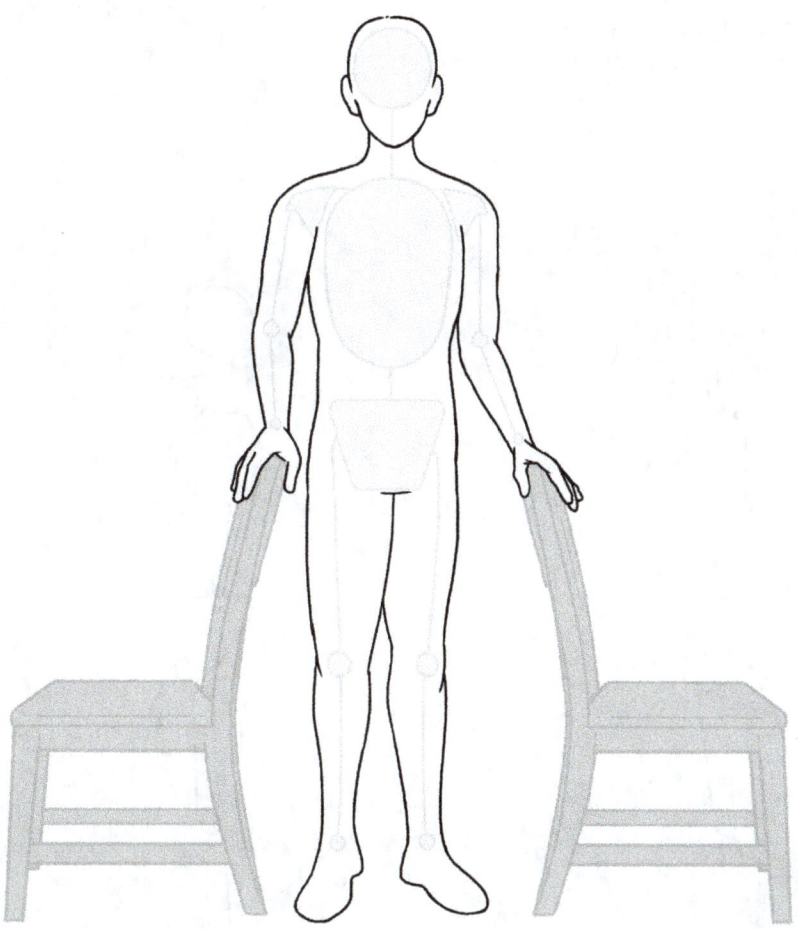

Fig. 15. *Exploring walking using chairs for support.*

Part 1: Inclining at the ankles to shift your weight forward

1. Standing with the two chairs on either side, place your hands gently on the chair rails and give your directions.

2. Gently shift your weight forward from your ankles, allowing both feet to remain fully in contact with the floor, and then bring your weight back (*Fig. 16*).

3. Shift your weight forward and back a few times until the movement is easy and comfortable.

We've seen that, when we take a step, we must first incline at the ankles in order to initiate the forward movement of the body as a whole—an action that is central to the act of walking. For this to happen, the lower leg—and the entire body with it—must be free to incline at the ankle. Notice that, when you incline forward, the center of gravity of your trunk has shifted forward over the front of your feet.

Part 2: Letting a knee bend without shifting weight

1. Stand with your hands placed on the chairs and your weight on both feet (*Fig. 17a*).

2. See if you can raise your right heel off the ground, being sure that you are not shifting onto your left side but keeping your weight over both feet.

3. Let your knee bend further forward, so that your heel is coming fully off the ground (*Fig. 17b*).

4. Let your leg straighten so that your heel comes back onto the ground.

5. Without taking your weight off your left foot, let your left knee bend slightly.

6. Let your knee bend further forward, so that your heel is coming up fully off the ground.

7. Let your leg straighten so that your heel comes back onto the ground.

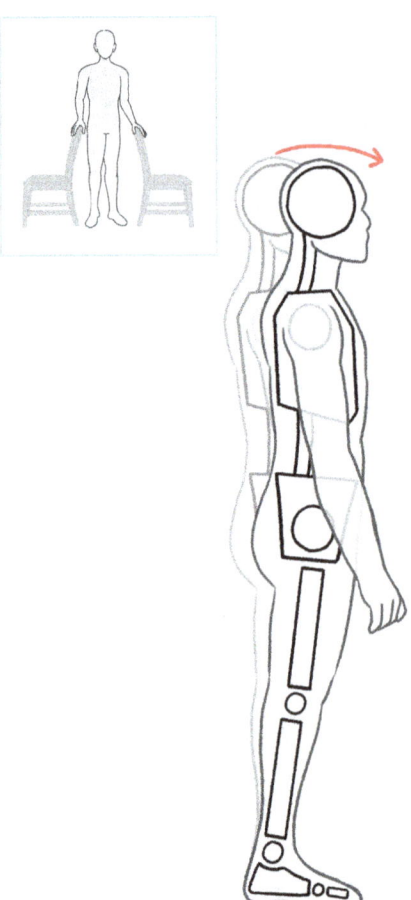

Fig. 16. Inclining at the ankles to shift your weight forward and back.

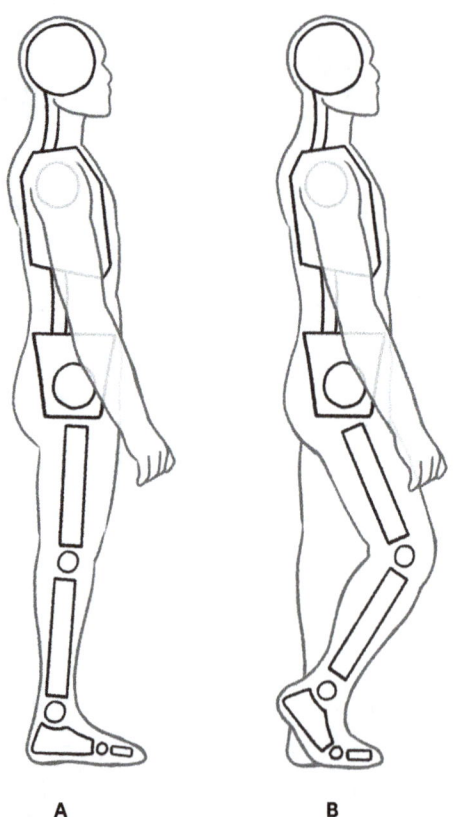

A   B

Fig. 17a-b. Letting a knee bend without shifting weight.

Sensorimotor Awareness

Part 3: Combining the weight shift with raising a heel

In this exercise, we will combine the two previous elements, shifting weight and raising a heel. Take time with this part of the sequence before going on to the final part.

1. Stand with your hands placed on the chairs and your weight on both feet (*Fig. 18a*).

2. Gently shift your weight forward from your ankles (*Fig. 18b*).

3. Let your right knee bend slightly (*Fig. 18c*).

4. Shift your weight back and come fully onto both feet.

Part 4: Taking a step without shifting weight to the side

In this exercise, we put all the elements together to take a step.

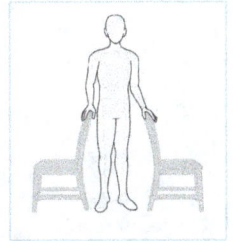

1. Stand with your hands placed on the chairs (*Fig. 18a*).

2. Gently shift your weight forward from your ankles (*Fig. 18b*).

3. Let your right knee bend (*Fig. 18c*).

4. Allow your right foot to advance so that it comes under your trunk (*Fig. 18d*). Your right foot should now be slightly forward of your left, with both feet fully in contact with the ground.

You have now taken a small step by focusing on the constituent elements that make up walking. The idea here is that, if your PNR system is working well as a whole and you incline forward at the ankles, a knee can bend and the leg can easily swing under the advancing trunk, making it possible to take a step without shortening in stature, sinking into the supporting leg, or using too much tension. If you have been able to successfully complete the exercise, you will find that taking a step can happen quite easily and that it is possible to remain fully poised and lengthened while walking.

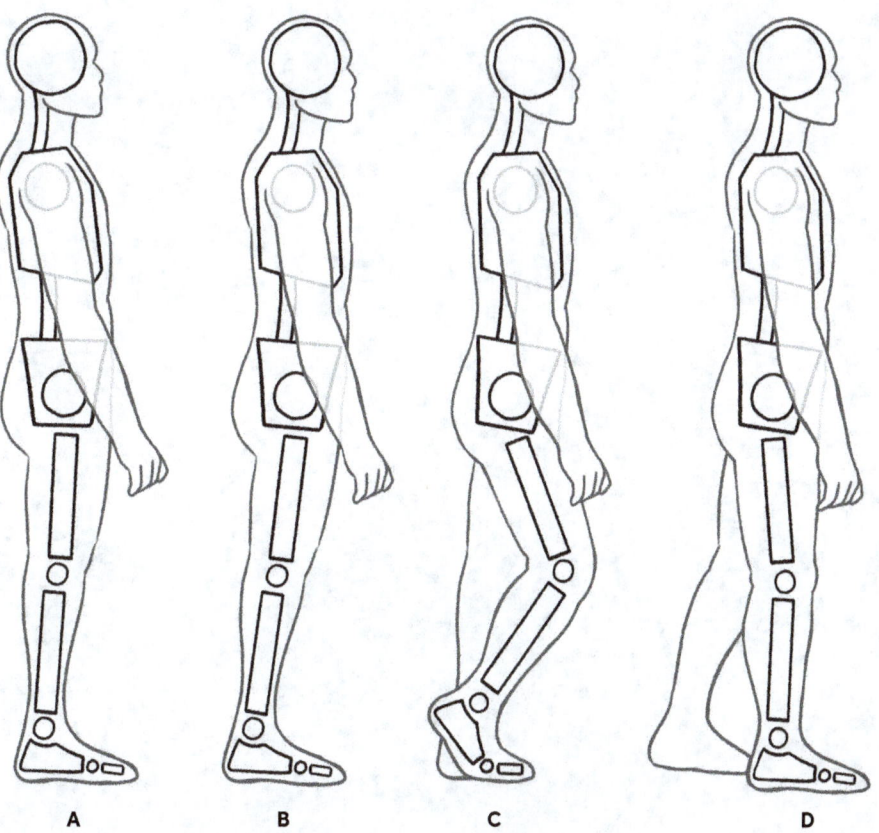

A   B   C   D

Fig. 18a-d. Combining the weight shift with letting the knee bend to take a step.

PART FIVE

Advanced Procedures

Paying Attention

Throughout this book we have looked at various aspects of movement as the basis for becoming more kinesthetically aware—how we perform actions, how to reduce muscular tension, how to "direct" particular parts of the body. It sometimes surprises people to learn that, to become more kinesthetically aware and to bring the body into better balance, we must also practice forms of mindful attention. That is what we're going to look at this chapter—how to pay attention, how to do this in a sustained way, and how to quiet the mind so that we learn how to become more focused and less distracted. We'll begin first with what I call "conscious intention"; after this, we'll look at the process of paying attention in a sustained way.

Conscious Intention

Conscious intention is the process of choosing consciously to do something, or paying attention to something, in a deliberate way. Because we have the subjective sense of being consciously in charge most of the time, most of us do not realize how little, and how rarely, we are actually in charge of our own thoughts and actions. Much of our behavior is dictated by circumstance and opportunity, our attention constantly diverted by trivial distractions. Because we are preoccupied with and caught up in the various demands of daily life—and because we have never been taught how to pay attention as a kind of deliberate skill—it does not occur to us that we have the ability to choose how to focus and how to do this as a constructive form of self management. Conscious intention is the name I give to the process of deciding what you want to pay attention to and carrying out this decision in a constructive and sustained way.

Conscious intention, as described here, is not the same as meditating on a single object (which is done while sitting quietly and not while engaged in activity) but is a kind of mindfulness practice that can be applied to various activities and faculties including vision, hearing, movement, sitting, and standing. When, for instance, we are aware of the contact of our feet on the floor while observing a visual scene, we are not meditating in the usual sense but expanding our awareness to include an aspect of ourselves while engaged in an activity.

Conscious intention is also not the same as being disciplined or focused in the usual sense. When children do their homework, or when we perform specific tasks at work, we are attending to what we are doing in a focused way, but we are motivated by the task itself and, if we are trying to get it done, are completely drawn in by it. We are performing a voluntary activity, but it is routine and mechanical and, even as we perform it, we become so immersed in it that we forget ourselves. Conscious intention, in contrast, involves deliberately and mindfully focusing on oneself or on some object of attention—usually something that has little inherent interest—in a sustained way. Learning to do this runs counter to our background and experience. We are used to becoming immersed in what we're doing—getting lost in a good story, entertained by a good film, or lost in social media or the internet. Paying attention consciously, in contrast, is neither pleasurable nor rewarding—at least not in the immediate sense. Here we must be motivated by our own sense of purpose. This is not a difficult thing to do in a momentary way, but most of us never learn to do this as a matter of discipline—that is, to pay attention to something not because it draws us in or because we find it entertaining but because we choose to pay attention to something for its own sake.

But how do we learn to pay attention in this sustained way? We are all capable of putting our minds on a problem or paying attention in a continuous way, as when we drive or perform desk work. This ability, however, is based on narrowing our focus so that, although we may be aware of what we are doing, we lose ourselves in the process. Conscious intention is aimed at paying attention in such a way that we remain present throughout the process. One example of conscious intention, which we will explore in a moment, is to pay attention to yourself while watching a movie or video. When we are watching a movie, we tend to get lost in what we are seeing and completely forget about ourselves. This is just what many of us want from a movie— to get lost in the action of the film and to forget

about ourselves. It is perfectly possible, however, to remain aware of yourself while viewing the film, so that enjoying the film is not associated with a loss of attention but with heightened mindfulness. Learning to do this takes time but, with practice, leads to an ongoing presence of mind that makes it possible never to become so absorbed in things that you become forgetful and inattentive. Having this sense of clarity and purpose will transform how you conduct yourself and how you approach your activities. You will be able to set your own goals, you will not easily get lost in thought or distracted by outside stimuli, and you will be able to stick to your set purpose. You will be poised and alert rather than taken out of yourself by circumstances. You will stop wasting time so that you will use your time constructively and, whatever the situation, you will always know what you are about.

Although this quality of purposiveness is based on making a decision and sticking to the decision you've made, it isn't the same as, and cannot be achieved by, simply making a resolution or deciding to do something in the usual sense. When we decide that we're going to, say, lose weight or exercise every day, we have resolved to make a lifestyle change. In a similar way, we may decide that we want to be a better listener and to make an effort to ask more questions, or to give the person we're speaking to a chance to express him or herself. In these cases, we have made a decision that reflects a change of heart or a felt need to address a particular problem, but it is not an attitude of mind that translates into actual practice. Conscious intention, in contrast, is a decision to engage actively in a process of paying attention or working on something in an ongoing way.

Becoming Your Own Teacher

Although the practice of conscious intention may at first seem unfamiliar, the truth is that we have all practiced some form of conscious intention when we learn a new skill such as acting, singing, or playing an instrument. Here the teacher asks us to carry out various procedures in a thoughtful manner, paying attention or observing ourselves in a deliberate way. Under someone else's tutelage, this process is easy to carry out because, in this context, we are motivated to learn and eager to follow the instructions given to us. Learning to carry out the same procedures on our own is more difficult for several reasons. First, when working on our own, we may not have as clear an agenda as when a teacher is directing us. Second, we tend to be more easily distracted on our own than with a teacher. Third, when we work on our own, we are more uncertain about the value of what we are doing. We tend to be less positive and, in many cases, will become positively negative and self-critical. To overcome this, we need to guide ourselves just as the teacher would. This may include using language to guide our progress, noting when we are taking positive steps forward and encouraging ourselves. In essence, we need to internalize the teacher, using the directive function of language as a guiding process just as the teacher does, and treating ourselves as nicely as we would treat someone else.

Exercise 1

Expanding your awareness

We pay attention to things outside ourselves all day long but, as we do so, we are usually unaware of ourselves. In this exercise, you will expand your awareness to include yourself as you are paying attention visually.

1. Sit comfortably in a chair.

2. Look around so that you are visually aware of the room you are in—the walls, the windows, the objects in the room.

3. Without losing focus on the room, notice your sit bones on the chair and your back resting against the back of the chair.

4. If you take a moment with this, you will find that there is no difficulty in maintaining awareness of your surroundings while at the same time being aware of the contact of your body against the chair as a kind of background sensation. These bodily sensations will not conflict with your visual awareness because it is quite possible to be visually or perceptually aware and, at the same time, to have bodily sensations.

You have now expanded your awareness in such a way that you are attending visually, while at the same time remaining aware of yourself.

Exercise 2

Taking time to visually observe

We pay attention to things outside ourselves all day long but, as we do so, we usually forget ourselves. In this exercise, you will expand your awareness to include yourself as you are paying attention visually.

1. Stand at a window where you have a clear view of the street or the trees outside.

2. Take time to observe what you see. Look at the street, notice the cars, the houses, whatever is happening.

3. Do not try to see what is in your field of vision. Allow your eyes to soften so that you are simply allowing them to see for you.

4. While continuing to observe, be aware of your feet on the floor so that, as you look, you are aware of the sensation of your feet contacting the floor.

Taking time to be quiet doesn't have to be unpleasant or forced. When you give yourself time to do something—and when you embrace what you are doing as a positive process—it becomes both easy and pleasant to take time to stop and pay attention to what is around you.

Exercise 3

Paying attention to tactile and proprioceptive feedback

When we suffer from bodily tension, we tend to become overly focused or worried. In this exercise, we begin by focusing outwardly and, without losing this outward focus, notice some aspect of ourselves, in this way being aware but without being fixated or worried.

1. Lie down in the semi-supine position with books under your head. Take a moment to be quiet.

2. Take a moment to look at the ceiling, the walls around you, and the sounds in the room or outside.

3. Without losing visual awareness, notice the contact of your head on the books and your back on the floor, taking note of this tactile information even while you continue to be visually aware.

4. When you are able to maintain visual and tactile awareness at the same time, see if you can be aware of your neck and head, your back on the floor, and your legs while continuing to attend visually.

In this exercise, you are taking note of tactile and proprioceptive feedback, without worrying over specific problems and without trying to relax or control specific muscles. This makes it possible to pay attention to yourself in a constructive way.

Exercise 4

Exploring how we move at our joints

In this exercise, we focus on moving at our joints in an exploratory way. When we perform exercises or move in some way, we are of course using various joints. But because we are focused on actively moving, we are largely unaware of the joints that make these movements possible and how they work. By taking time to do the following movements in an exploratory way, we discover where some of our key joints are located and how they work. In the process, we allow movement to happen more freely, increasing our mobility in the process.

1. Standing with your feet slightly apart, take a moment to come up to your full stature.

2. Gently nod your head up and down. Do not move quickly or force your head to move but go slowly, exploring how much freedom there is to move in each direction.

3. Rotate your head gently from side to side. Again, do not rush the movement but slowly and gently turn to one side and then the other, seeing how far your head can move without forcing it in any way.

4. Swing your arms gently at the shoulders, seeing how easily they can move at the shoulders.

5. Look to one side and gently turn your head to follow your gaze. Continue to turn, allowing your trunk to follow the movement of your head until you are rotating your entire body right from your feet up to your head.

Although we move at our joints all the time, we rarely take the time to identify exactly what movements are possible, or how the joints actually work. Taking time to explore these simple movements—and doing this consciously and thoughtfully—is a useful way of bringing about greater freedom and mobility in the musculoskeletal system as a whole.

Focusing Your Attention

Directing parts of the body in order to bring about improved coordination requires the ability to pay attention for periods of time without becoming mentally distracted, preoccupied, or worried about specific problems. For most of us, this is far from easy. When sitting or lying quietly, we become lost in trains of thought and, when we try to focus on ourselves, we become fixated on parts of the body or worried about tensions or discomfort we may be experiencing. To overcome this, we need to learn to maintain our attention—and to know what to attend to—without becoming distracted. Being able to do this requires the ability to be mindfully or consciously aware, which is what we're going to talk about now.

MINDFUL AWARENESS

At the most basic level, mindfulness refers to the act of paying attention to something at a conscious level, as when we enjoy a sip of coffee or eat something sweet and savor its taste. There is no difficulty in doing this; when we pay close attention to something, we are by definition being mindful. Sustaining mindful attention is another matter. We all inherit the ability to be attentive in the normal way, but learning to be mindfully attentive requires conscious work. When this state can be maintained in activity so that one is undistracted by outside stimuli, it goes to a higher level and thus functions as a higher stage of awareness. Understood in this way, being mindful is not simply a practice or goal in itself but leads to a higher stage of consciousness.

But how do we maintain a state of conscious or mindful attention? Mindfulness is a kind of alertness that is interfered with when we become mentally distracted by outside thoughts or lost in what we are perceiving or doing. What this means, in simple terms, is that the key to being aware is to notice when you lose awareness. This cannot be achieved by trying to get oneself into a state or by some other mechanical means. Mindful awareness takes place in the active present, and the only way to maintain this state is to notice when you lose it. By bringing your attention back each time it wanders, you will soon be able to notice when you lose attention, leading eventually to the ability to remain completely focused and alert.

Because the goal in meditation is to be more present in ourselves, it is natural to assume that the primary focus, when paying attention, should be on ourselves. But attention begins with perception, and focusing on yourself—by closing your eyes, turning inward, or going into a relaxed state— leads not to heightened attention but to inattention. Paying attention to what you are seeing or hearing means that you are focused outwardly, yet in a peculiar way it means that, at the same time, you are attentive to yourself. This is because, in attending to something wholeheartedly, we are also remaining present or aware of ourselves; perceptual attention, actively attending to some thing, implies awareness of oneself. When you stop attending to the object and become lost in a train of thought, you are no longer aware of yourself.

One very useful way of learning to pay attention in an extended way, which we'll try out in a moment, is to see if you can listen to a piece of music without losing focus. To do this, you want to see if you can listen very actively to the music, staying in the moment, hearing every note, and noticing when you become distracted—that is, when you stop hearing the notes. Listening to music is a good way to stay focused on something outside yourself so that, if you have a tendency to become worried about what is happening in your body, you stay focused externally. At the same time, if you are listening mindfully you will be present within yourself so that you are being both aware of yourself and attentive. When doing this, your attention will wander; when you come back to the music, you will not be entirely sure whether you were consciously listening to the previous section of music or had lost concentration. Each time this happens, notice when your attention strays and bring your attention back to the music. At first, you will find that you simply cannot pay attention for more than a short period; after a period of days or weeks, you will notice when your mind begins to stray so that you won't lose yourself. If you are diligent, you will find that, after a period of several months, you will be able to listen to an entire piece without any loss of attention.

Exercise 1

Visual awareness and the peripheral field

Because we spend a great deal of time looking at computer screens, we tend to use our eyes in a limited way, becoming habitually fixated on what we're doing at the expense of being aware of our environment. If we want to be more mindfully aware—and to take better care of our eyes in the process—we have to learn to pay more attention to what is around us and to be more broadly aware of our surroundings. The following exercise, which focuses on peripheral vision, is a simple and pleasurable way of exploring our visual sense and of heightening our awareness in the process.

1. Sitting in your chair, look at something across the room—a window, a picture or some other object on the wall. Pay attention to what you are looking at, noticing specific details of what you're looking at.

2. To become aware of your peripheral field, continue to look at the object and, without looking away, see if you can now become aware of what is around the object. The object you are looking at will be very distinct; in contrast, objects in your peripheral field will be rather indistinct. As you continue to look, however, you will soon be able to make out some of these objects—a chair, a lamp, the floor—as well as color and shade.

3. If you continue to explore your peripheral field, you will find that it is very wide and includes your awareness of the walls to either side of you, as well as the ceiling above and floor below. Keeping your eyes focused on the object in front of you, see if you can now be aware of the entire space around you. If you are sitting in a room alone, there may be no movement but, if you are sitting in a classroom, on a bus, or in a crowded cafe, you will soon become aware of movement all around you.

4. See if you can now shift your gaze to another point in the room. Are you still aware of your peripheral field or, when you focused on a new object, did you lose awareness of your peripheral field? Take a moment to allow your peripheral field to come into your awareness.

5. Stand up and take a few steps. Are you still aware of your peripheral field?

6. Pick a location across the room and walk toward it, continuing to notice what is in your peripheral field as you move. What do you notice about the objects to your side as you move? Do stationary objects remain stationary, or do they move as you move and, if so, how? Can you continue to move around the room, while being peripherally aware?

In this exercise, you have expanded your awareness to include a heightened sense of the space you occupy as well as your visual field. This heightened awareness includes a sense of yourself, which means that you are learning to maintain self-awareness in the act of being perceptually alert. The next time you are riding a subway or relaxing in a cafe, see if you can become aware of your peripheral field in this way. Looking at an object in front of you, begin to take in information about your peripheral field, allowing your awareness to expand to include the entire space around you.

Exercise 2

Listening to music without losing awareness of yourself

When we listen to music, watch a film, or just observe people around us, we tend to become absorbed in what we are seeing. In this exercise, we focus on listening to a piece of music, but in such a way that you maintain an awareness of yourself.

1. Sit in an armchair with your feet flat on the floor and arms resting on the arm rests. Notice the air going in and out through your nostrils.

2. Play some quiet music. This will be your initial focus of attention.

3. Be aware of your feet on the floor, seeing to it that you are not tightening your legs.

4. Be aware of your back resting against the back of the chair, seeing to it that you're allowing your back to get its full support so that your trunk is supported and you do not have to slump.

5. Be aware of your head, allowing it to nod forward and to come up in space.

6. You now have three parts to be aware of while you listen to the music: your legs, your back, and your head. While listening to the music, go over these three areas so that they begin to get clear in your awareness. There's nothing to do here except to notice these three areas while you listen.

7. If you find that you become absorbed in the music to the exclusion of your bodily awareness, start over, reiterating the parts of your body that you want to be aware of.

8. Keep doing this until you find that are able to listen to the music, while at the same time maintaining a background awareness of the three areas of your body.

We are often drawn in by what interests us so that, when we attend, we lose ourselves. If you learn to listen to music while maintaining an awareness of yourself, you will find that you are not only able to listen better but will also gain the ability to remain present and self-aware even while attending to other things.

18

Integrating the Whole

In this book, we have looked in detail at the problem of muscle tension and the process of utilizing awareness to address it. As we've seen, a muscle that is tense and constricted is not simply "tight" but is constantly receiving messages from the nervous system to contract. To address this, it was necessary to send messages to "tell" the muscle to stop contracting and return to its normal length. We also saw that muscles function within a larger whole so that, when they stop contracting, they don't simply relax but lengthen between their bony attachments. To explore this, we looked at the forearm muscles that act on the hand. The forearm muscles, which form meaty bundles that taper into tendons that attach to the wrist and fingers, are the main muscles that act upon the hand and fingers. If the fingers are curled up, the forearm muscles will be shortened, and direct attempts to relax these muscles will be futile. To reduce tension in the forearm, it was necessary not only to stop tightening the forearm muscles but, in addition, to support the fingers so that, with the fingers extended, the muscles could lengthen or release between their origins and attachments.

Even when we have understood how to direct muscles, however, we must remember that the purpose of directing is not simply to bring about specific improvements but to restore the coordinated working of the PNR system as a whole. When we suffer from a particular problem, we are often so focused on what we think is wrong that we forget that the body is designed to work as a coordinated whole. Knowing how this system works represents a truly educational approach to kinesthetic awareness that can be applied in daily life. In the following exercises, we will focus on directing as an intentional process aimed at restoring muscle length throughout the body. We will also look at how to direct in such a way that the different parts of the body can link up and work together as a coordinated whole.

Opposition and Muscle Length

To make sense of how the dynamic relation of parts plays a central role in directing, let's look first at what happens when you're lying in semi-supine position giving directions for your neck to release so that your head can go out of your back and your knees can go away. As the neck and back muscles let go, the head moves in such a way that it comes out of your back. When that happens, the head begins to exert stretch on the muscles. Muscles let go of parts, but parts, in turn, begin to "act" on muscles.

But why do parts move in a particular direction, and why do muscles lengthen between body parts? The answer is that muscles and bones form a dynamic partnership to produce bodily support, and this relationship—otherwise known as "tensegrity"—is based not on muscle tension but on muscle length. The muscles on the nape of the neck, for instance, must maintain the support of the head, which will otherwise fall forward. But they don't perform this function simply by tightening, which would cause the head to be constantly pulled back and fixed in place. Instead, the head is weighted in front so that it exerts an opposing force on the neck muscles and keeps these muscles lengthened. The neck muscles are able to contract, but they do so in the context of length. Some variation of this tensegrity architecture exists in virtually every part of the musculoskeletal system. Instead of simply contracting, muscles are suspended within a latticework of bones, working in a kind of partnership with the bones to produce a network of support that is highly economical and efficient, with all the muscles working together even when we are moving just one part of the body or contracting individual muscles.

To produce support and movement, then, muscles don't simply pull on bones; bones "push" on muscles even as muscles pull on bones. This creates a polarity of forces that produces directional support in space with a minimum of fixation and effort. Because we are concerned with muscle tension so much of the time, it is easy to think that release of tension is the main quality we're looking for in muscles, as if muscles are simply happier when they let go than when tightening. But muscles work in partnership with bones to produce directional support, as we can see when we carry weight on our heads, in which case the head naturally counteracts the downward force of the weight with an upward force, producing energetic support or movement in a particular direction.

Directing Is a Dynamic and Intentional Process

So what does this dynamic relationship of muscles and body parts tell us about the process of sending directions or messages and about how we should use our awareness to bring about an improved working of the PNR system? To counteract the shortening of muscles, we must send inhibitory messages to muscles, allowing time for the muscles to let go and for the musculoskeletal system to quiet down so that muscles that are chronically contracted can become less active. But muscles do not simply let go; they lengthen between parts that are dynamically opposed to each other. For muscles to lengthen between bones, we have to think of where the parts go and see to it that they go that way. What this means in practice is that, when you direct, you are not simply doing nothing but must also direct body parts to move in a particular direction, and see to it that you are giving yourself the help and support needed to let this happen. In doing this, the goal is to establish a condition in which muscles that are contracted and pulling on skeletal parts can let go so that they are dynamically stretched or lengthened *between* skeletal parts. When this happens, the head will release out of a lengthening back; the back will fill out and widen; the shoulders will spread apart; and the hips and legs will let go so that the knees will actively go away from the hips. Instead of muscles pulling on bones, muscles let go of the bones and all the parts let go into expansion. This is the real purpose of directing, which is aimed at restoring a coordinated working of the PNR system based on the principle of muscle length.

Exercise 1
Not tightening to "direct" parts away from each other

In this exercise, we will explore the process of directing by focusing not on muscles but on parts. This diverts our attention away from muscle tension so that we think instead about the head going up, the knees going away, and the back lengthening and widening in between.

1. Lying in semi-supine, begin by noticing the air going in and out through your nostrils. Don't do anything except simply to notice this.

2. Be aware of your neck, seeing to it that you're not holding or pulling on your head. As you do this, you may notice that, because you're not tightening your neck muscles, this allows your head to move. Don't focus on the movement; just notice it.

3. Now be aware of your back on the floor. See to it that you're not tightening in your ribs or holding your breath, allowing your back to have its full support on the floor at the shoulders and pelvis. You may notice that, as you leave your back alone, it can fill out on the floor.

4. Be aware now of your hips and thighs, seeing to it that you're not tightening or holding so that your knees can go out of your trunk.

5. Go over the three directions again—not tightening your neck to let your head go out; not tightening your trunk to let your back lengthen and fill out; and not tightening your legs to let your knees go away.

6. You are now thinking of your head going out of your trunk in one direction, your knees going our of your trunk in the other, and your back lengthening and widening in between.

Learning to "direct" parts of the body is a key aspect of restoring the PNR system. As muscles release, we can think increasingly clearly about the parts to which they attach—in particular the head and the knees—and how muscles let go so that these parts can go away from each other.

THINKING OF SEVERAL PARTS AT ONCE: THE FUGUE

Let's turn now to another aspect of directing—namely, the ability to think of several things at once. When we give the direction for the neck muscles to release so that the head can go forward and up, we do not want to focus on just one part but on several at once. In this way, we are coordinating the various parts as a whole and, at the same time, diverting our attention away from specific tensions or problems.

A simple analogy for the process of "thinking" of several things at once is the musical fugue. A fugue is a musical form in which a melody or theme is played in one voice and then repeated by subsequent voices, creating a layered and three-dimensional effect. A fugue typically begins by introducing a melodic theme that is followed, soon afterwards, by the same theme starting at a different point. Each melodic line is called a "voice" because it could be sung like a melody—in fact, many fugues written for instruments have been performed with voices, as in the famous Swingle Singers from the 1960's, who performed a number of Bach fugues with individual singers representing separate voices.

Projecting mental directions is similar to the fugue. When we give mental directions to parts of the body, we are layering our thinking by establishing one voice and, without forgetting this first voice, adding new voices, making it possible to think of several parts at once until they create a whole that is greater than the parts. That's going to be our theme in this exercise: thinking or being aware of one direction, or "voice," and then layering new voices over that until we are giving several directions at once.

Exercise 2

Thinking in three voices

1. Lying in semi-supine, begin by noticing the air going in and out through your nostrils. Don't do anything except simply to notice this.

2. Be aware of your neck, seeing to it that you're not holding or pulling on your head, which can rest freely on the books.

3. After thinking this for a minute or so, your neck and head will come into your awareness. This is your first voice.

4. Now be aware of your back on the floor. See to it that you're not tightening in your ribs so that you are allowing your back to have its full support on the floor.

5. After thinking about this for a minute or so, you should be generally aware of your back on the floor. Don't worry about anything specific that might be wrong; simply be aware of this general part of your body and notice that it has come into your awareness now on its own. This is your second voice.

6. Be aware of your back on the floor but, before you do this, reiterate your first voice so that, as you introduce the second one, you will not forget the first.

7. You will now have two parts, or two voices, in your awareness. Before going on to the third, don't forget to reiterate these two.

8. Be aware now of your hips and thighs, seeing to it that you're not tightening or holding. Don't worry about anything specific, or if you're not fully aware of anything that might be wrong; just be aware of this area.

9. After a minute or so, see if your thighs have come into your awareness. This is your third voice.

10. Be aware of your legs going away but, before you do this, be sure to reiterate the first two voices.

11. Three areas are now in your awareness simultaneously—your neck and head, your back, and your legs—so that you have expanded your awareness to include all three.

You now have three directions going—a fugue in three voices. By becoming consciously aware of one area and keeping it in your awareness as you add a second, and then keeping the first and second in your awareness as you add a third, you can think several things at once, expanding your awareness to include all the parts, which begin to work together as a coordinated whole.

DIRECTING AND INTEGRATING THE WHOLE

We have seen that, when we give directions, we are telling muscles to stop contracting, allowing them to let go so that the head can come out of the back, the shoulders can widen, and the knees can come out of the pelvis. When this happens, the various parts can begin to work together to produce lengthened support of the body as a whole. This linking up and coordination of parts is critical to the proper working of the PNR system. When, for instance, the thigh muscles release, this allows the knees to come out of the pelvis and trunk. When this happens, the legs begin to work as an extension of the trunk and, in this sense, link up with the trunk to form a more complete whole. This linking up of parts isn't just about length and release in muscles but involves the connecting up of parts into a coordinated whole that is designed to produce effortless, lengthened support against gravity.

Exercise 3

Direction, release, and linking up the parts

Let's look now at how the directions begin to work together so that the different parts begin to work as an integrated whole.

1. Lying in semi-supine, take a moment to be quiet, noticing the contact of your head on the books, your trunk and your feet on the floor.

2. Focus for a moment on your knees. Think of the top of your knees going to the ceiling. Take some time with this, repeating the thought of your knees going to the ceiling until you begin to feel your thighs.

3. As you continue to think of your knees going upward, you may begin to feel your thighs tone up, so that it becomes clear that they are more responsive to your thought and begin to let go.

4. The thought for your knees to go upward will now include an awareness of your thighs letting go, so that for your knees to go up, you must remember to let the thighs go.

5. Think this for another minute or two until it is quite clear that, to let your knees go upward, you must allow your thighs to release.

6. Now turn your attention to your head. Be aware of the top of your head and think of it going toward the wall behind you, or out of your trunk.

7. As you think of your head going out, see to it that you're not holding or pulling on your head, which can rest freely on the books.

8. After thinking this for a minute or so, your neck and head as a whole will come into your awareness.

9. The thought for your head to go out of your trunk will now include an awareness of your neck so that, to think of your head going out, you must include this awareness of your neck.

10. Now see if you can think of your knees and your head together, allowing your thighs to release so that the knees go up, and your neck to release so that your head goes out.

11. Now be aware of your back on the floor, allowing it to fill out and open up.

12. Now see if you can be aware of all three areas at once—your knees and thighs, your head and neck, and your back—as if they are becoming one connected whole.

It is easy to think, especially when we suffer from chronic muscular tensions, that removing tension is an end in itself, as if the only problem with muscles is that they get tight and that we somehow need to relax them. But muscles function as part of a coordinated whole, and the goal of directing, as we've seen throughout this book, is to bring about the automatic working of the PNR system by organizing our thinking so that the parts begin to work as a coordinated whole.

19

Habitual Action and Conscious Control

We have seen that, when we perform an action, we engage the muscular system at a largely unconscious level, even though we would describe the action itself as conscious or voluntary. To address this, we must understand how the musculoskeletal system is designed to work as a whole, identifying how it is interfered with and restoring its natural function. We must then apply this knowledge to various activities, learning how to use the legs, shoulders, arms and trunk in a new way.

But muscle tension is not simply a matter of relaxing or releasing over-tightened muscles or even of restoring the PNR system. Let's say, for instance, that you habitually tighten the muscles of your back when sitting, have brought about an improved working of the system, and want to maintain these improvements while working at your computer. This seems simple enough: just make sure you don't tighten your back muscles when you resume typing. What will happen instead is that, once you begin to type, the muscles will tighten up against your wishes, and you simply won't be able to control or even to notice what you are doing. This is because, to perform an action, we must first make a decision—whether at a conscious or unconscious level—about what we want to do, while the details of how the action takes place are automatically carried out. If we

are employing the muscular system in a harmful way, we will not only be unaware of this but will be unable to do anything to prevent it. The old messages persist because they are inseparably linked to the very intention to act.

The harmful pattern we have been observing, then, is not purely physical but is part of a larger psychophysical process that takes place in response to the thought to do something. Because we can control muscles directly, we assume that, when we experience harmful bodily tension, we can directly prevent the tension. But the tension is not simply a harmful form of muscular activity; it is an inherent part of our natural and instinctive way of performing the action and can no more be stopped, once we think about acting, than the act itself. Learning how to prevent this harmful activity, as anyone who has studied this subject knows, is much more than a method for reducing tension or controlling movement but represents a new stage in action.

Awareness in Action and the Act of Vocalizing

How then do we gain control over our actions, if they take place at an almost entirely habitual level, and if the very effort to perform actions in a new way triggers this habitual activity? To make sense of this, we're going to look at what happens in two activities: vocalizing and walking. Vocalizing, as the first of the activities we will look at, is a very good test case for looking at stopping because most of us, when we vocalize, will tend to suck in air, pull the head back, and arch the back. Now of course we need to take breath to vocalize, but I am speaking here about an audible, noticeable increase in tension involving pulling the head back and lifting the chest. When we are doing nothing and just sitting quietly, breathing happens automatically and none of this interference happens; the breath simply comes in and out on its own. This is very different from taking a breath, which involves actively sucking in air by lifting the chest and ribs, tightening the neck, and so on—that is, by pulling the head back and shortening in stature. That's what I mean by taking a breath. And we want to see if we can stop doing all this, as the basis for vocalizing in a new way.

So how can we stop pulling back the head, if the very act of vocalizing involves pulling the head back? We must recognize that, if we go ahead and speak, we will pull back the head and, conversely, if we want to prevent the pulling back of the head, we must refrain from speaking. This is not just a matter of pausing or stopping; we must recognize that the decision to speak involves our harmful habitual use and that, to prevent this harmful use, we must refrain entirely from speaking. This is different than just holding yourself back from doing something, or waiting for the right moment to speak, in which case you are still fully intending to speak and just postponing your habitual reaction. What I am speaking about here is refraining in the sense of actually deciding not to speak as the basis for performing the action without any interference and in a completely new way.

Although the idea of stopping, as described here, is simple in theory, it is in fact difficult to put into practice. One of the main reasons for this is that we do not realize that we are doing something harmful and, because we don't see that we're performing actions in a harmful way, we locate the problem in the body—that is, we

describe the problem in purely physical terms and do not believe we are in any way causing the problem. Because we believe the problem is physical, we assume we need to reduce or release the tension and see no need to actually stop what we're doing. When we realize that the pulling back of the head is caused by the decision to speak, it then becomes clear that the only way to stop this is to put aside the idea of vocalizing and to reconsider how to achieve our end in a new way.

A second reason is that, even when we recognize the need to stop, it is easy to assume we're stopping when we're not. Let's say, for instance, that you try pausing before speaking and, after trying this, you find that you have taken breath and stiffened your neck and ribs. It is easy, at this point, to become frustrated or confused—after all, you have stopped and given attention the process. But paying attention to the process and going slowly isn't really stopping. The purpose of stopping is to prevent the habitual, misdirected activity from taking place, which requires that you make a clear decision to refrain entirely from speaking. If you simply pause before speaking but, during this whole time, you have really decided to speak and are thinking about speaking, how can you expect the harmful habits associated with speaking to disappear? Stopping means putting aside entirely the idea of speaking as a way of preventing the harmful activity associated with speaking.

Exercise 1

Observing habits of speech in the semi-supine position

I said a moment ago that, when we pull back our head and take a breath to speak, these actions come into play as a result of the decision to speak and that we must therefore learn not only to direct but also to stop, or refrain from action. The harmful activity that comes into play in response to the decision to speak can be easily demonstrated on a student when, for instance, you adjust the student's head so that it is no longer pulled back, and then ask him or her to speak and to observe what happens. With a teacher's help, the student will be able to notice what happens. Without such help, however, it is not easy to see what we're doing. This is why, to begin with, we need to spend time giving directions and bringing about improvements. By doing this, we create a new standard against which we can begin to see when we revert to our habitual way of speaking, as we'll now see.

1. Lying quietly in the semi-supine position, allow the air to flow in and out through your nostrils.

2. Give your directions to free your neck, to let your head go forward and up, to allow your back to lengthen and widen, and to allow your knees to point to the ceiling.

3. Using a poem you're familiar with, recite one line and notice what happens to your head on the books. Did you pull your head back? Did you tighten your chest or arch your back?

4. After you stop reciting, allow your head to rest fully on the books and your back to lengthen and widen. Did you notice that your neck muscles let go slightly, that your ribs let go, or that your back stopped arching—in other words, that you had tightened unconsciously while reciting?

5. Recite another line and this time notice what happens to your breathing. Did you prepare to speak by lifting the chest and taking breath? Did you hold in your ribs, and did this affect the contact of your back on the floor? Any slight intake of breath means that you have reacted or responded to the stimulus to speak by pulling back your head and shortening in stature.

When lying quietly in the semi-supine position, the tendency to shorten in stature is fairly easy to identify. This tendency is not an aberration, nor is it the result of harmful tensions—after all, harmful tensions cannot be the cause of harmful tensions! The pattern of tension is initiated by the decision to speak, and the first step in preventing this response is to see it happen, in real time, and thus to recognize the need to stop as the basis for preventing these harmful tensions.

Exercise 2
Non-doing and speech movements

If the harmful pattern of shortening is initiated by the decision to speak, the next step is to find a way to speak without actually having the idea of speaking. In this exercise, we produce some of the elements involved in speaking, without making the decision to actually speak.

1. Spend a few minutes lying in the semi-supine position, making sure that your neck is free, your head is resting on the books, and your back is fully supported on the ground. Notice the breath going in and out through your nostrils.

2. When you're satisfied that you are leaving the system alone nicely, see if you can open your jaw while continuing to breathe through your nostrils. Notice if you have stiffened your neck muscles, tightened your throat, or held your breath. Opening the jaw is, of course, one of the elements of speech and is therefore closely associated with the basic pattern of misuse; learning to open the jaw without interfering with your head balance and without disturbing the flow of breath in and out of the nostrils is critical to coordinated speech.

3. When you can move your jaw comfortably without interfering with the flow of air through your nostrils, try moving your tongue, lips, and the muscles of your face. See if you can do this without holding your breath and while continuing to breathe through your nostrils.

Using your jaw, lips, tongue, and palate to form words is associated with our habits in speaking. Learning to employ these structures in a way that is not associated with speech and vocalizing will help the transition to vocalizing in a more coordinated way.

Exercise 3
Inhibition and nostril breathing

We now come to the most challenging part of the process, which is to convert the elements of speaking into actual speaking. We have seen that, when we breathe normally, air flows into and out of our lungs via the nostrils and that, when we speak, we interfere with this process by actively taking in breath. An effective way to prevent this tendency is to notice the air going in and out through your nostrils as a kind of baseline against which you can perceive the tendency to take a breath in preparation to speak. When you have seen to it that you are doing nothing, consider speaking only after the air has come in through nostrils and you have done nothing to prepare.

1. Lying in the semi-supine position, take a few minutes to give your directions for your neck to be free, your back to lengthen and widen, and your knees to go forward and away.

2. Notice the breath going in and out through your nostrils. Make sure your lips are together and your tongue is naturally arching in your mouth.

3. Without interfering with this natural flow of air, think of the first line of your poem but do not actually say it. If you notice that you have pulled your head back or taken a breath, stop and give your directions.

4. Taking more time to give your directions, see if you can simply open your mouth as if to speak. Can you do this without pulling your head back and taking a breath?

5. Notice the air going in and out through your nostrils and, if you have come to a complete stop, try reciting the first line of your poem.

Here we have structured the situation in such a way that, by breathing through our nostrils, we can monitor what happens when we prepare to speak. If you are focused on vocalizing itself, you are missing the point of the exercise, which is to understand the nature of our harmful habits and how to prevent them. The idea here is to observe what you do to interfere with vocalization. When you see clearly that the interference comes about as the direct result of the decision to vocalize, it will also become clear that, to stop this habit, you must refrain entirely from vocalizing and focus instead on the directions for the improved working of the PNR system. This forms the basis for performing the act in an entirely new way.

Walking with Poise:
To Take a Step or Not to Take a Step

Let's now look at the process of stopping in relation to walking, which is another very good test case for observing our habitual and harmful ways of doing things. When we walk, we have the same problem as in speaking: we shorten in stature as part of how we walk, which means that, to stop shortening, we must refrain from walking. This, as we saw when we explored speaking, is not a matter simply of pausing but of understanding how the system works as a whole so that, when we take a step, we can see how we interfere with the system.

But what replaces our harmful way of walking, if all we do is stop and then, while thinking of our directions, go ahead and walk? The answer is that, by stopping, we are able to prevent the old signals or neural messages from being sent and to replace the old signals with new ones. We inhibit, or stop, not only to prevent the old habit from operating but, in addition, to create the space within which we can send the new messages. So in reality the inhibition does two things: it stops the old habit from operating, and it creates the space within which something new can happen. If we stop in a desultory fashion, or forget to stop altogether then the old messages will be sent and there will be nothing new to replace them. This is why, when we stop, we have to be clear on what we want and what we don't want. We don't want to perform the action in the old way, which means that we want to prevent the old directions from being sent. And we want to create space for allowing the system to work in the new way, which means we have to take time to give the new directions, and see to it that they are working. If we have done all this, and if the system is working nicely as a result of all the preparatory work we have done, we can then perform an intermediate action—say, bending a knee or hinging at the ankles—while continuing to inhibit the old direction. In this way, we achieve our end without actually thinking of the end but by attending only to the means.

All these elements—the practice of non-doing, the giving of directions to restore the PNR

system, the act of stopping or refraining from performing the action, and breaking the action down into steps—are now applied in action so that, if we are able to put this into practice, we will be able to achieve our end in a new way.

Exercise 1

Identifying the problem: Taking a step

In this exercise, we take time to simply observe what happens when we take a step. As in the last exercise, it is important, before trying to solve the problem, to identify what the problem is.

1. Go into vertical stance and give your directions.

2. Come up gently out of vertical stance.

3. Now take a step and notice what happens.

4. Did you shift your weight over one leg?

5. Did you notice an increase in pressure over this leg?

When we initiate walking by shifting our weight over the supporting leg and sinking into that leg, we are interfering with the system as a whole. To prevent this, we must refrain from walking and achieve our goal indirectly.

Exercise 2

Intermediate action to taking a step: Shifting your weight forward

The next step is to perform an intermediate or partial act of walking such as shifting your weight forward from the ankles, which we explored in the earlier chapter on walking. Remember to take time with this, and to see if you can perform this act without actually thinking about taking a step.

1. Stand normally and give your directions.

2. Gently shift your weight forward from the ankles and then come back.

3. Try this a few times, seeing if you tighten in your ankles or legs.

You are now performing one essential element of walking, but in a way that is completely divorced from the act of walking itself.

Exercise 3

Intermediate action to taking a step: Letting a knee bend to raise your heel

Another intermediate step in walking, which we also explored in the chapter on walking, is to let a knee bend and to raise the heel, but without shifting weight or taking a step.

1. Standing with your feet shoulder width apart, give your directions for your head to go up, your back to lengthen and widen, and your gluteal muscles to let go.

2. Bend your right knee so that the heel of that foot comes off the ground, allowing your weight to go onto the ball of that foot so that you are not shifting your weight onto your left foot but keeping your weight evenly divided between both feet.

3. Bring your right heel down so that you are again standing normally on both feet.

4. Do this with your left foot and then bring the heel down.

If you are able to perform this action comfortably, see if you can combine the action of raising the heel with shifting your weight forward, without actually taking a step. You will see, when you can do this, that you have come very close to actually taking a step; yet it is possible to do all of this without actually thinking about, or deciding, to take a step.

Exercise 4

Shifting your weight forward to take a step

The final step is to perform the earlier actions, without deciding to take a step, and then to allow your leg to come forward, in this way taking a step without actually having the idea of doing so.

1. Stand normally and give your directions.

2. Bend your right knee so that the heel of that foot comes off the ground.

3. Gently shift your weight forward from the ankles so that your weight is supported on the whole of your left foot and the ball of your right foot.

4. Allow your right foot to advance so that it comes under your trunk. Your right foot should now be slightly forward of your left, with both feet fully in contact with the ground. You have now taken a step and, if you have been successful in putting these elements together, will have done so without actually deciding to take a step, without shifting your weight and without shortening in stature.

Recognizing how action takes place at a subconscious level forms the foundation for a new kind of awareness or consciousness in action. When the PNR system is restored, we create a new standard of perception that makes it possible to detect when the old habitual pattern comes into play. Becoming aware in this way is not simply a matter of using one's kinesthetic sense to be aware of muscles or of being mindful during activity but of learning to pay attention—and to perform actions—at a more conscious level. In this sense, the study of action is not merely a way of addressing bodily tension but of identifying the wrong and habitual activity of the muscular system, operating in response to the intention to act, as a fundamentally automatic process. This is not just improving bodily function or reducing tension or even cultivating awareness but learning the much more fundamental skill of becoming more conscious in action. By exploring the instinctive and unconscious nature of action, we become more aware in activity and open the door to a new level of conscious perception, a new state in which the various functions—proprioceptive, muscular, perceptual—are integrated, awakening a new level of balance and mental quietness and a new faculty of awareness and control in activity.

Index

Page references followed by n indicates footnotes, and page numbers referring to figures are in *italics*.